HIGHEST PRA[...] [...]LPS

"M. William Phelps dares to tread where few others will: into the mind of a killer."
—*TV Rage*

"Phelps is the king of true crime."
—**Lynda Hirsch**, Creators Syndicate

"Phelps treads dangerous ground like an Amazon jungle guide—fearless, compassionate, insightful."
—**Geoff Fitzpatrick**, Executive Producer
of *Dark Minds*

THE KILLING KIND

"In this true crime book, Phelps focuses on unrepentant killer Danny Hembree . . . [who] seizes the chance to take center stage with lurid confessions of a decades-long career of violent robbery, assault, rape, and murder. . . . Fans of the author's Discovery TV series, *Dark Minds*, will be rewarded."
—*Publishers Weekly*

"Phelps presents in-depth research and interviews that allow for vivid descriptions of characters and events. . . . Fans of true crime, forensics, and serial killer activities will all find something of interest here."
—*Library Journal*

OBSESSED

"True-crime junkies will be sated by the latest thriller from Phelps, which focuses on a fatal love triangle that definitely proved to be stranger than fiction. The police work undertaken to solve the case is recounted with the right amount of detail, and readers will be rewarded with shocking television-worthy twists in a story with inherent drama."
—*Publishers Weekly*

"Phelps infuses his investigative journalism with plenty of energized descriptions."
—*Publishers Weekly*

DEATH TRAP

"A chilling tale of a sociopathic wife and mother . . . A compelling journey from the inside of this woman's mind to final justice in a court of law. For three days I did little else but read this book."
—**Harry N. MacLean**, *New York Times* best-selling author of *In Broad Daylight*

I'LL BE WATCHING YOU

"Phelps has an unrelenting sense for detail that affirms his place, book by book, as one of our most engaging crime journalists."
—**Katherine Ramsland**

IF LOOKS COULD KILL

"M. William Phelps, one of America's finest true-crime writers, has written a compelling and gripping book about an intriguing murder mystery. Readers of this genre will thoroughly enjoy this book."
—**Vincent Bugliosi**

"Starts quickly and doesn't slow down. . . . Phelps consistently ratchets up the dramatic tension, hooking readers. His thorough research and interviews give the book complexity, richness of character, and urgency."
—**Stephen Singular**

MURDER IN THE HEARTLAND

"Drawing on interviews with law officers and relatives, the author has done significant research. His facile writing pulls the reader along."
—*St. Louis Post-Dispatch*

"Phelps expertly reminds us that when the darkest form of evil invades the quiet and safe outposts of rural America, the tragedy is greatly magnified. Get ready for some sleepless nights."
—**Carlton Stowers**

"This is the most disturbing and moving look at murder in rural America since Capote's *In Cold Blood*."

—**Gregg Olsen**

SLEEP IN HEAVENLY PEACE

"An exceptional book by an exceptional true crime writer. Phelps exposes long-hidden secrets and reveals disquieting truths."

—**Kathryn Casey**

EVERY MOVE YOU MAKE

"An insightful and fast-paced examination of the inner workings of a good cop and his bad informant, culminating in an unforgettable truth-is-stranger-than-fiction climax."

—**Michael M. Baden, M.D.**

"M. William Phelps is the rising star of the nonfiction crime genre, and his true tales of murder are scary-as-hell thrill rides into the dark heart of the inhuman condition."

—**Douglas Clegg**

LETHAL GUARDIAN

"An intense roller-coaster of a crime story . . . complex, with twists and turns worthy of any great detective mystery . . . reads more like a novel than your standard non-fiction crime book."

—**Steve Jackson**

PERFECT POISON

"True crime at its best—compelling, gripping, an edge-of-the-seat thriller. Phelps packs wallops of delight with his skillful ability to narrate a suspenseful story."

—**Harvey Rachlin**

"A compelling account of terror . . . The author dedicates himself to unmasking the psychopath with facts, insight and the other proven methods of journalistic leg work."

—**Lowell Cauffiel**

Also By M. William Phelps

Perfect Poison
Lethal Guardian
Every Move You Make
Sleep in Heavenly Peace
Murder in the Heartland
Because You Loved Me
If Looks Could Kill
I'll Be Watching You
Deadly Secrets
Cruel Death
Death Trap
Kill For Me
Love Her to Death
Too Young to Kill
Never See Them Again
Kiss of the She-Devil
Bad Girls
Obsessed
The Killing Kind
She Survived: Melissa (e-book)
She Survived: Jane (e-book)
I'd Kill For You
To Love and To Kill
One Breath Away
If You Only Knew

DON'T TELL
A SOUL

M. WILLIAM
PHELPS

PINNACLE BOOKS
Kensington Publishing Corp.
http://www.kensingtonbooks.com

PINNACLE BOOKS are published by

Kensington Publishing Corp.
119 West 40th Street
New York, NY 10018

All Kensington Titles, Imprints, and Distributed Lines are available at special quantity discounts for bulk purchases for sales promotions, premiums, fund-raising, and educational or institutional use. Special book excerpts or customized printings can also be created to fit specific needs. For details, write or phone the office of the Kensington special sales manager: Kensington Publishing Corp., 119 West 40th Street, New York, NY 10018, attn: Special Sales Department, Phone: 1-800-221-2647.

Pinnacle and the P logo Reg. U.S. Pat. & TM Off.

ISBN-13: 978-0-7860-3726-1
ISBN-10: 0-7860-3726-1
First Kensington Mass Market Edition: March 2017

eISBN-13: 978-0-7860-3727-8
eISBN-10: 0-7860-3727-X
Kensington Electronic Edition: March 2017

10 9 8 7 6 5 4 3 2 1

Printed in the United States of America

For My Readers . . .

PART ONE

The voice of your brother's blood is crying to me from the ground.
And now you are cursed. . . .

—Genesis: 4:10–11

1

SHE HAD A SOUTHWESTERN CHARM that people adore: calm disposition, a Texas twang, a relaxed outlook on life, an admirable Christian manner. Since 2002, sixty-eight-year-old Rueon had been married to Gethry Walker, eighty-three years old, a man pretty much set in his ways by now. Gethry was a gentle spirit—one of those rare men that listened more than he talked. He was an old-school, churchgoing Texan who almost every day wore suspenders, dress shirt and slacks, along with a subtle, elegant tie. When Gethry did have something to say, he spoke it at the altar behind a lectern during services at the Greater Love Temple Church in Tyler, Texas.

Both Gethry and Rueon were God-fearing people. They believed in Jesus Christ, redemption of the cross, penances paid for wrongs committed, justice, and facing demons and coming to terms with who you are under the guidance, influence and faith of God.

On Saturday, June 19, 2010, when Gethry and Rueon had not heard from Gethry's daughter, thirty-nine-year-old Cherry Walker, they felt something was wrong.

Where is Cherry?

Perhaps she had simply decided not to call. Cherry was entitled to her own life. Plus, she could be absentminded. Cherry had suffered from "learning disabilities" all her life and had just gone off to live on her own. She was almost thirty-nine, her birthday four months away. Classified as MR, "mentally retarded," by her doctors, she'd made great progress.

That Sunday morning (which also happened to be Father's Day), as Gethry and Rueon got ready for church, Rueon wondered again why Cherry had not called. She would always call before church to check in or ask what time the van was coming to pick her up. But as the morning wore on, there was still no word. Almost two full days now and not a peep.

Totally out of character for Cherry.

Rueon fixed her hair and figured the church van, which Cherry's brother drove, had picked her up for services and they'd meet her at Temple Love. She told Gethry not to fret. They'd go to church and run into Cherry there. No worries. Rueon could kindly scold Cherry and remind her that calling Rueon and Gethry once a day, if not every other day, was what they expected from her. They could explain to Cherry she needed to take responsibility, be done with it, and enjoy Sunday service, praising Jesus.

Gethry and Rueon, Cherry's stepmother, looked for Cherry as they walked into Temple Love. Cherry had her favorite seat down in the front row of pews, her name on it. But when Rueon reached the front by the altar, she looked around and Cherry was nowhere to be found.

Rueon sought out Cherry's brother. "Where's your sister?"

"I thought she was with y'all," he said.

"No, we thought she was coming with you."

Throughout that Sunday service, as anxiety turned more into a deeper concern, Rueon called Cherry at her apartment and Cherry's cell phone number.

"We got no response," Rueon said later.

If there was one thing about Cherry that Rueon and Gethry and anybody close to Cherry knew, it was that the girl did not go anywhere without two things: her money purse and cell phone. These two items were part of her, attached.

For Rueon and Gethry it was easy to tell themselves that Cherry probably just went to church with someone else.

"She sometimes did," Rueon explained later.

When Rueon and Gethry got home, Rueon called Cherry several more times, but got no response.

"You know," she told Gethry, "I'm going to git her."

Cherry had struggled, but worked hard, and she'd managed to overcome many difficulties and disabilities to carve out a life for herself with a small studio apartment across town in Tyler, not far from Rueon and Gethry's home. She had help from an aide, who came to see her every day, but Cherry was living on her own, doing things for herself. They could think of no reason for Cherry to fail to call them for this long. It just did not make sense.

"Call her again," Gethry suggested.

No answer.

"Let's go eat, and if we don't hear from her by the time we're done, then we can stop by Cherry's apartment and check in on her," Rueon suggested.

Gethry nodded.

They ate lunch and still heard no word from Cherry. Leaving the restaurant, they stopped back at home to grab the spare key to her apartment and headed out to East Houston Street in Tyler, the Citadel apartment complex.

Rueon walked in first. She couldn't believe it. The place was in "disarray," which was entirely unlike Cherry, a neat freak who fixated on cleaning and cleaning supplies in an obsessive-compulsive way. She'd never, under her own will, leave her apartment with "everything" all over the place. "Her ironing board was up. . . . Her bed was unmade . . . and things were just kind of scatter-y," one source later recalled.

"This is not Cherry, ain't it, Gethry?"

"Sure ain't," he said.

In addition, Cherry would have never walked out of her apartment without taking a bath, changing her clothes—all of which needed to be ironed before she'd wear them—or tidying up. Everything in her apartment had its place, and there was a place for everything. That was how Cherry lived her life.

Structure.

Focus.

Detail.

"This was the first thing I noticed," Rueon later explained. "And you just kind of get a feeling, you know."

A sense. That sinking pit in your gut. A woman's intuition—something was off.

Rueon looked in Cherry's closet. In her kitchen. All over. She searched for Cherry's cell phone or the coin purse Cherry always carried with her. Not finding either gave Rueon a bit of comfort, because there was no chance Cherry would leave the house without both of them. With both being gone, there was a bit of relief in knowing that she wasn't whisked away in some sort of home invasion or kidnapping.

Still, walking around the apartment, Rueon couldn't shake the feeling: *Something's wrong*.

The comb was on the vanity counter, the mouthwash by the faucet, the spray bottle of tile cleaner on the floor by the shower, where Cherry always left it, the smiling kitty cats on the ironing board apron underneath of pair of socks waiting to be ironed, two cases of water on the floor by the wastebasket, a roll of paper towels on the kitchen table, Cherry's favorite poster—from the horror film *Shutter*—taped to her wall, her velvety red chair against the wall, stacks of DVDs, mainly horror and other R-rated movies around the television, and the TV remote sitting on the bed.

Everything in Cherry's life was there waiting for her, but she was missing.

Rueon didn't see it then, but on a calendar on Cherry's wall, two dates stuck out: June 18, the previous Friday, and the following Wednesday, June 23. On both days, in pen, somebody had written, *Babysit*.

Another possibility existed, Rueon thought. One of Cherry's closest friends or even her caseworker, Paula Wheeler, a woman who saw Cherry almost every day, may have come by and picked her up to go out to eat or to shop. Rueon had been getting on Cherry lately, in a motherly way, "Girl, you know . . . you're [thirty-nine years old] now, and you need to grow up."

They had been trying to show Cherry what Rueon called "hard love," based on the idea that Rueon and Gethry could not be with Cherry forever—she'd need to spread her wings and go off on her own. Was this

Cherry doing that very thing, going it alone? Had she taken Rueon's advice?

There was another side of Cherry, however. Her collection of DVDs. She liked to watch horror films such as *Saw, The Texas Chainsaw Massacre* and her favorite, *Paranormal Activity.* Yet she played with children's toys and could not read or write much more than her name and a few numbers and letters. She was very much a child in an adult's body.

Rueon and Gethry decided to go home and wait for Cherry to call.

2

BOBBY LEWIS WAS ON HIS way back to work. Such a common, routine task that so many perform each day. Waking up, heading off to a job, collecting that paycheck on Friday, then enjoying a weekend of rest and relaxation.

On Saturday, June 19, 2010, the day before Rueon and Gethry Walker grew concerned that Cherry had not called or shown up at church, Bobby was driving along an area near Smith County Road, known locally as the CR 2191, in Whitehouse, a small town north of Houston and east of Dallas, Texas. It was just outside Tyler, directly west of Lake Tyler, a massive body of water shaped like a cluster of clouds.

Bobby had the radio on. The windows rolled down. That familiar hot and heavy, wet Texas air was blowing into his face. It was a peaceful ride on a lovely day—and should have been nothing more.

Somewhere just before three o'clock, however, Bobby Lewis's rather predictable life took a turn into the Twilight Zone. He worked at Domino's Pizza in Tyler. He was in Whitehouse on this afternoon to pick up a coworker before heading back into the restaurant for more deliveries.

Passing the 15900 block of CR 2191, after pulling into a driveway and turning his car around, thinking he was lost, Bobby saw something off to the side of the road.

What in the hell?

He pulled over and stopped his vehicle.

Bobby got out. There was a dirt area, "overgrown with weeds," in a thickly settled part of town—mostly red clay, some sand, trees and forest on all sides, save for several buildings and a few homes to the southwest. It was a semisecluded area, just to the west of the famed Piney Woods section of the state. Whitehouse is small-town America: About seven thousand souls resided there in 2010. The median household income fell in the neighborhood of about $70,000 per year, with Texas, overall, coming in at about $50,000. So there was some money here in Whitehouse. Most people, 85 percent of whom the recent census termed as "white," weren't poor by any means.

From his vehicle Bobby Lewis saw a charred black patch of land. After stepping out of his car, curious, he walked closer. It was probably the residue of some kids burning up an old mattress or a campfire from a keg party. Maybe even a load of trash some knucklehead had tossed out and set on fire. The charred remains spread over a small area of the sandy and red clay ground. The pile had not burned entirely, however, and the pizza man noticed that something about it beckoned a closer look.

Bobby went in for a more personal view.

Getting within about fifteen feet of the debris, he could clearly see that, in fact, it wasn't a pile of trash, an old campfire or the remnant of an ordinary fire. Approaching the pile from about three yards away, he did not want to get any closer, Bobby later told police, because in that moment he realized what he was looking at.

Anxiety throbbed as Bobby Lewis stepped back, pulled out his cell phone and, with index finger shaking, dialed 911.

3

SHE WAS LYING FACEDOWN ABOUT fifty feet off the side of CR 2191, where Bobby Lewis waited for police to arrive. "I knew what it was," he said later. "So there was no need to go any closer."

It was a dead body (DB)—probably a female, by the look of what little clothing was left and the feminine shape of her body. It was difficult to say for certain, because the person was lying on her stomach. Still, the contour appeared to be that of a large female.

The DB had one arm at her side pointed downward, and the other was pointed up above her head as though she was raising her hand in class to ask a question. Her legs were about a foot apart, toes pointed into the dirt. She wore black Capri pants (what was left of them), white sneakers with black oily stains and no dirt on the bottoms, indicating that she had not walked to this location on her own, but had been dumped here. (Her shoes, otherwise, would have been caked with the same red clay that was on the ground all over the place.)

It was unclear what type of shirt she had on because

it had melted to her charred skin, which had peeled and creased in some sections, spotted in others, burned entirely off in small areas. The shirt, best Bobby could tell from the pieces still intact, was green with a floral pattern—another indication that the body was female. Even more horrifying: All of her hair was gone. Her face, pushed into the ground, appeared to be nearly burned off. The entire area of her neck was burned. She was unrecognizable. Bobby did not know from looking at her how old she could be. Best estimate from him was that she was young, maybe late teens to early thirties.

She had no name.

No identification.

Bobby had no idea where she had come from or who had put her here.

Much less, why.

He waited, staring at "the ash all around [the] body," not touching her or anything within what was now, he realized, a crime scene.

Whitehouse police (sometimes referred to as "peace") officers Joshua Brunt and David Roberson arrived at 3:03 P.M. They surveyed the scene, secured it and unspooled a roll of yellow police tape, tacking the plastic rope up around the immediate area and closing most of it off. Preserving a crime scene as quickly as possible might be the most important action any cop can take within this type of investigation.

Outdoor crime scenes pose so many inherent problems from the onset that safeguarding the scene is as important as combing through it with a magnifying glass. It was imperative to have a scene protected from footsteps, passersby, animals, untrained cops, the elements and anything else that might contaminate the scene and its surrounding area.

Officer Roberson, per protocol, started a crime scene log, a notebook detailing time, date, action, personnel. Soon the entire area, which had otherwise been quiet, would be teeming with cops and crime scene investigators (CSIs) and detectives and sheriffs and Texas Rangers, all looking to unravel what had happened—that is, after the most important task began: identifying the girl, contacting family members and beginning to learn "who, what, where, when and how."

Whitehouse Police Department (WPD) officer Rod Langinias arrived and spoke to Roberson and Brunt, who stood with Bobby Lewis, and talked about how Bobby had come across the scene. The first suspect in any case was the person who found the body.

Bobby explained how he had pulled into that driveway, turned his car around, and there she was. He said he didn't realize at first what he was looking at, but after getting out and surveying the scene, it hit him. She was dead. Someone had lit her body on fire.

No, he had not touched anything.

A sergeant arrived. After talking to Bobby Lewis, Officer Langinias asked his sergeant, "You want me to take some photos until the boys from [CSI] arrive?" Langinias mentioned that he had spotted some tire tracks in the red clay and skid marks on the road closest to where the body was located. That sort of stuff needed to be documented before it was contaminated or, even worse, destroyed.

"Stay out of the crime scene area and wait for the crime scene people to come," the sergeant ordered.

"Got it," Langinias said.

Langinias and several other officers blocked off the road, so no one could drive down it. There was a rolled-up carpet nearby, some charred ashes just north of the body. Between the victim's legs was a grade-A, homogenized, half-and-half Dairy Fresh creamer cup, one of those tiny plastic containers you get with your coffee at McDonald's or, in this case, Dairy Queen. The item was used, crumpled up. It had no age to it.

Other latent trace was visible right away, mainly those tire tracks and some carpet fibers and other small pieces of what looked to be potentially important evidence. For CSIs the best thing about red clay was that it acted as a mold. Footprints and tire tracks had left solid imprints. There was some sand around the area, too, and they wouldn't get much from that, but the red clay was a bonus. It might not lead to finding out the identity of the woman, but it would certainly help at some point in the investigation when suspects were identified and their cars and shoes were examined.

Ultimately, this was a Smith County Sheriff's Office (SCSO) investigation, with the Tyler Police Department (TPD) and the local WPD, along with the Texas Rangers, lending assistance. In Texas everyone understands his or her role when solving crimes: to find and arrest the bad guy.

Around 4:00 P.M., with the scene overrun by law enforcement personnel, word spread around town that something was going on near CR 2191, south of Tyler. The local media was alerted. Many would hop into their satellite trucks and little cars with the broadcast banners written in bright blues and reds on the doors and head out to the location to see what could be reported.

SCSO detective Ron Rathbun took a call to head down and find out what he could. Rathbun was an old-school, by-the-book guy. He was on scene by 4:55 P.M. Bobby Lewis was still there, sitting, shaking his head in disbelief, ready and willing to answer any questions he could. Rathbun located him not long after arriving. Rathbun asked him where he worked.

"Tyler," Bobby said. "I was trying to find a coworker out here. I turned around in that driveway"—he pointed—"because I thought I had passed the address I was looking for."

From there, Bobby explained the rest.

Texas Ranger Brent Davis arrived with a Bublcam Sphere 360 and the supplementary software technology needed to employ it, a sophisticated photography unit used to take aerial photos, among other uses. The local district attorney's office (DAO) had purchased the expensive piece of equipment with more than $250,000 in drug money seized from several recent high-profile busts. The aerial images, once they came back, would give everyone a good indication of where possible evidence was located beyond the range of the naked eye. The camera had the capability to take photos with twenty different lighting levels, giving detectives a much clearer picture of minuscule pieces of evidence that could be otherwise overlooked by CSIs searching the ground. Using the Bublcam was a high-tech way to get the upper hand on a case and give it a shot of adrenaline out of the box.

Detective Rathbun walked down to where the victim

was still lying. Beyond a number of factors he noticed while studying the scene, Rathbun was interested in the idea that the victim was facedown. She wore white Ralph Lauren tennis shoes, with that familiar polo pony emblem on the sides, and that she was a black female, whose "pink panties" were showing only because the Capris she had on were nearly burned off her body. There was a subtle, almost intrinsic indication within the entire scene—if only by a cop's intuition—that her killer had left a trail directly to his or her doorstep. Not that this was going to be an easy crime to solve—but as long as the SCSO took it one step at a time, it was going to come together.

Rathbun noticed there was something on her shoes, so he squatted down to have a closer look.

The shoes appeared to be very clean (maybe recently purchased), he wrote in his report. *I noticed that the bottom soles appeared to have a black-colored substance on them.* It was faint, almost like a film. Rathbun wrote, *At one point, walking around on a surface that had black soot . . .* He leaned toward *[a] mechanic's shop that had grease, oil, and other materials on the floor.*

It was an interesting calculation that opened up specific investigatory possibilities. Considering that there was red clay all over the area around the body, the residue—if it was, in fact, oil—seemed like an important clue to this intelligent, intuitive cop. It said to him, rather clearly, that she had not walked by herself onto the surface where she was lying—someone, probably driving the car whose tire tracks were left nearby, had dumped her here.

Righting himself, Rathbun stared at the woman. She had not been there, he thought, for very long.

Maybe a few hours at most.

Between her legs, Rathbun observed a drinking straw contained in a wrapper from Chick-fil-A, which was left not too far from that plastic, empty, crumpled-up Dairy Fresh creamer cup. The creamer cup, especially, Rathbun surmised, had not been on the ground long. He could tell by looking at the way it sat there.

After taking a walk around the area and seeing other pieces of garbage, Rathbun was certain the items near the body were fresh—and perhaps left by the killer. The other garbage looked weathered, as though it had been part of the landscape for some time.

SCSO detective James Riggle was on the Loop 323 when he took a call to head over to the Whitehouse crime scene. He arrived near four-thirty to have a look and locate Rathbun and other members of the SCSO team.

"You're going to be the lead on this," one of the sergeants told Riggle after his arrival. He was then briefed on the situation.

Riggle found Rathbun after meeting with Brent Davis to verify the Bublcam imagery was in the process of being completed. Banking on the notion that the Chick-fil-A evidence was potentially explosive, the immediate plan was to find any Chick-fil-A locations in Tyler and Whitehouse and get to the surveillance equipment inside the restaurant to have a look before they erased the tape for that day.

Restaurants generally did not keep copies of surveillance tapes—even if it was recorded digitally—unless they were robbed or something happened. They'd record over the previous day with the next. Riggle knew the potential was there to see his victim possibly purchasing her last meal—and with any luck, which was something every murder investigation depended on, standing by her side might be a viable suspect or, at the least, someone the SCSO needed to find and speak to.

4

IDENTIFYING THE YOUNG WOMAN WHO had been found dead and burned, abandoned off to the side of the dirt road, near the CR 2191, became the primary task for the SCSO as Detective James Riggle took over as lead in the case. Somebody's daughter had been murdered and dumped in a field of dirt and debris, before being lit on fire. Her family deserved to know where she was, what had happened and who was responsible. Moreover, any cop can tell you that your best chance to solve a homicide lies within the ring of people circling the victim the closest, and it pays to get to those people within a day or two of finding the body.

Riggle and Rathbun stood studying the victim. She was about eighteen to twenty-five," Riggle guessed. "Around two hundred forty pounds."

No identification.

No tattoos.

No noticeable scars.

It was hot, a wet 90 degrees. Detective Riggle knew by those conditions that she had not been at the scene very long and had probably been placed there within the past twenty-four hours, at the most. Otherwise, her body would have been decomposing, bloated and rotting. Within decomposition there are five stages the body goes through: The first is considered "fresh," whereby a body has just been found (within hours of death). The second would be a body that has begun to "bloat" and has become puffy as a chemical reaction takes place inside the organs (beginning in the intestines and colon). The third consists of "active" enzymes beginning to rot the tissue and organs and skin from within. The fourth is an "advanced state of decay," a stage of decomposition in which the victim has been deceased for a longer period of time and her body has become a soupy mess of gruesome, foul-smelling liquids and solids. The corpse has begun literally to melt because of the bacteria escaping from the intestinal tract (sometimes clinically referred to as "putrefaction," sped up and slowed down by extreme heat or cold). The fifth is that final "dry" corpse (usually in the form of skeletal remains) that is nothing more than bones and possibly hair and clothes. Of course, all of this depends on the elements (weather, where the body has been found, any wildlife in the area, the temperature) and even the clothing the person was wearing at the time he or she died.

Detectives Riggle and Rathbun could tell this particular victim was still in the earliest—or "fresh"—stage and had not decomposed much at all.

This fact would help them.

After a local judge came to the scene and signed off on all that had been done, CSIs were allowed to turn the victim over and take a look at her face—or what was left of it. A set of "small studded" earrings were found on the victim's ears, jewelry that could become important once they tried to identify her through flyers and pleas to the media and community.

Riggle and a sergeant called into the SCSO and asked for a team to go through missing person reports from the local area. Maybe somebody had reported a woman missing and she fit the description of their DB. Sometimes it was that easy.

Other times there was much more involved.

A report went out: *Young black female, 18 to 25 years old, studded ear rings, black Capri pants, white Polo tennis shoes.* That should be enough information to generate a response from the public.

Within an hour or so, Riggle and Rathbun were told by Smith County that "dispatch did not have anyone matching this description entered" into the system, but they were still waiting on word from other counties and surrounding jurisdictions. Maybe it was too early for anyone to have filed a missing person report. The woman wasn't a child. She could have lived by herself and had not been expected to be anywhere.

"Okay," Riggle said. He got with Rathbun. "Chick-fil-A?"

"Probably the best place to start."

They left the crime scene bound for the local Chick-fil-A restaurants in the area.

The Chick-fil-A they had in mind was due north on the 2964, which connected with the 110 in Tyler, about ten minutes away from the crime scene. It was the closest Chick-fil-A, which seemed to be the obvious starting point.

Riggle introduced himself to the assistant manager and explained what they needed, without going into detail. Last thing they needed was the rumor mill to begin. Facebook and Twitter could clog up investigatory time if they had to put people on monitoring those sites, not to mention tracking people down via their social media accounts.

There was a problem, the manager said. "I'm not sure how to download the videos."

This was a good problem to have; it meant the video surveillance was still in the computer system and that the computer (or a human being using the computer) had not erased it.

"I can have someone do it for you if you want to come back tomorrow," the manager explained.

They made plans to meet up at ten o'clock, the following morning, June 20, 2010.

Riggle and Rathbun drove to the Chick-fil-A eight minutes away on South Broadway in the same town. It was more unlikely, considering the out-of-the-way location of the restaurant as compared to the crime scene, but they needed to check every possibility.

This Tyler area was built up and loaded with your standardized, corporate retail stores and strip malls, gas stations, convenience stores, check-cashing windows, banks, elementary schools, apartment buildings, condos and cookie-cutter homes, surrounded, of course, by that distinctive Texas acreage. Named after President John Tyler, because he had supported admission of Texas into the United States, the town of Tyler had seen its economy go from boom to bust to a solid balance as the corn and cotton fields gave way to a peach crop, which eventually succumbed to a blight outbreak, paving the way for a rose industry. Tyler's medium income is about $9,000 below the state average of $50,000; but with a population hovering around 100,000 any given year, there is plenty of money to go around.

"Monday," the manager of the South Broadway Chick-fil-A told Riggle. That was when the SCSO could come back. "We'll see about what we can do to get you that video."

So it wasn't going to be as easy as the first hunch a cop had. It never was. However, this sort of case, Riggle and Rathbun knew, was not going to go cold. There was too much evidence at the scene. The dumping of the body was hasty and not planned out. The key was going to be identifying the victim. There were prints and dental traces left behind. Most killers who don't want you to know who it is that they killed will leave the scene with the heads and the hands of their victims, if they cannot get rid of the bodies altogether, taking with them any means of identifying their victims—if he or she is not part of the national DNA database. With this victim, it was obvious from the way in which she had been placed there—out in the open, facedown, for anyone to come upon her corpse—that her killer was not worried about the victim being identified, or she hadn't thought of this particular contingency.

It might take a while, but the SCSO was confident it would be able to locate her relatives and begin looking into family and friends.

On Sunday morning, June 20, 2010, Riggle took a call to head out to a "residence off Highway 31 east," a roadway that cut directly through the center of Tyler, running east to west. Word was that they might have an identification on their victim. A girl thought to fit the description of the DB had not returned home. She had been gone for several days.

Riggle showed up and spoke with the girl's parents. Nice people. Worried and concerned for their child. He spent thirty minutes with them.

As they talked about their daughter and showed him photos, it was clear they were talking about two different people. After he left the home, Riggle got a call that they had located the missing girl: she was alive and well and on her way home.

Good for that family, Riggle considered. *Bad for another.*

Riggle went back to that first Chick-fil-A. The manager informed Riggle the detective could sit in the office inside the restaurant, if he wanted, and watch the videos on the manager's computer.

And so that's what he did.

5

LATE ON JUNE 20, 2010, Rueon and Gethry Walker were at home, nervous and worried, waiting for Cherry to call, hoping for word from somebody that she was okay. Neither the Walkers nor Cherry's brother, cousins, nieces, nephews, any of her friends—including Cherry's neighbor—had heard from her in close to two full days. During the leading up to Cherry going missing, Rueon had been trying to break Cherry away from depending on her and Gethry—and now she was questioning that decision.

"Let me say this. The . . . main reason was for her, because she had a quality of life, she could function—and her father being in his eighties and I'm in my sixties, and we wanted to see from a distance . . . how she could maintain if we wasn't there."

Cherry was ready. Rueon and Gethry could not take care of the girl her entire life. She was able to function on her own. She could take care of herself with the help of her aide, Paula Wheeler. She was able to make decisions. Somebody just needed to cut the cord so she could grow even more.

Something had happened. Rueon was certain of it. It was past five o'clock on Sunday evening. Rueon was calling Cherry's cell phone number every thirty minutes, but there was no answer. They had gone to Cherry's apartment. Nothing was out of order other than the apartment not being its usual immaculate space, cleaned and tidied up. However, the apartment had an air of finality Rueon could not shake.

Rueon took to the couch and then to her bedroom to think about what their next move might be. It was going to get dark in a few hours. Cherry was still not responding to text messages and calls.

When the nightly news came on, Rueon felt she needed to watch. It was being reported that a body had been found about fifty feet off the road in Whitehouse, just over the Tyler town line. These early reports had a few of the facts wrong, but there was enough information to jar Rueon into sitting up and taking notice.

". . . And when the news person was talking about it, they were saying they had found a person, a young woman . . . ," Rueon recalled.

Rueon didn't need confirmation after watching the report. A mother or father doesn't need proof. She knew, right then and there.

Cherry is in trouble. . . .

Rueon decided not to tell Gethry right then. He was sleeping, anyway. No need to rustle him awake and get his blood stirring, his heart racing, his nerves in a state of unrest.

After Rueon saw the number on the TV news, she "eased" herself out of the bed, she later explained, being sure not to wake Gethry, and wrote it down. Then she made a decision. If she had not heard from

Cherry by morning, she would tell Gethry about the news report and call the number.

The following morning, June 21, a Monday, town residents began to talk about what might have happened outside Tyler on the CR 2191. A Smith County sheriff released what the entire team of investigators had agreed was the most accurate description of the woman the pizza deliveryman had found, with the hope that someone would come forward to say my daughter, wife, friend, sister, mother, has not been home in a few days and fits the description:

> [A] *heavyset black woman . . . dressed in a black and green floral shirt, black Capri pants, white shoes and socks. . . . [Her age is estimated to be] from 18 to 34 years old. . . . Foul play may have been involved in her death.*

Notably missing from this early report was the fact that the woman's body had been set on fire and burned horrifically. This omission was by design. Cops held back certain crime scene elements in a case because they would need the information down the road when questioning suspects and witnesses. They knew the fact that someone had tried to burn the victim's body would eventually come out, but the longer they kept this fact from the public, the better off everyone would be—namely, the victim's friends and family, who did not need to hear this shocking, gruesome detail from a news account.

Rueon said later that when this latest report was made public, it confirmed her suspicions. There was only one thing in the world that would have stopped Cherry from calling them by now, Rueon said. "A tragedy."

Indeed.

After talking with Gethry, Rueon had the feeling that the girl found on the side of the road had to be Cherry.

"We knew her size and her age and it seemed like that was . . . Well, it might be, could be, *can't* be," Rueon later told a local television station. The tragic situation was in strong contrast to how well Cherry had been doing the past year. She was evolving beyond a learning disability and was becoming her own person. Her move out of the Walker residence into an efficiency apartment was the result of hard work and determination on Cherry's part. If it *was* Cherry on the side of that road, who in his or her right mind could have wanted to harm someone like her? Somebody so innocent and sweet. Why?

"Please, please, please let me move out on my own," Cherry had told Rueon many times before Christmas 2009. For months they had been discussing her entry into adulthood, beginning with her own apartment. Rueon and Gethry believed Cherry, with the help of an aide, was ready to be on her own. It was such a hard decision, but Cherry was the type to make a promise and work toward keeping it.

Cherry was still struggling with certain tasks, and Rueon and Gethry were a bit nervous, but they had taken her to see that studio/efficiency apartment on East Houston Street in Tyler one day and Cherry fell in love with the place. The smile on Cherry's face as she walked around the small apartment showed she was "elated," Rueon later explained. Cherry could picture herself here, alone, living a life.

It was perfect.

They discussed the situation and decided to move Cherry in. It was an apartment Rueon and Gethry thought was ideal for Cherry to start out in: small kitchen, with a bedroom and living area all in one, a small bathroom off to the side of the kitchen, a tiny closet.

"Small" was the key word here, and "what she could handle," Rueon said.

Right away Cherry showed that her parents had made the right choice. On her own she was going to the Laundromat to wash her clothes and going to the bank. She had been able to accomplish routine life chores that many of us do every day without a second thought. These were big obstacles Cherry had taken on and had overcome with the help of Paula Wheeler, who visited Cherry every morning. Cherry lived between a Papa John's Pizza and Church's Chicken and "loved both of them," Rueon recalled. Her quality of life had gone from being sheltered and at home all the time, whisked to one doctor's appointment and the next, to being out in the world on her own, learning how to be the thirty-nine-year-old adult she was.

Rueon and Gethry were excited for their daughter. The restaurants and Laundromat were close by. Cherry was happy about being able to do things for herself.

The Dairy Queen was a bit farther away from her apartment. One night Cherry called her stepmother, "I'm going to try it tomorrow. I just love those [Blizzards]."

After building up the courage to venture off to the Dairy Queen, Cherry was confident enough to walk to the Dollar General, which was even farther away. Cherry had an affinity for cleaning supplies and air fresheners and she always bought more than she needed. This was okay, Rueon and Gethry felt. The girl wanted what she wanted and it kept her focused. She was building self-esteem, self-confidence and self-assurance. One day at a time.

The Andrews Center in Tyler, a behavioral-health facility, helped people like Cherry integrate into society. A part of Community Access, a nonprofit, state-run operation, Andrews calls itself a "comprehensive mental health and mental retardation center." Rueon and Gethry had been working with Andrews for years. Cherry was part of the system, receiving disability, Social Security and welfare benefits. She was also given government assistance wherever she needed it. Andrews had always, it seemed, been a part of Cherry's life. In just the past ten years, from the time Cherry was twenty-nine until her death, she had made significant strides in overcoming her disability. In 1995, Cherry had tested with an IQ of near 60 (significantly below the average person, 100). In 2000, one of her psychologists from Andrews, who had worked in the mental retardation department of the facility, claimed Cherry was age equivalent to someone between five and six years old. Her "communication domain," or the ability she tested at communicating with other people, came in at about four years, four months; her "daily living skills" were about nine years; her "adaptive behavior" measured at six years, six months. Since then, Cherry had made considerable advancements.

As she developed new skills through the years, someone from Andrews had called Rueon and explained how they could offer Cherry a caregiver to teach her more about living on her own than Rueon or Gethry ever could. This was what had sparked the idea that Cherry would one day be able to move out of the house and into an apartment.

The one problem Rueon and Gethry had been working with Cherry on was the ability to count money. Cherry had an issue with it. She understood what a $5, $10 or $20 bill was, but adding them together became something Cherry struggled with. Still, she would master it—as long as she had a little help. Thus, with everything heading in the right direction for Cherry, her outlook was positive and full of excitement for where life could take her. Cherry had even considered a man she saw from time to time to be her boyfriend.

Once the SCSO identified Cherry Walker positively as their DB, they were quite interested in speaking to that man.

6

GETHRY AND RUEON KNEW THAT with Cherry missing all weekend, their daughter's sudden disappearance was not by her own will. Cherry "lived in the Lord," Gethry said. She would be in church no matter what—that was what had done it for him. With Cherry not sitting that past Sunday in the same pew she had for years, Gethry needed no additional proof that something bad had happened.

Unable to turn away from what they believed was the inevitable, Rueon called the SCSO and faced whatever it was the Lord had in store for them.

Rueon explained that the woman on the side of the road mentioned in recent news reports fit a description of their missing daughter. She described the clothing Cherry had been wearing last time they saw her: "Black Capri-style pants, white tennis shoes, Polo." Rueon said she could not recall what type of shirt Cherry had on.

"We'll send someone right over," an officer told the Walkers.

Detective James Riggle showed up at the Walker

household not long after the call came in. He sat down and asked the Walkers to talk about Cherry.

"Last time we heard from her was Friday," Gethry said.

"Gethry picked her up at the beauty salon," Rueon added.

Gethry explained further that he picked Cherry up at the salon, dropped her off at her apartment, and then returned home by about 4:00 P.M. It was like any other ride, any other normal day, any other errand.

The Walkers had not seen her since.

Rueon remembered this was the last time anyone had seen Cherry, further telling Riggle, "Cherry needed me so much more than any other child I had ever had, that's why we bonded. On that Friday I was talking to my [other] daughter that lives far away." As they spoke, Rueon explained, another call beeped into the line. It was Cherry. "She called me by my name, Rueon. She said, 'I'm ready—I'm at the beauty shop, and I'm ready to go.' And I said, 'Okay, your daddy is on his way.'"

Riggle took notes.

"She would always call, but especially on Sunday mornings so we could pick her up for church. But she never called," Rueon added. She told Riggle about one distinguishing characteristic that could perhaps help identify Cherry. She'd had a hysterectomy three years back—an important factor that would help a medical examiner (ME) make a positive identification.

When they had not heard from Cherry, Rueon said, they went over to her apartment. She said they'd kept an extra key to the apartment for this very reason.

"What'd you find there?"

Rueon explained that the door was locked, so they let themselves in. Cherry was nowhere to be found.

"How did the apartment look?" Riggle wondered.

"Nothing was out of place. Cherry liked to keep that place very neat, in good order, very clean."

"Can we get a phone number for her apartment, any cell phone numbers she might have had, and perhaps a release of her medical records?"

The Walkers said they would help with all of those things and anything else the SCSO needed.

The detective could not get over the thought that everything he was being told seemed to fit. It was her. No doubt.

"Dental records, too?" Riggle added.

"Yes, of course."

"We cannot confirm that it's Cherry, I want you to know this," Riggle said, explaining that the dental records were the standard way of positively confirming a person's identity.

The Walkers said they understood.

"I'm sorry, but it could take several days."

Again, the Walkers were a patient couple.

Riggle asked if the SCSO could have a key to Cherry's apartment; it would help if they could get in there and look around. Cops are trained to see things others might overlook. There could be a telling clue or something alerting them to where Cherry had gone off to.

Rueon gave the detective the key and told him the SCSO was welcome to have a look.

"Has anybody [else] been inside?"

As far as they knew, nobody else.

Riggle wondered if there was anybody the Walkers could think of that the SCSO should speak to—friends, other family members, neighbors, anyone that might help.

"Paula Wheeler," Rueon said right away. "She's Cherry's caseworker and friend." Wheeler was probably the closest person to Cherry. She saw Cherry every workday, even sometimes on weekends. She worked for Community Access. She helped Cherry cook, clean her apartment, shop, make it to her appointments on time; she took Cherry to the doctor, the store, just about anywhere she needed to go. "If anyone might have seen or talked to Cherry, it's Paula," Rueon said.

"Did she have any other friends?" Riggle asked.

"Cherry did not really have a lot of 'friends,'" Rueon explained, Gethry nodding in affirmation. "She does have a white boy she sees, Ron . . . or, um, Rob?" Rueon wasn't certain of the name. "He borrowed some CDs from her and I recall she had a problem getting them back. I don't think she has spoken to him in a long time, though."

Killing a woman and torching her body over a few CDs didn't seem at all probable—but cops know that human beings kill each other for far less. Perhaps there was another layer to the relationship between Cherry and this man the Walkers were unaware of. One had to include any motive, any suspect, any situation at all, despite how insane or inconceivable it looked. If Cherry had a young man she was seeing, the narrative of their romance went deeper than some borrowed CDs.

Rueon talked further about an upstairs neighbor of Cherry's, "who kind of kept an eye on her and might have talked to her."

"How did Cherry get around town?" Riggle wondered.

"Usually, Paula and Gethry took her everywhere she needed to go. She walked, too." Rueon then seemed to remember something she needed to share.

"That . . . boy, his name, I remember now . . . Joe Mayo. It wasn't Ron or Rob. It was Joe!"

Riggle wrote it down.

"Did Cherry have any favorite places she liked to go?"

"Church's Chicken, Papa John's and Whataburger," Rueon said. The thought brought a slight smile to her face. It was her enjoyment of the simpler things in life that helped to make Cherry the special person she was to those who knew her.

Riggle thanked the Walkers and told them the SCSO would do their best to find Cherry. If the body found on the CR 2191 was not Cherry, they would certainly begin searching for her.

Leaving, however, Riggle knew the outcome was not going to be a happy reunion for the Walker family.

Of course, they would wait for the autopsy results and dental records to make it official, but all signs pointed to the CR 2191 DB being thirty-eight-year-old Cherry Walker.

The good news about meeting with the Walkers was that Detective Riggle had two names, Paula Wheeler and Joe Mayo, which meant he had people he could talk to about Cherry.

7

MARCIE FULTON LIVED IN THE Citadel Apartments in a unit above Cherry Walker's. She knew Cherry well beyond a "hello" in the hallway or bumping into her on the front stoop. Once in a while the two even hung out. Marcie would take Cherry to the store to buy groceries, rent or buy DVDs. "She liked scary movies," Marcie said of her neighbor. Later, in court, Marcie described Cherry as someone who "liked to eat." Cherry was a fan of Burger King and other fast-food restaurants.

Marcie also seemed to suggest that Cherry had a bit of an OCD (obsessive-compulsive disorder) issue with regard to keeping everything in her apartment "neat and clean." It was to the point that if something—anything—wasn't clean, it bothered Cherry. For example, she'd step in Marcie's truck to head off on a shopping or food trip and complain to Marcie that she wasn't keeping her truck clean enough. Even when she visited with Marcie, Cherry held nothing back in letting her neighbor know when she thought Marcie's apartment needed a good cleaning.

That's what friends were for, right? To look out for each other.

Marcie had watched a little boy for a woman she knew. He was four years old. The mother would drop him off "two or three times per week." Sometimes she would leave him and not return for two, three or even more days. But the boy had gotten to be too much to handle for Marcie, not to mention how rude and inconsiderate his mother was, and so Marcie decided to ask Cherry if she wanted to watch the child.

"You interested?" Marcie asked one day. It was a babysitting gig. She explained to Cherry that the woman would pay her.

"Yes," Cherry replied.

Ever since, Cherry had watched the boy when the mother asked. The mother knew Cherry was a special-needs person, but she didn't seem to mind. She'd dump the boy off, at times leaving him with Cherry for days, usually without ever checking in.

Before speaking with Marcie, Detective Riggle and another investigator walked through Cherry's apartment without touching or moving anything, to see if they could come up with any answers. By now they had matched a photo of Cherry up against the DB and were 99.9 percent certain Cherry Walker was their victim. The SCSO had initiated an autopsy, but the results for manner and cause of death, as well as toxicology, were not yet available. The coroner had even identified the DB as *Cherry Walker, 39, Black Female.*

Yet, "positive ID" was "still pending." Before telling the Walkers their daughter was dead, they had to be scientifically certain. However, the SCSO was investigating the case as a homicide.

Inside Cherry's apartment, Riggle later noted, they found it "intact and in place." An officer had already gone in and photographed the entire apartment, in order to preserve the integrity of the scene. There didn't seem to be any sign that an altercation had taken place. This was an early thought: Someone might have murdered Cherry inside her apartment, then dumped and burned her body on the CR 2191. That didn't seem to be the case, at least not from any early, outward appearances. Forensics would have to come in and make that determination, spraying luminol (to check for the presence of blood) and sprinkling fingerprint powder. But it didn't seem to be a second crime scene.

On one of her counters Riggle noticed a photo of Cherry with a white male. They looked happy, like a couple.

Joe Mayo?

The detective took the photo.

Riggle saw that Cherry's answering machine was blinking; there were "several messages," he later reported, still waiting to be heard. One was from Cherry's caseworker, Paula Wheeler. She was looking for Cherry and "checking up on her." Another message was from a woman who called herself "Kim" (she left no last name), who said she was "on break" and needed Cherry to call her back. The date and time of the messages, unfortunately, had been turned off. They had no idea when these messages would fit into the timeline between the moment Gethry said he dropped Cherry off at home and when Bobby Lewis found her. They could ask Paula Wheeler when she remembered leaving her message. The "Kim" woman would need to be tracked down as well.

Marcie was home when the SCSO knocked on her door. The SCSO had to be careful, because anybody at this early stage of the investigation could be a suspect.

"Sure," Marcie said. "Excuse the place. Come in." Marcie confirmed that she and Cherry were friends and spoke all the time, saw each other almost daily.

Riggle asked Marcie when she had last seen Cherry.

"Oh, geez," Marcie answered, "it's been a couple of days." She explained that she had not seen or heard from Cherry, and that nobody she knew of had been over to Cherry's apartment over the past few days, save for Mr. and Mrs. Walker.

Riggle showed Marcie the photograph he'd taken from Cherry's place. He asked her if she recognized the man in the photo.

"Yeah, that's Joe Mayo," Marcie confirmed. He was Cherry's so-called "boyfriend."

Riggle got with his investigators and it was decided they needed to locate Mr. Mayo. Had Joe and Cherry gotten into a fight? Had he seen Cherry this past weekend or on Friday night? Had he been over to her apartment recently? Could he account for his whereabouts on Friday?

Joe Mayo had a bit of explaining to do, if only because he was the one viable suspect thus far with even a smidgen of a motive. In addition, the stats were not on Joe Mayo's side. One of every three female murder victims in the United States is murdered by her spouse, boyfriend, ex-boyfriend or ex-spouse. What is even more shocking is that three women a day are murdered by the same group.

It didn't take long to track down Joe's house by running his name through the system. His vehicle license plate number popped up.

Joe was tall and lanky. He was about six inches taller than Cherry. In the photo Riggle had shown Marcie, Joe wore a ball cap (backward), a football jersey (several sizes too big) and a gold chain around his neck, with a medallion hanging from it. He hugged Cherry, who was, in the same photo, smiling, wearing a white sweater. Cherry was pretty; she had long, dark hair, past her shoulders, and round cheeks that accentuated her girl-next-door charm. Joe made a duck face in the photo and the two seemed like they were hamming it up for the photographer.

Joe Mayo fancied himself an entertainer, a singer, and had been, he later testified, "since I was three years old." He'd auditioned for *American Idol* and *The X Factor.* Near the time when he dated Cherry, he'd performed at places like Carreta's and the Highway 155, small restaurant/clubs in and around Tyler that offered open mic and karaoke. Generally, he'd go in on those nights, though Joe thought putting it that way was an insult to his talent. He hated when someone mentioned that he "sang karaoke" or did "open mic." Besides singing, Joe did impressions of celebrities.

The SCSO didn't know it then, but Joe and Cherry had known each other since 1997, when they met at a local Goodwill center, where they both had worked. It was part of what Joe later referred to as an "O.I.T. program" (Opportunities in Tyler) for people with disabilities. Joe said he loved Cherry.

"She was a very special person to me, *very* special," he stressed.

He'd take her to the movies, out to eat, regular date nights. One of Cherry's favorite cuisines, he said, a "weakness" Joe Mayo also admitted, was Mexican. With those types of restaurants being in abundance in Texas, he liked to treat Cherry to it whenever he could afford to do so.

Joe had even sung at Cherry's church and attended services there regularly for a while, he later claimed. He adored singing for Cherry and the rest of the congregation, saying, "Oh, it was amazing." He'd play the guitar up on the altar with other musicians backing him up. He'd sing an "original song . . . and people got saved," Joe testified. "I mean, that's the power of the Lord. He's amazing!"

If there was one source of entertainment Joe and Cherry liked more than any other (especially Cherry), it was movies. *Paranormal Activity* had scared Joe so much, he said, "I actually thought it was real . . . especially when the Ouija board caught on fire. . . . I had never seen anything like that before."

According to Joe, Cherry's favorite movie was *Saw.* The clown in the film had scared Joe "half to death," he said, so he told Cherry he was not watching the sequels with her. But Cherry seemed unaffected by these types of movies, regardless of how scary or gory they were—and in that regard, it seemed, more was always better as Cherry saw it.

* * *

SCSO detective James Riggle put a cop on Joe's house. He first needed to secure a search warrant for where Joe lived, before they went in. Joe might come across as charming and kind and scared of horror movies, but that did not mean he and Cherry got along. In fact, one report claimed Cherry was upset with Joe for some reason and that they had not seen each other for well over a month.

Riggle and his colleagues knew that sometimes a case just came together: A lead developed; you secured a warrant; you shined a light in the person of interest's face; he gave it up. As a cop you go to bed that night knowing one less scumbag is off the street, one more murder victim's family now has at least part of the answer.

The next twenty-four hours would tell that side of the tale for the SCSO—and if Joe Mayo had anything to do with Cherry Walker's disappearance.

8

DETECTIVE JAMES RIGGLE CALLED PAULA
Wheeler on Sunday evening. As Rueon Walker had
explained, Wheeler was Cherry's eyes, ears, wheels,
teacher, friend, mentor and caseworker, the one person
Cherry depended on daily. The one aspect of living on
her own that Wheeler recently had been working with
Cherry on was her spending. Cherry did not, as Rueon
had told the SCSO, have a good concept of counting
money, or what things cost in relation to her budget.
She would go to the store and buy "eight, ten, twelve"
bottles of Pine-Sol, for example—with a closet full of
the stuff already.

"She didn't understand that she didn't have to have
eight [bottles] of Pine-Sol," said a source. "Every time
she went to the store, she wanted Pine-Sol."

One time, Wheeler brought Cherry to Walmart.
Her bill rang up to nearly $300—all cleaning supplies.
Standing inside Wheeler's house one afternoon, the
first time the caseworker had invited Cherry over,
Cherry took a look at the walls and said, "Girl, you
need to clean this house." It was Cherry's way: She said

what she felt. There was no barrier between what she thought and said.

"I want to stop at Whataburger," Cherry told Wheeler not long before she went missing.

"Why?" Wheeler asked. It seemed random and a last-minute decision. They were almost at Cherry's apartment.

"It's my favorite thing," Cherry answered.

"You're going to have to save your money," Wheeler explained.

Cherry lived on a fixed government income and welfare benefits. It was something Wheeler was working on getting Cherry to understand.

"She didn't have much," said a source, "but I'll tell you what . . . she loved to get her hair done."

Something else Cherry was fond of had been a cute monkey toy that crashed cymbals in front of itself and played music.

Cherry never had enough money to buy the monkey, so Paula Wheeler would take her to the store and Cherry would play with the toy there.

Cherry had often purchased food and clothes for other people, Wheeler recalled. Cherry cared deeply and passionately about human beings. She especially cared about Timmy (pseudonym), the boy Marcie Fulton had watched until he became too much for her to handle. Cherry would babysit the four-year-old several times during the week and sometimes on weekends. It seemed odd that a woman with Cherry's disabilities, who herself needed a caretaker, would be hired to babysit a young child. However, the woman she worked for, Kim, apparently believed Cherry was capable.

One day when Kim was slated to pick Timmy up,

Wheeler happened to be there with Cherry. The boy was, in fact, sitting in Wheeler's car. Kim was late. They waited and waited. Finally she showed up, giving both a story and an apology.

After that, Wheeler regularly asked Cherry about Timmy. There were times, Cherry told her caseworker, when the boy would have to stay overnight at her apartment because the mother failed to show up at all (or call). Kim was hardly ever on time for the scheduled pickups. She never sent the boy over with food, and Cherry was concerned about his clothing being worn and dirty. She fed the boy and bought him things. Cherry believed Timmy was not being taken care of properly by his mother—a reason why Cherry wanted to watch the boy as often as she could.

"She would feed him," Wheeler said. "She would give him baths. . . . They played puzzles together. They played with little toys. She would sit on the floor [with Timmy] and they would play."

Like two little kids.

Wheeler noticed that whenever Cherry "got really nervous," she would shake. The anxiety she experienced turned visible and obvious, manifesting into her becoming, as the old-school term went, a "nervous wreck." It happened around people who raised their voice or scolded Cherry in any way. Her head and body would shake. She would sit and stare straight ahead until the anxiety passed.

Cherry loved to iron clothes. At the Laundromat she'd take all of her clean laundry out of the dryer and stuff it into a bag.

"You know, if you hang your clothes up, you won't have to iron them," Wheeler would tell her.

"Don't worry about it," Cherry would say. "I'm going to iron them, anyway."

Cherry would clean her bathroom before a visitor to her apartment said they needed to use it—and then right after they were done.

As Paula Wheeler and Detective Riggle spoke about Cherry, the detective learned how compassionate and thoughtful Cherry Walker was, despite some social issues Wheeler was working on with her. Then an interesting piece of information emerged. Wheeler said something about a subpoena.

"What subpoena?" Riggle asked.

Wheeler explained that it happened on that Friday morning. Just a few days ago—the last day anyone had seen Cherry. She and Cherry were out shopping. A man showed up in the parking lot after they walked out from a store. He approached them.

"Are you Cherry Walker, ma'am?" the officer asked Wheeler.

"No, I'm her caregiver," she said.

After sorting out who was who, the man handed Cherry the subpoena. Cherry had no idea what it was.

Wheeler took it and read it. Then she explained to Cherry what a subpoena was, before reading aloud. "Cherry, it says, 'This subpoena is issued at the instance of the Department of Family and Protective Services. . . .'" Cherry was being served with a subpoena to testify in a family court matter on the following Wednesday.

Apparently, Cherry wasn't the only one who thought Timmy was being mistreated by his mother. The father of the boy must have figured out that Cherry had been watching him, among a host of other factors that played into his taking Timmy's mother to court. The Department of Family and Protective Services (DFPS) was investigating Timmy's mom, Kim, and was asking Cherry to make herself available to testify in a family court about the question of Kim being competent enough to take care of the boy and if, in fact, Kim had abused the boy in any way.

Cherry still didn't understand what was being asked of her. Something about it made her feel icky. She didn't want to face it.

"If you don't testify," Wheeler explained to Cherry, "you're going to get a fine or get locked up."

"I have to call Kim," Cherry said.

Kim Cargill was a forty-three-year-old, three-time divorcée, mother of four kids (all boys, and all from different fathers). Born in Mississippi, Kim had moved to Texas after college. In her CV, Kim described herself as "self-motivated, reliable and organized." She lived in Whitehouse, on Waterton Circle, not far from Cherry's apartment. A licensed vocational nurse (LVN), Kim said she was "dedicated to the nursing profession." She had worked at several Texas hospitals, for the city of Dallas and at a few nursing homes, along with several other patient care facilities.

During that time when Cherry was watching Timmy for her, Kim had somehow held on to a youthful beauty: long and flowing dark-blond hair, deep blue eyes, clear skin and thin red lips. Kim spoke with intelligence when she needed and kept her family business to herself. She did not involve Cherry in most of what was going on, either by design or for privacy.

With Kim there always seemed to be a drama taking place with a lover or an ex-lover, one of her children or somebody at work. Generally, it was the same old domestic problems many estranged couples with kids find themselves involved in. Yes, it only hurts the kids. But Kim Cargill never got that. Or she didn't care. With this recent problem with the state, Kim realized she had the fight of her life ahead of her—a battle to keep her youngest son. (Her oldest had already been removed from the home many years before.) If she lost a second child, what about the other kids? It would open a Pandora's box of issues for her. Not to mention the fact that Kim would have to pay child support to two ex-spouses—something she claimed she could not afford and would never do.

Cherry had a conflicting appointment for that Wednesday, June 23, the same day she had been subpoenaed to testify. Wheeler asked the officer who served Cherry about that appointment and what Cherry could do with regard to the conflict.

"Tell her to cancel her appointment," the officer told Wheeler. The hearing was, of course, more important. Cherry needed to be in court or she would be held in contempt.

When the officer left, Cherry called Kim. Wheeler stood and listened to the call.

"Don't tell no one," Kim told Cherry. "Don't tell your daddy"—about the subpoena. Cherry related the conversation to Wheeler afterward.

"[She] says I don't have to go to the court, Paula," Cherry said.

Wheeler nodded her head. "Yes, Cherry—yes, you *do* have to go."

This was around 10:50 A.M. on that Friday before

Cherry went missing, Wheeler explained to Riggle as the two spoke over the phone on Sunday night. The subpoena had been delivered to Cherry at 10:18 A.M., records later proved, so the timeline given by Paula Wheeler, which would prove to be important in the days to come, turned out to be spot on.

"What else happened?" Riggle wanted to know. He was curious about the subpoena. This Kim person, whose kid Cherry had been watching. Had Kim seen Cherry? Had Kim dropped Cherry off somewhere? Had Cherry called Kim that night or on Saturday? Kim was someone the SCSO needed to interview right away.

"She handed me the phone," Wheeler said. Cherry was overcome with anxiety as she spoke to Kim and felt she couldn't continue, so the caregiver took the telephone from her.

"I didn't know what to think," Wheeler said, recalling what had transpired.

"Yes," Wheeler said into the phone. Cherry stood in front of her, looking on. She was becoming more anxious as each moment passed.

"What is your name?" Kim asked.

"This is Paula Wheeler," said the caregiver.

"She was very arrogant," Wheeler later remembered, describing the phone call in detail. Kim's nerves were surely fraying as she scrambled to come up with a way to keep her child. She probably just realized that having Cherry watch the boy was not the best decision she had ever made. Her former husband, fighting for custody, was going to use what he could—and that included the fact that a clinically diagnosed mentally retarded woman, regardless of how nice and kind she was, not to mention how gentle and pleasant she was to the child, had been watching Timmy. As soon as he found out, he and the court were going to use Cherry against Kim.

"They want to make Cherry go to court and they want to make her look bad," Kim said to Wheeler. Kim claimed to be worried about Cherry's welfare. She said the court was going to make Cherry out to be a freak and that it was going to devastate her. Being on the witness stand was not going to be good for Cherry's psychological well-being. "They want to make her come to court," Kim reiterated, "but she doesn't have to—she doesn't *have* to go to court!"

Kim was obviously upset. She asked that Cherry not show up to testify against her. Couldn't Cherry just do her that one favor?

Wheeler didn't know what to tell Kim. Cherry wasn't going to be held in contempt of court for not answering a subpoena, pay a fine or go to jail. Not for Kim. Not for anyone. That wasn't the right thing to do, nor was it the proper message to teach Cherry about responsibility.

"Look," Kim said. "Wednesday (June 23) is the last day of the trial—I can take Cherry to my house and hide her all day there."

Now Kim was asking Wheeler to sign off on Kim and Cherry committing a crime.

As Wheeler spoke to Kim, Cherry began to shake nervously in front of her, Wheeler explained to Detective Riggle. Cherry had a blank look on her face, staring straight ahead. Cherry was beyond terrified, likely getting the feeling that she was doing the wrong thing, maybe even betraying a friend—even though she did not understand what was happening. She sensed the situation was becoming unglued and she was in the middle. She didn't know what to do.

"Was that it?" Riggle asked.

The caseworker explained that she and Kim hung up, but Kim called right back.

"What did she want?" Riggle wondered.

Kim, Wheeler explained, went into a rant about Cherry not telling anyone that she had received the subpoena and how she didn't want Cherry to "show the paper" to anyone else. It was nobody's business but hers and Cherry's. They'd figure it out together, Kim said to Wheeler.

"Have you told anyone?" Kim asked the caregiver.

"Well, I need to tell my supervisor about it because I need to tell my supervisor about *everything* that goes on with Cherry. I'll also have to write it in my notes."

"You're some kind of friend!" Kim snapped, apparently trying to make Wheeler feel bad. "If you were a real friend to Cherry, you wouldn't take her [to the court date]."

"I have to tell my supervisor, ma'am. I have to report what goes on with Cherry. I have to let my case manager know everything."

Why wasn't Kim getting this? Was she that desperate? Didn't the court already know about Cherry? Or maybe not? Was this why they had subpoenaed Cherry in the first place, to learn more about who she was and what she knew?

"They're just going to try and make her look incompetent, and they're going to confuse and upset her," Kim repeated.

The aide explained that she had to do the right thing. She had to teach Cherry the correct way to handle life's challenges. The court would be sympathetic to Cherry and her mental issues; Kim need not worry about that.

"I can come and pick her up," Kim then suggested, sounding as though she'd had an epiphany. "She doesn't have to go to court."

Wheeler said once again that Cherry had to answer the subpoena.

As Cherry stood nearby, listening to the phone call, the aide could tell by looking at her that Cherry was becoming increasingly upset over the whole thing. She continued to shake and stare. Kim didn't have to worry about the court upsetting or confusing Cherry because it was already happening, Wheeler considered.

"Well, let me tell you," Kim lashed out, realizing she wasn't getting anywhere with the caseworker, "if they find out something's wrong with Cherry, they're going to . . . They're going to take my baby from me."

They hung up.

Riggle was interested in this conversation, not to mention the subpoena.

There was more, Wheeler said.

"More?" Riggle asked.

Much more.

9

AFTER KIM CARGILL AND PAULA Wheeler hung up, the caseworker consoled Cherry, who was torn up over the idea of not being able to make everyone happy, while at the same time unsure about what she had done wrong. The confusion. The stress. The unsettling feeling of disappointing people. Cherry sensed that Kim, Timmy's mom, was mad at her, but she didn't fully comprehend what had just happened.

"It's going to be okay," Wheeler reassured her.

"I don't want to go."

"Go where?"

Cherry meant court. "I'm nervous," she added.

Standing inside Cherry's apartment, Wheeler realized this was the first time Cherry had verbalized being nervous. She'd never come out and said it before— at least not to Wheeler. The caregiver could see that Cherry was suffering anxiety because of the way she acted, but now Cherry was telling Wheeler how she felt. Was it a good sign? Had Cherry crossed a threshold? Was she beginning to understand her feelings?

Wheeler explained to Cherry that they needed to take a drive downtown to the Community Access offices to report what was going on, make copies of the subpoena for Cherry's file, and perhaps speak with Wheeler's supervisor regarding any next steps. There was no way Wheeler could just leave Cherry in the state she was experiencing. Cherry needed to understand the importance of what was going on in her life; she was obligated to show up in court and tell the truth.

Wheeler went to see her supervisor, Pertena Young, who also happened to be her sister. Community Access, which both sisters worked for, fell under the Adult Human Services banner of the Home & Community-Based Services of the state. Young knew of Cherry Walker and her case because, as Wheeler's supervisor, she would have to meet with Cherry once a month. Young had also taken it upon herself to help Cherry when she could, giving her rides, answering questions, consoling her. She adored Cherry. The one thing Young noticed about Cherry was how softly she spoke. Her voice had a dulcet quality, a nonconfrontational tone, innocent, perhaps needy.

Cherry was still shaken up. This was clear as she sat down with the two sisters inside the Community Access offices.

"Calm down, Cherry, it's going to be okay," Young explained. This had become a common way to address Cherry when she seemed nervous. "It's going to be all right." Sometimes this tactic worked, sometimes it didn't, Young later said. It all depended on how close Cherry was to the person trying to settle her down. If she knew and trusted you, Cherry generally took your advice.

Cherry had been on medication for what one law

enforcement official later described as "controlled" seizures. The episodes in which Cherry began to shake and appeared nervous were in no way associated with her seizures. A seizure was an entirely different matter.

In so many ways Cherry was "like a child," especially when she became upset and did not know what to do with a swell of emotion. The support of family, friends and professionals, like Paula Wheeler and Pertena Young, was essential to her maintaining a balance and settling down. Cherry needed caring people to stay focused on her goals and to live as normal a life as she could.

When Young had heard that Cherry was watching little Timmy, she had a sit-down with Cherry to talk about it. It was some months before Cherry went missing. Young had gone over to see Cherry one day and Timmy was there. Young was shocked. In fact, the supervisor had gone over to pick Cherry up for an appointment, but Timmy's mother was late again. As a result they had to bring the boy with them and Young had to watch Timmy while Cherry saw her doctor. Right after that, during one of their monthly meetings, Young told Cherry, "Can you have Kim . . . call me, please? I . . . need to speak with her."

"Sure," Cherry said. Community Access could not stop Cherry from watching the child, not as a disciplinary matter. They could suggest that Cherry not babysit, they could report what they knew to DFPS and the boy's father (if they chose), but in the end it was Cherry's decision. She lived on her own, and was an adult. She made her own choices.

A day after Young sat down with Cherry, Kim called.

"Hi," Young said, introducing herself. "I'm Cherry's case manager." Young was under the impression that perhaps she could speak with the mother and explain the situation. As adults they could come to an agreement that Cherry was probably not the best choice in a babysitter.

"Okay, *and* . . . ," Kim snapped.

"Well, I was told that Cherry keeps your son once in a while and I have some concerns about that."

"Concerns?" Kim cracked in a nasty tone.

"Cherry is MR." Young had used the clinical acronym because she had been told that Kim was a nurse. As an LVN Kim must have known that MR meant "mentally retarded" and that Cherry was in no position to be watching a four-year-old.

Young wanted Kim's last name, something Cherry could not give her. The case manager's plan was to get Kim's last name out of her on the phone and then call DFPS and "turn her in" for having a mentally challenged person babysit her child. It wasn't right. Young and Wheeler were dedicated to helping families and people in the community; neither could sit by and do nothing with regard to Timmy. Not to mention how emotionally disastrous to Cherry the situation could be if something ever happened to the boy while in her custody. It would set her back, possibly even destroy all of her progress.

"That's what I was going to do," Young explained later. "Turn her in."

"One of Cherry's case managers I spoke to," Young further told Kim, "does not want Cherry watching the child. It's not good for her and it's not good for [Timmy]," Young said. Why wasn't Kim understanding such a simple issue?

They went back and forth, Young trying to get Kim to give up her last name, which she was not willing to do. At one point Young said, "Look, I am going to turn you in to the [state]."

"Well, you do whatever you need to do," Kim said, then in an ominous tone, "I have friends down at the DA's office."

"Are you threatening me?" Young wanted to know. It sure sounded like it. "Because I don't threaten very easy."

Intimidating pushback was nothing new to Young. In her role as manager of her department at Community Access, she'd heard people say similar things: *"I know this person. I know that person. I'll make a call, and you'll lose your job."* It did not faze her one bit. She had a job to do. Baseless, idle threats would not deter Young from always doing the right thing. "She was kind of making . . . like I was going to be afraid of her," Young recalled. "Like she could make me *do* something . . ."

Not a chance.

Pertena Young made it clear she wasn't standing for it. She knew what to do.

"So I hung up in her face," she later explained in court.

On that Friday, June 18, after Cherry Walker and Paula Wheeler spoke with Kim, and Wheeler brought Cherry down to the office to photocopy the subpoena papers, they sat down with Young. Cherry had a beauty shop appointment scheduled for that early afternoon (the one from which her father, Gethry, would later pick her up). Cherry never wanted to miss one of her beauty appointments. She liked getting her hair done. It was important to her.

"She loved looking good," Wheeler remembered.

It took some time, but they were able to calm Cherry down. Young put in a call to the office number on the subpoena and spoke with someone there at the office, letting the woman know that Cherry was considered MR. It appeared the office in charge of handling the case had no idea of the extent to which Cherry had a learning disability, or even that she had one at all.

Cherry made it to her hair appointment at one o'clock. Wheeler dropped her off—or, rather, tried to. As it turned out, Cherry had some trepidation about going into the salon on this day, which in itself seemed strange to Wheeler.

After pulling into the parking lot of the salon, Cherry said she didn't want to get out of the car.

"Cherry, what's wrong?" Wheeler asked.

She had pulled the car under a shade tree so they could talk. They sat with the vehicle turned off. They were early, but as it got nearer to one o'clock, Wheeler said, "Cherry, you have to get out now. You have to go to your appointment." Keeping Cherry on schedule was important to her progress. Wheeler couldn't understand Cherry's misgivings about going into the salon, because she had always adored this appointment. This was one time Cherry could relax with no pressure, no one asking her uncomfortable questions.

"Okay," Cherry said. She opened the door and began to get out of the car. She was still shaky, just not as much as she had been most of that day. She hesitated. "But I want to stay with you, Paula."

It was as if Cherry knew she was never going to see her caseworker again.

"I know you do," Wheeler said. "But you need to go inside now. Listen, you call me when you get home, okay?"

Paula Wheeler said good-bye to Cherry, watched her walk into the salon, and then drove away.

Gethry Walker picked Cherry up that afternoon when her hair appointment was over. He drove her home to her apartment. They discussed the following day, a Saturday. Pizza, maybe. Church's Chicken, perhaps. Cherry and Gethry didn't need to say it, but they would talk tomorrow, maybe meet up for lunch or dinner at one of those places. Gethry told his daughter he loved her and he'd see her on Sunday morning at church service.

By 7:00 P.M., or thereabouts, Cherry Walker was back inside her apartment. She seemed to be calm and recovered from all that had happened earlier. An hour later, just before eight o'clock, on Friday, June 18, the last day anyone saw or spoke to Cherry Walker, she was at home. Alone. Cherry had told nobody about any plans to go out or leave her apartment. As far as anyone knew, Cherry was in for the night.

"How do you know that?" Detective Riggle asked Wheeler as he interviewed her. How could she know that Cherry was home at 8:00 P.M. on Friday and not planning to go anywhere? A victim's timeline for the last day of her life was gold. You get a timeline on a victim, and you can question witnesses and suspects with authority to determine who is hiding (or holding) information and who is not. Although Paula Wheeler worked for the state and was, by all accounts, a person who cared for others, she also needed to explain her whereabouts and how she knew Cherry was at home on Friday evening. Had Wheeler gone over to visit Cherry that night?

"She called me about eight o'clock [on Friday]," Wheeler told Riggle.

And, boy, did Cherry Walker have something important to tell Paula Wheeler.

10

ONE COULD ARGUE THAT JOE Mayo was part of a healthy support system Cherry Walker depended on to make her life as fulfilling as it could be. Joe adored Cherry. They had been friends for almost fourteen years, according to Joe. Although he had not been seeing Cherry as often as he had in the past, they still talked on the phone and went out to eat once in a while. They remained friends.

By 3:30 A.M. on June 21, early Monday morning, still without a warrant for Joe's house, investigators from the SCSO decided to "regroup," as Detective James Riggle explained in his report of the night, and would rendezvous the following morning at eight o'clock, after securing the necessary paperwork to have a look around Joe's house and speak with him.

Paula Wheeler was providing a litany of facts for Riggle and his investigative team, giving them a clear indication of Cherry's comings and goings.

"She called before eight P.M.," Wheeler explained to Riggle. Cherry phoned, as she had promised, to tell her that her father had driven her home from the salon. It was near four o'clock in the afternoon on Friday when Cherry had first called Wheeler.

"My daddy brought me home," Cherry told her.

"She was so excited that her daddy had brought her home," Wheeler recalled.

It seemed that the day's events had been forgotten and Cherry was getting back to her old self. The simple things in life, those routine occurrences throughout most people's days that felt mundane, were high points for Cherry. She appreciated the interaction with family and friends. Calling her aide to explain that her father had driven her home brought Cherry comfort.

"Right before eight P.M.," Wheeler explained to Riggle further, "she called me again." Cherry was different this time. Not the same relaxed, happy woman who had been phoning earlier. Something had happened between the two calls.

"What was that?" Riggle asked.

Wheeler explained.

"I'm nervous . . . ," Cherry had said.

"Why, what's wrong, Cherry?"

Cherry expressed how upset she was, adding, "Kim called me."

"What did she want?"

"She said she's coming over to take me out to eat. . . ."

"When?"

"Tonight . . . tonight," Cherry said. Her anxiety grew as they spoke. Wheeler needed to keep Cherry talking, keep her calm by allowing her to explain herself, while making her understand that it was going to be okay. Everything would work out. Cherry just needed to relax, take deep breaths.

"Don't go," the caseworker said. "You take your

medicine . . . and you do her like you do me. Don't answer the phone. Don't answer the door. You take your medicine and you go to bed. You understand, Cherry?"

Cherry said yes.

"And, oh yeah . . . Miss Paula . . . she said something else, too."

"What else did Kim tell you, Cherry?"

"She said she would pay me a lot of money to come over and clean her house."

Wheeler worried about this because she knew that "Cherry had the mind of a child and could be easily misled" and manipulated by an emotionally stronger person. Cleaning and eating were two of Cherry's favorite things—Kim knew this. Was Kim trying to use two of Cherry's passions to control her?

"I don't want to go out with Kim, Miss Paula," Cherry said.

"You do not *have* to, Cherry. Do what I told you. Don't answer the door or the telephone."

Cherry mentioned that she didn't feel good. "I'm nervous."

"It's going to be okay, Cherry."

"I just ate my dinner," Cherry said.

The situation bothered Wheeler. "Cherry loved to eat," she said. Everyone knew that. So when she said she didn't want to go out with Kim to eat that night, that she was nervous and wanted to stay home, Wheeler knew Cherry was serious.

As the aide explained that last conversation with Cherry to James Riggle, she expressed how concerned she grew after phoning Cherry later that night, the next day (several times) and all day Sunday, but not getting any response.

Riggle asked if he could get a copy of Cherry's file—including the subpoena—from Community Access. Wheeler said she'd check with her supervisor, but didn't see why not.

Detective Riggle now considered Kim Cargill a strong "person of interest," since she had been one of the last people to have spoken (or maybe even seen) Cherry Walker.

Still, could Kim, a petite woman (at five-three) compared to Cherry's size, commit the crime, hoist Cherry's body into her vehicle and then dump her out on the CR 2191?

It didn't seem possible.

11

DETECTIVE JAMES RIGGLE WAS INFORMED that the search warrant for Joe Mayo's 2000 Buick Century and place of residence had come in, and several detectives and uniformed officers were in the process of serving the warrant.

Riggle headed over to interview Joe himself.

By now—early morning, Monday, June 21, 2010—Cherry had been positively identified. There was no more wondering for the Walkers: Their child was dead, likely murdered. Her body had been set on fire, postmortem, according to the ME. If there was a silver lining within the evidence they had uncovered thus far, it was that a mentally retarded woman had not been set on fire while alive.

Joe lived with two friends. He said, "Yes, I borrowed a DVD"—not a CD—"from Cherry and she called me about bringing it back. It took me a month or so to return it." Cherry had called Joe, over and over, asking for her copy of *Paranormal Activity*. "She blew up my phone," he recalled.

Joe told Cherry he had been busy. He was responsible

for taking care of his eighty-five-year-old grandmother and equally old grandfather. The grandfather was on oxygen, struggling with emphysema. The grandmother had fallen. Joe said he had his hands full and he'd get her the DVD when he had a chance. Cherry could be relentless, Joe seemed to suggest. Within the past month, Joe explained, he had seen Cherry only once. It wasn't as if they were going out every weekend, hanging out every night. They had been good friends. Joe took Cherry out to eat once in a while.

That was it.

As they spoke, other investigators talked to Joe's roommates, a friend of Joe's and the friend's girlfriend. Joe had given an alibi that these two could back up or shoot down. The SCSO was looking for someone who had a window of opportunity—from 8:00 P.M. on Friday to just before 3:00 P.M. on that Saturday.

Joe talked about his car and how excited Cherry was that he had purchased the new vehicle some months back.

"This is nice," Cherry said while sitting in it one day with him. "It's better than that piece of crap you had before."

You could always depend on Cherry to be honest and tell you *exactly* how she felt.

The car he owned before that, Joe explained, was a clunker. He'd taken Cherry out one night. They broke down. "This thing, you cannot take us *anywhere* in it," Cherry complained. They were on the side of the roadway. "Really?" Joe had said aloud to himself; he couldn't believe the car had broken down while on a date. Cherry went on, "You mean, I am going to have to sit here . . . because [the] car broke down, and you ain't got no jumper cables to help us!" Joe thought about it later, the memory a bit funnier now in hindsight, and had wondered to himself that night: *Could this be more awkward than anything?* He recalled this event because it was the night he had returned Cherry's DVD of *Paranormal Activity,* which the SCSO knew was sitting beside Cherry's television.

Riggle asked Joe to talk about that previous Friday, June 18, where he was, what he had done that day, if he had seen or spoken to Cherry.

"A friend came into town," Joe said. "It was like three o'clock in the afternoon. . . . Later that day," Joe added, he had to go and pick up his roommate's girlfriend from work. It was around five o'clock. His other roommate, the girl's boyfriend, got out of work at nine that same night, returned home, and Joe said he was there with his friend and the girl at the apartment. Joe was heading out to go sing. Later, when asked about this, he became perturbed when the question insinuated that he was merely heading out for a night of "doing karaoke" at a local bar, not necessarily fulfilling an obligation to perform. Joe considered himself an entertainer. He wasn't some hack who showed up at the local bars to belt out familiar tunes after a few beers, messing up the lyrics and singing out of key.

All four went to the local Carreta's and Joe sang that night. He had not spoken to Cherry, he insisted.

His roommates backed up his alibi when they spoke to Riggle's colleagues.

Riggle asked about Cherry. Joe said he could talk about Cherry all day long. She was a lovely human being, one of those people who could bring joy to others.

"She liked to clean?" Riggle asked.

"Oh, my gosh," Joe answered. "She was a neat freak. I mean, you could not go into her apartment without it being just absolutely spotless. If I left a glass on the table, she'd say, 'Uh-uh! You know what to do. You better put that in that dishwasher, boy.' And I'm like, 'Yes, ma'am, I will.'"

Years later, as Joe Mayo talked about Cherry, he became overcome by emotion. It was hard to talk about her in the past tense. She was such a sweet person, so generous and forgiving, someone who touched your soul. He recalled that Cherry would sometimes come out to see him sing. Seeing her there in the audience had always given him courage and confidence.

"I need to tell you something, Joseph," Cherry said one night. They were alone. Cherry had watched Joe sing earlier that night. "Joseph, I am so very proud of you for doing . . . for pursuing your dream." Joe Mayo had appreciated this so much: "After all the people in my family telling me, 'You're not good enough. Your daddy didn't make it, so what makes you think *you* are going to make it,' I mean . . . she *believed* in me."

The SCSO would still have to tear into Joe's life, search through his vehicle and ask some uncomfortable questions, but Detective Riggle could tell: Joe Mayo had no more killed Cherry Walker than he had won *American Idol*.

The SCSO confiscated Joe Mayo's Buick; they needed to run it through forensics. Policy and procedure dictated protocol in this situation.

"We'll need your cell phone, too," Riggle said.

Joe had consented to the search of his residence and his car. He put up no resistance. He had nothing to hide, he said. In the back of his mind, however, as cops went through his things, took his cell phone and prepared his car for towing to the forensic lab, Joe didn't feel he had any choice in the matter.

"Well, if you don't do that, you're going to jail—you're going to be handcuffed," Joe later said he had thought as he spoke to Riggle and realized he was a suspect in Cherry's murder—a fact the SCSO had not yet related to him. Nobody had ever said, *"Cherry was murdered and we need to speak with you about it."*

Joe would have been relieved to know that after Riggle had spoken to him at length, and his colleagues had interviewed his roommates, Riggle wrote in his report, *We were able to exclude Joseph Mayo as a suspect in the death of Cherry Walker.*

There was one other person on the SCSO's list they needed to speak with, a woman who had some hard questions to answer.

Kim Cargill.

12

LATE MONDAY MORNING, JAMES RIGGLE went through Paula Wheeler's file on Cherry Walker, while other members of the SCSO's investigative team devised a plan to track down and speak with Kim Cargill. Autopsy results were still pending. Who knew if the ME would determine homicide as a manner of death?

Paula Wheeler had kept meticulous records of her visits to see Cherry, including those times when Cherry had babysat Timmy and when Cherry had interacted, from Wheeler's perspective, with Kim Cargill.

Wheeler's first notation of seeing Timmy at Cherry's went as far back as November and December 2009. On December 14, she ran into Timmy at Cherry's apartment. Cherry had moved in several weeks before. The following morning, December 15, Wheeler went back to pick Cherry up for an appointment and saw Timmy there again. She found out he'd never left.

"She was getting ready to fix his breakfast," Wheeler later explained.

Timmy had spent the night. As the caseworker would

soon learn, this was not unusual. Timmy had been spending many nights at Cherry's.

The following morning Wheeler arrived to take Cherry out shopping and to a few appointments. When she walked in, there was Timmy, sitting on the floor in the living room, watching cartoons. Timmy had been at Cherry's for three days.

"I need to go out to the store," Cherry said. The implication was that she'd had Timmy too long. Cherry said she had a difficult time getting hold of Kim.

Wheeler told Cherry it was not a good idea to take Timmy with them to the store. They could wait and go shopping another day. As for Cherry's appointments, she'd have to reschedule.

The next morning Wheeler showed up at her usual time—between eight-thirty and nine. There was Timmy, once again, parked in front of the television, watching cartoons as Cherry made him breakfast in her little efficiency kitchen.

Four days in a row. No Kim.

"I need to do laundry," Cherry said. It was piling up.

"We can't take [Timmy] with us, Cherry," Wheeler explained again.

The next time the aide saw Timmy at Cherry's was December 21, a few days later.

"He was in bed," having slept over *again*. It was unclear if Kim had ever come to pick Timmy up since December 14, when Wheeler had first seen him. "Cherry was ironing his clothes." The two of them were like brother and sister.

Timmy was there the following day, December 22. Wheeler noticed Cherry was "upset" because of a conversation she'd recently had with Kim, not going into detail about what had been said.

"She was a little shaky . . . ," Wheeler reported.

On December 23, two days before Christmas, Wheeler arrived to find Timmy and Cherry at the table, eating breakfast together. It seemed by now that Cherry had taken care of Timmy for half the month of December.

As James Riggle read through the file on Cherry Walker, he could see that Kim Cargill was not going to win any Parent of the Year awards. But did her behavior point to a motive to want to kill Cherry and savagely burn her body? If anything, Kim should have put Cherry up on a pedestal. Moreover, it seemed that Kim depended on Cherry. She needed her.

On the morning of Christmas Eve, Wheeler walked in to see Timmy and Cherry again eating breakfast together at Cherry's small table in front of her bed. The boy loved to eat with Cherry. Kim had still not come by to pick up her son, or see him, or even call to check in on him.

"I'm giving him water," Cherry told her caseworker. It seemed like an odd statement. But as Wheeler later explained, "[Cherry] said his mom didn't bring him any food." Because of that, Cherry felt the need to explain that she was not only feeding the child, but also was providing him with fresh water.

One had to wonder: Could a mother be any more neglectful? Wheeler and Cherry only knew the half of it.

December was not the only time Wheeler reported seeing Timmy with Cherry for an extended period of time. It seemed that whenever Kim dropped the child off, she would not pick him up until days later. He was always hungry when he arrived; he wore dirty clothes and appeared to be upset. He never came with extra clothes, toothbrush or anything for an overnight stay. Cherry would feed him instant oatmeal and box cereal. The kid would scarf it up as though he had been starving.

One morning Wheeler showed up and found Timmy eating his oatmeal while Cherry was sitting nearby playing with one of her dolls on the floor. It was as though two children had been left by themselves. When Timmy finished his breakfast, he picked up one of his toy cars and joined Cherry on the floor. The caseworker watched them play together as though they'd met on a playground.

It became a regular occurrence, once every few weeks or sometimes in the span of a few days, for Wheeler to stop by to pick Cherry up and see that Timmy had spent the night.

The first time Wheeler met Kim was when the aide had shown up to take Cherry for a doctor's appointment. Cherry was fixing bacon and eggs for her and the boy. Kim arrived to fetch Timmy, and Wheeler said hello. Kim looked at her, snatched her child and left. She must have known the outsider had posed a threat to her situation.

"Can I have something to eat?" Timmy asked Cherry one night when Wheeler was there. He had just arrived.

"His mom should have fed him," Cherry told Wheeler. Cherry was upset that Kim wasn't feeding the child. It was something Cherry said she dealt with constantly.

January and February 2010 came and Wheeler routinely ran into Timmy at Cherry's apartment. Cherry was always feeding him, cleaning and ironing his clothes. She played with her toys as the boy played with his. She bathed him. When he was sick, Cherry nursed him.

By late February, Wheeler decided it was time to speak with one of Cherry's doctors and tell him that Cherry was taking just about complete care of the child.

Cherry Walker was in no position—emotionally or otherwise—to take care of a child. She had a hard enough time taking care of herself.

The doctor spoke to Cherry about watching Timmy. It wasn't healthy for her, he explained. Nor was it the right thing for the boy. Cherry didn't need any extra stress in her life. There had been times when Kim dropped Timmy off and the child was ill, with a runny nose, cough and fever. Cherry didn't need to be watching someone's sick child. She had enough to deal with on her own. Cherry had several quirks that some of Timmy's behavior aggravated. If Timmy took a bath, for example, Cherry would make the boy stay inside the tub until all the water drained and then he would have to be completely dry before stepping on her floor because Cherry did not want one drop of water to land on the floor of her bathroom.

But well into March and April, Cherry was still watching Kim's child. She did not know how to say no and Kim was very schooled by then in the art of manipulating and controlling Cherry.

It became a common sight for Wheeler to show up and see Cherry ironing Timmy's clothes, with Timmy standing by her side, saying, "I'm hungry. . . . Can I have something to eat?"

Another good example of why Cherry was not equipped to watch Timmy was Cherry's choice in films to watch with him. More than any other type of film, Cherry favored scary movies, the hard-core stuff, such as her all-time favorites, *Saw* and *Hostel*. Some other titles she owned and liked to watch, over and over: *Dark Floors, Alive or Dead, Séance, Rancid, Panic Room, Guys Gone Wild, Table Dance* and so on. There was not one in the bunch that would have been appropriate for a four-year-old. A boy Timmy's age did not need to see this type of violence and bloodshed, rape and murder, sex and nudity. He could not discern fact from fiction, real from fake. The images would embed themselves into his developing psyche, which at that age was eager to absorb all that was around him. Watching these movies could have a detrimental, negative effect on the boy later in life. Cherry did not realize any of this, and Wheeler would find them on the couch or floor, watching some unsuitable movie together.

Timmy's stays with Cherry ended in late March, according to Wheeler's later testimony and notes. Just like that, he stopped coming, and Cherry did not hear from Kim for several weeks. There was an indication that Kim had an episode of some sort with one of her other children—which ultimately led to the court date in which she was fighting for custody—and Cherry might have heard about this from Timmy.

Wheeler showed up one morning in mid-May. Cherry "seemed" happier than usual. The aide asked Cherry what was going on. Why the bouncy mood and the big smile on her face?

"Timmy's coming over today," Cherry answered. She had missed him. She was excited.

That one visit sparked a new wave. A week later,

Timmy was back—and staying over. Cherry was iron-ing his clothes, feeding him, bathing him. Kim was disappearing without word of where she had gone, or for how long. She failed to call when she said she would. She didn't show up on the days or times she had promised.

Little did Cherry know how serious it was. However, there was a second narrative playing out on Kim's end that Wheeler soon became aware of. At first, Cherry had not shared any of it. But then she broke down one day and explained.

On May 20, 2010, when Kim dropped Timmy off, she told Cherry, "You do not open the door for anyone that knocks, you understand me, Cherry?"

"Yes," Cherry promised.

"There's a bad man who lives in this apartment complex," Kim explained, as though talking to one of her own kids.

Kim said this bad man was out to get Timmy and Cherry. She scared Cherry into submission.

"Yes, Kim," Cherry said.

"And, most important, Cherry, do not open the door for the police, okay?"

Cherry said she understood.

It was easy, later on, to see that Kim had played off Cherry's horror film fixation, using the term "bad man," as if Cherry had somehow gotten mixed up in the plot of one of the movies she liked so much.

Detective James Riggle and Paula Wheeler did not yet know several secrets Kim Cargill was keeping from Cherry and, by mere involvement, Wheeler.

Kim Cargill did not even have custody of Timmy when she had been dropping him off at Cherry's.

DFPS had stepped in back during that period when Kim stopped bringing Timmy to Cherry's. On May 20, Kim had picked Timmy up at day care, violating a DFPS agreement, and was hiding the boy at Cherry's—without Cherry having any idea what she was getting herself wrapped up in. Kim knew that she could easily manipulate and use Cherry, and that was what she did. Kim's reason for not wanting Cherry to testify in the family court matter wasn't based on Cherry being mentally handicapped and ill-equipped to watch the boy. She knew Cherry's testimony would focus on all the dates Timmy had stayed over her apartment, proving that Kim had been, in effect, kidnapping her own child.

Additionally, there was a relationship between Kim and Cherry that went deeper than Cherry babysitting Kim's son. Cherry explained to Wheeler, alluding to that "bad man" comment Kim had made.

On June 3, 2010, two weeks before Cherry went missing, Wheeler arrived to find Timmy watching cartoons, Cherry ironing his clothes. Nothing had changed.

It had to stop, Wheeler knew. As Cherry's caretaker, she went to her supervisor and reported everything.

Detective Riggle knew after learning all of this that he needed to look deeply into the relationship between Kim Cargill and Cherry Walker. Was there a motive for murder there? Perhaps all that Cherry knew about Kim and could testify to was enough to make Kim capable of murder. But the SCSO was a long way from serving an arrest warrant up with Kim Cargill's name on it. After all, the medical examiner had not even weighed in yet regarding whether Cherry had been murdered or had died of natural causes. The fact that someone had lit her corpse on fire did not mean she had been murdered. That one fact alone could be an investigatory black hole. If the SCSO fell into it without evidence to support its claims, it could destroy a future case against any suspect they hauled in.

13

DR. MEREDITH LANN WAS IN charge of determining how Cherry Walker died. A graduate of the University of Texas at Austin, Dr. Lann completed her graduate work at the Southwestern Institute of Forensic Sciences (SWIFS). This was the same facility where she now conducted as many as five to seven autopsies per day with colleagues in Smith County's crack team of medical examiners. Board certified, Dr. Lann was qualified in clinical pathology and forensic pathology.

Studying Cherry Walker's charred, burned and blistered body to make a determination of manner and cause of death was going to be a difficult job. Medical examiners such as Dr. Lann, however, were highly trained in this arena. Where manner of death was concerned, Dr. Lann had five choices: natural, suicide, accidental, undetermined and homicide.

"Cause of death," Lann later explained, "specifically is a physiologic abnormality, something that sets into motion a series of events, which eventually terminates in the death of a person, without any intervening factors."

Manner and cause of death can be obvious: a gunshot wound to the head, a knife to the heart, a jump from a building. Or it can be a long process of connecting the medical and investigatory dots to draw an educated conclusion backed up by science and interviews with witnesses. Many times medical examiners will rely not only on their findings during autopsy, but on police reports, suspect and witness statements, along with what the overall picture—all of the information collected—showed. SWIFS had its own team of medical examiner investigators that helped with those hard-to-figure-out cases. In some deaths it, indeed, took a village.

In her office, before receiving Cherry's body inside the morgue, Lann reviewed Cherry's chart and file, learning everything she could about how Cherry had been found, where, by whom, the conditions and elements, the evidence collected at the scene and so on. It gave her a solid primer for what she would see in the autopsy suite. Well versed, she entered the suite and began her work under the slow hum and heat of the overhead fluorescent lights. As she conducted an initial, cursory inspection of Cherry Walker's body, a less frequently used phrase came to mind: *"Mechanism of death."* This clinical way of explaining the means by which a person had expired became important almost immediately.

"'Mechanism' is a little bit more medical," Lann said. It is a term that "we use as doctors" essentially describing "how a person died." Fundamentally, "mechanism of death" is a "variable" on cause of death. "For example, 'exsanguination,'" Lann added, using an uncommon word that means "loss of blood," much as "asphyxia" means "loss of oxygen to the tissues, the vital organs."

"There are other mechanisms [that] create a broad picture of how that person died, like a gunshot wound being a cause of death usually leads to exsanguination."

Unzipping the body bag Cherry Walker had been delivered in, Lann noted a red tag tied to her toe, which meant she had not been "officially" identified as of yet. Lann and her assistant took photos of Cherry's body as it lay on the table, being sure to document every step along the path to finding out what had happened to her. This part of the receiving procedure is a good opportunity to look for hairs, trace evidence or other debris, carpet fibers and anything else that might be a candidate for future forensic testing.

With the bag open the intense smell of burned flesh became overpowering.

Lann carefully cut off Cherry's clothing—or what was left of it from the fire. Her skin was split open in some sections and Lann described those injuries as "thermal burns"—which look a lot like a hot dog on a grill, the skin tightening up and tearing open. As the surface of the skin burns, the skin desiccates (dries out); because of that, it stretches and splits. It was so prevalent on some sections of Cherry's body, the splitting looked like slash marks, as if someone had cut Cherry open. At this stage of the investigation everything and anything was possible, so Lann had to rule those types of wounds in or out. After all, Cherry's body had been set afire for a reason—and that reason was to cover up something her killer did not want law enforcement to learn.

Upon further examination Lann could tell that the "slits" were surface wounds and there had been no hemorrhage or bleeding underneath, as would be the case if they were cuts or slashes. Lann's opinion was that all of the splitting on Cherry's skin was due to thermal burns.

This was, in a sense, good news. It meant one less avenue investigators needed to consider going down.

Every move on Lann's part was scripted, a practiced and dignified ceremony of respect for the dead that Lann's profession took on with deference and integrity whenever a human being arrived in a morgue for autopsy. Lann understood her word was not final, as per the protocol that was important to the overall veracity of the autopsy. Jeffrey Barnard, the chief medical examiner, and Joni McClain, the deputy chief medical examiner, along with every one of SWIFS's nine additional pathologists, would have to sign off on Lann's work. Each autopsy was scrutinized to the fullest extent by the entire staff. Doctors at SWIFS took their jobs seriously. A medical examiner needed to come to the right conclusions the first time around. Exhuming bodies—weeks, months, even years later—was not what medical examiners liked to do. It meant they had missed something.

The medical examiner's "field agents" make phone calls, speak with family members and wage war on the "front lines" of any investigation into a suspicious death, looking to gather all the information they can for the medical examiner and later a prosecution, if there is to be one. Cherry Walker's death scene and the condition of her body certainly suggested a homicidal death. But there were far too many questions at this point to say that yes, Cherry Walker was murdered.

Another doctor at SWIFS "positively identified" Cherry Walker through dental records, just as Lann was preparing to start her autopsy, allowing her to strip Cherry's toe of that red tag. At last the victim had an identity. She was Cherry Walker, thirty-nine, not just a DB with a number attached to her toe.

Cherry's medical records would play an important role in Lann's autopsy. The doctor received a file from one of Cherry's physicians that provided all of the pertinent information Lann might need in figuring out manner and cause of death. The most telling fact Lann learned was that Cherry had been, according to her medical records, "mentally retarded." Also of note was that Cherry had suffered from seizures. Lann learned how one doctor noted that on January 22 and February 4, 2003, Cherry had two seizures. But then on September 1, 2004, the same doctor reported: *She's not had any seizures since I saw her for one, and this was when she was placed on Wellbutrin.* (Wellbutrin is an antidepressant—with the common side effect being seizures.) In June 2006, some three years later, another doctor noted that Cherry had not had any seizures since 2003. And in 2007, her doctor reported: *I've been following her for seizures. She's not had one in quite a while.* Perhaps when she stopped taking Wellbutrin, the seizures went away. By April 2010, a few months before Cherry was found dead, she had reported to her doctors that she had not had any seizures in a long period, but she had been experiencing "tremors."

Lann considered this information to be vitally important within her final analysis—especially the "tremors," which Lann later attributed to "shaking of some sort of the body," a condition Paula Wheeler had noted on several occasions in her reports. What seemed even more relevant to Cherry's case as Lann studied her history was that on April 24, 2010, the last time Cherry had seen this particular doctor, she had not reported seizures in years and had even denied having "transient paralysis, weakness." She had not been faint, had no vertigo, no memory problems, no clumsiness: *[No] shift in gait, no poor balance, no poor coordination, no trouble walking, no concentration difficulty, confusion or drooling.* These were all potential symptoms that could be experienced by mentally retarded patients suffering from seizures and other more serious conditions. Apparently, though, from all reported accounts Lann had at her disposal, Cherry had gotten her condition under control with medication. This was incredibly important: ruling out the idea that Cherry might have died from a seizure.

One of the first tasks Lann did during the autopsy was to take X-rays of Cherry's entire body to see if it contained any gunshot wounds or bullets. This, again, was a vital part of the body inspection, based in part on the supposition that Cherry's body had been set on fire for a specific reason: to cover up a crime.

Lann reported that Cherry's body was in the "early stages of decomposition," and had not been out in the elements long, maybe overnight at the most. Equally important to those in law enforcement waiting for the results of this autopsy, Lann confidently concluded that Cherry had died as result of "homicidal violence."

The means by which she had been murdered, however, remained elusive as Lann conducted a more complete autopsy.

After opening Cherry up with a scalpel and studying her organs, tissue and muscle, Dr. Lann encountered a few not-so-specific "findings." This intrusive but crucial procedure indicated that someone much stronger than Cherry had killed her in a horrific, violent, personal way. One possible means of death was asphyxiation. During Lann's autopsy, she found: *[Cherry Walker] might have had a compression to the neck or some sort of portion of her body, which allowed for . . . small capillaries in her eyelids and eye lining . . . which covered her eyes called the conjunctiva [to have] small hemorrhages in them.* It wasn't a slam dunk for Lann, but she added, *When I see those little hemorrhages or bleeds in the membrane, I wonder.*

The caveat was that these same type of asphyxialike injuries in the eyes can also occur "in the process of decomposition" or "breakdown of tissue" and "with positioning of the body"—so one had to be careful before jumping to any conclusion that the person had been asphyxiated.

Lann ruled Cherry Walker's manner of death as homicide and cause of death as homicidal violence through a means that, at the time of autopsy, would have to be considered "unknown." The coroner walked a thin line here, because Cherry suffered from seizures on occasion, sometimes intense ones. Still, as Lann read through Cherry's medical history: *What etiology or what caused these seizures is unknown.* No one could say, in other words, what had caused Cherry to have seizures.

Trumping any of the latent, speculative opinions regarding Cherry and her seizures that would come up later, indicating a potentially new and overlooked cause of death, was the fact that Cherry's body had been burned. This one fact said a lot about the likeliness of a seizure being responsible for her death. In Dr. Lann's extensive experience as a medical examiner, she knew that people generally burned bodies to hide identities and other evidence that would point in the direction of a killer. On top of that, Lann took into account that Cherry's body had been dumped in a field a distance from where she had lived, as well as her being a mentally challenged woman.

Whoever had burned Cherry's body made sure to pour the accelerant all over Cherry's neck, making examination of this area almost impossible.

Someone had murdered Cherry—Dr. Lann was certain of it. There was no possible way she could have had a seizure, fallen into that field and caught on fire by herself. It sounded ridiculous, of course, but Lann and her colleagues knew that once a suspect was identified for this crime, all scenarios would have to be considered and ruled out with evidence—if the case was to go anywhere.

Lann went through several scenarios that could have led to Cherry ending up in that field, set on fire. One included the possibility that Cherry could have had a seizure and died while riding around with someone, and then that person tossed her body in the field and lit it on fire to hide her identity—this might have been someone who was scared and did not know what to do. This seemed possible, if only in theory. Yet, for this medical examiner, based on what she found during the autopsy, it did not seem at all probable or even reasonable.

Why?

The most telling piece of evidence against this scenario was the evidence that Cherry Walker was probably strangled to death. That alone told Lann this was a case of premeditated murder with a potential cover-up.

An additional potential scenario of Cherry going for a walk and having a seizure and falling over and dying in that field off CR 2191 was struck down by common sense. For it to be true, it would have to mean that someone had come along afterward, found Cherry's body, then set it on fire for no other reason than to watch her burn. That wasn't likely. On top of that, there were no other footprints around the immediate area of Cherry's body. Just tire tracks.

Equally important, before arriving at the dirt section of the field—that heavy clay—where Cherry's body had been found, you would have to pass over a gravel road. If someone had taken Cherry in a car or truck and dumped her, they'd had to travel on the same gravel road. What Lann found interesting as she studied Cherry's body was that Cherry had "very irregular, haphazard scratches" on her forehead "that were somewhat dried." At first, this seemed puzzling to Lann. But after further examination, it appeared that the scratches were consistent with a person having lifted Cherry's body out of a vehicle, perhaps then allowing it to fall under its own weight onto that gravel road before dragging it to the place where it was found. The wounds were subtle, Lann noticed, as if at one point Cherry had something covering her head, or her entire body was wrapped, shroudlike, and that covering had protected her forehead from being completely cut open and gashed by the scraping, leaving only minor wounds.

As Lann looked at this, she thought of one item: *bedsheet.* Someone might have wrapped Cherry's body in a sheet of the sort found in any household.

Other evidence supported the theory of a premeditated plan to kill Cherry Walker.

Cherry had been found lying on her stomach. It would seem that she had been lit on fire where she was found, because there was a "unique distribution over primarily the back, and then the upper portions of the torso, to include the right flank and lower right extremity on the back of the thigh and then shoulders as well." From the position of Cherry's body in situ, it appeared that her killer had dumped her and she landed face-first on the ground. From there a flammable liquid was poured over her as she lay on her stomach. Then her body was set on fire.

Lann found a few minor abrasions in the area of Cherry's head. These injuries, the doctor was almost certain, took place right before or during death, because "there was no healing" and "blood was stilling pumping" at the time those injuries—superficial as they were—had occurred.

Lann couldn't say definitively if Cherry Walker was dead when she was lit on fire and burned over nearly the entire back portion of her body and her neck. The only medical certainty Lann could conclude—and she wasn't 100 percent certain about this, either—was that Cherry Walker "wasn't breathing" when her body was on fire. A look inside the lungs told the doctor this. However, that finding could be deceiving. Horrifying as it sounded, Cherry could have been unconscious when she was lit on fire.

Without having to say it, Lann and the SCSO knew that only a sadistic psychopath could pour gasoline or some other accelerant on a human being, strike a match and set that living, breathing human being—unconscious or not—on fire. The object of this autopsy was to find that person as quickly as possible and understand the "what, where, when and why," so a case could be built and justice served for Cherry Walker.

14

TO FIND OUT HOW DEEP the relationship between Cherry Walker and Kim Cargill went, detectives needed to have a chat with Kim. Kim was in serious trouble with DFPS and had used Cherry in more ways than just as a babysitter and caretaker for her child. Yet, all of that, as bad as it seemed, did not mean Kim Cargill was a murderer. In fact, to call her such would be a leap: How does one go from a mother and wife to a predator that strangled a mentally retarded woman before lighting her body on fire? It sounded impossible—especially since Kim didn't have any police record to speak of.

Sure, there were domestic issues, fights with her husbands and partners, but there did not seem to be any indication that Kim Cargill was capable of such a gruesome, violent act. Of course, she could have hired someone to do it for her. However, if she had done that, the case was going to be easier to solve. The more people involved in a homicide, the more likely it is that one will talk about it sooner or later. Additionally, if this was a murder-for-hire killing, the death penalty would most certainly be part of the prosecution. In Texas, if the accused was sentenced to death, after his or her appeals were exhausted, the execution chamber was put to use. Convicts did not sit on death row for life in Texas.

Kim Cargill could have a good alibi and might even be able to help their investigation, pointing detectives in the direction of the perpetrator. Kim had interacted with Cherry in those days (and hours) before Cherry went missing and was murdered. Perhaps Kim had valuable information.

There was only one way to find out.

Before knocking on Kim's door, SCSO detective Ron Rathbun wanted to find out as much as he could about her from independent sources. Know your subject and her movements surrounding your timeline better than she does and you have the upper hand walking in.

Detective Rathbun headed out with a colleague to 4801 Troup Highway in Tyler, a nondescript one-floor office complex near a Food First fuel-and-convenience store. Across the street were a paint company, a family-owned cleaners and a Volkswagen dealership. As he pulled up onto Troup Highway, the landscape of rural Texas was vivid: the plush green grass, fertilized and cut with a surgeon's precision, the white-lined parking spaces in front of the redbrick building with plate glass windows and stenciled company signs on the doors. Similar strip-mall-like complexes are scattered all across Texas—and across America.

The SCSO was working on a tip that Kim Cargill had worked for Excel Staffing, a business that supplied nurses to local hospitals. An LVN, Kim was considered to be a "skilled health care worker," someone that aided nurses and doctors throughout the course of their workday. It's an "entry-level" health care position. Some take it on, love it, and stay, never going further, while others use it as a stepping-stone toward becoming a registered nurse (RN) or other career goals.

For Excel, Kim was making about $24 per hour. Rathbun and his colleague sat down with staffers Gina Vestal and Paula Maris. Both knew Kim personally and had effectively "staffed" her at numerous local East Texas hospitals: Athens, UT (a host of facilities under the University of Texas Southwestern Medical Center banner), Quitman, Pittsburg and Gilmer. These were all facilities Kim had worked for periodically. In fact, after they looked it up in the computers, Vestal and Maris confirmed that Kim had worked at Athens back on that previous Friday, June 18, 2010, the day on which Cherry went missing. Athens was a forty-five-minute drive from Tyler. It wasn't Kim's favorite gig, but it provided the dollars she needed to take care of her family.

"How long has she been here?" Rathbun asked Vestal.

"Oh, three months or so—since March 31, 2010, it says right here in her file."

"Can we get a copy of her schedule over the past several days?"

"Absolutely, Detective."

Vestal provided the SCSO with "copies of [Kim's] time sheets." It appeared that Kim had worked on Friday, June 18, at the East Texas Medical Center (ETMC) facility in Athens, between the hours of 7:00 A.M. and 7:30 P.M.

Kim Cargill had been close enough to the

Tyler/Whitehouse area to have met up with or at least spoken to Cherry Walker beyond those phone calls the SCSO could verify.

After she had worked in Athens on that Friday, one of the Excel staffers said, "They called asking me to call [her] because she—they didn't know if she had given an antibiotic to a patient or not. It wasn't documented."

This was fresh on the minds of the Excel staff because Kim had always been someone whom they never, *ever* had trouble reaching. She always answered her phone.

Rathbun wanted to know what they meant by that.

Anytime they called Kim, no matter when, she'd either pick up the phone or call them back immediately. Yet, on that Friday, when this important question came up, Vestal called Kim, over and over, but could not reach her. Protocol required that no matter what hour of the day or night it was, if there was a patient issue, Excel would call the nurse repeatedly until they connected. Records indicated Excel staff members had called Kim incessantly that Friday night, and did not stop until 11:56 P.M. Kim had not picked up during that entire time.

At 12:33 A.M., Kim called back.

"I've been trying to get hold of you all night, Kim," the Excel staffer had told her. "You need to call over to Athens immediately and tell them whether you gave a patient an antibiotic or not."

"Oh, sorry . . . I've been sleeping," Kim responded.

This seemed odd, because they had called Kim at all hours of the night over the past few weeks since she'd starting working at Excel and she had always picked up, sound asleep or not, within a few rings.

Kim did call the hospital right after she got off the phone.

Later that morning, a staffer then recalled, which would have been Saturday, June 19, Excel called Kim first thing. They needed someone to work. Kim was a go-to in a sudden situation because she was always asking for extra hours.

Except on this day.

"I can't," Kim said.

Looking deeper into her schedule, Detective Rathbun found that Kim was not scheduled and did not work on Saturday, June 19, but did return to work in Athens on Sunday, June 20. This opened up the opportunity—that is, unless Kim could show she was somewhere else—for Kim to have been with Cherry on Friday night and into Saturday.

Further supporting this theory, Rathbun later connected with the Athens hospital and obtained security footage, which showed Kim arriving at the hospital late at 7:04 A.M. on June 18 and leaving the hospital later that same day (early) at 7:08 P.M.

Maris explained that she knew Kim had Monday and Tuesday and Wednesday off.

Rathbun wondered if she had vacation days or plans, as these were not her normal days off. What had made her take those specific days off?

"She told us she'd need those days off to prepare for a child custody hearing. She did come here on Monday [the day preceding Rathbun's interview], though, to pick up her check," Maris said.

They talked more about Kim's work ethic and how often she was able to fulfill her duties and work a full week.

"Kim liked to work," Vestal said. Kim had no trouble doing lots of hours for Excel, even fifty or sixty per week. She always appreciated the extra hours.

Just not last Saturday, Rathbun thought. *Knowing she was going to take three days off in a row, she still refused that Saturday gig.*

Interesting.

There were times, Vestal explained further, when Kim was forced to find a babysitter on the spot if she wanted the hours, but it never seemed to be a problem. Excel could call her at four in the morning and Kim would find a babysitter within the hour.

That babysitter had to be Cherry Walker, Rathbun knew.

Evidence was mounting that Kim was likely the last person to see and/or speak with Cherry. Clearly, she had a window of opportunity to have been involved on some level in Cherry's disappearance and death. Rathbun met with Riggle and they decided it was time to knock on Kim's door.

15

THE SMITH COUNTY SHERIFF'S OFFICE on 227 North Spring Street in downtown Tyler is a stuccolike-textured white building. Two giant stars painted on the front glass doors greet people as they walk in. Just a few steps outside is a road made of tightly packed, shiny red bricks. It's elegant and nostalgic, reminiscent of what the city might have been like 125 years ago as horses pulling buggies trotted down the avenues under the gaslights of the day. Across the street is a parking garage attached to a tall building with glass windows, rising into the Texas skyline.

Early the week of June 21, SCSO detectives James Riggle and Ron Rathbun had Joe Mayo come in and meet them for a second interview on the seventh floor of the building. They wanted one more conversation with Joe before they wrote him off entirely, while part of his alibi was still being investigated.

"We were good friends," Joe said of his and Cherry's relationship. He didn't know what else he could add that he hadn't said already.

Rathbun and Riggle wanted Joe back in this environment to break the news to him that Cherry had been murdered. They wanted to gauge his reaction firsthand. Seasoned detectives simply know: You lay important information from a case on someone. If they haven't been involved in any way, they show a certain involuntary, visceral response without even trying. Whereas, you tell a man who has killed a woman about his crime, and his denial generally includes a certain arrogance—a feigned compassion, which he tries to manipulate into the conversation.

Joe Mayo was stunned as the news was relayed to him, according to both Rathbun and Riggle. Rathbun later wrote in his report: *He seemed genuinely shocked and surprised.*

"Where were you, Joe, last Friday?" one of the detectives asked again.

"I told you. I was singing at the Caretta's."

The SCSO cut Joe Mayo loose. Then both cops sat and talked about where they stood at this point in their investigation—but also, most important, where they needed to go. Any murder strikes caring cops, like Rathbun and Riggle, in the heart. They feel a need, which they cannot explain, to solve the case.

As they discussed the case in detail, there really was only one other place left for these detectives to take their investigation: Waterton Circle, Whitehouse, Texas.

16

YOU DRIVE SLOWLY DOWN THE gravel and concrete roadway of Waterton Circle, which surrounds the neighborhood where Kim Cargill lived, and it appears to be a toymaker's vision of a small plastic community, handpicked and perfectly crafted for the landscape of a child's train set. The houses are all kept up to date, red and/or white brick; the lawns manicured, green as Irish pastures; the trees, mostly maples and spruce, are planted in locations chosen to accentuate the beauty and family-oriented atmosphere of everything around them.

This is rural Whitehouse, Texas, in its essence: Young working couples. Husbands and wives. Two-point-two kids. A boat, a dog, a cat. Children's toys in the front yards and on driveways. Playscapes and slides and aboveground pools out back. Basketball hoops, garbage and recycling bins alongside the two-car garages. Boxwoods and evergreens curving up the front walkways, leading to the doors into the homes where suburbanites lived the American dream.

It all seems tranquil on the outside. Yet, there are no white picket fences here. It's not that type of community. It is almost as though, driving around, you've somehow been teleported into the back lot of Universal in Hollywood to the set of a crime drama. You sense that underneath the perfect neighborhood façade, something sinister, something menacing, is lurking in the shadows, unseen. It is much more devious and violent than anyone could have ever imagined.

Criminal Investigations Division (CID) sergeant Mike Stinecipher, with James Riggle and Ron Rathbun, rolled up to Kim's house on the early evening of Tuesday, June 22, 2010, without a search warrant. The feeling was that Kim was in enough trouble with DFPS and would allow them inside her home to have a cursory look around, answer a few questions; then they could be on their way. If Kim had nothing to hide, they figured, what was the problem? They wanted her help to find the killer of her babysitter. Why *wouldn't* she want to help find Cherry's killer?

"We went there to see if we could get a consent to search the residence," Stinecipher said later in court, explaining how this night unfolded.

For the SCSO this was a turning point. Some detectives had a feeling that Kim Cargill had a lot to hide. Others thought, *Why not give this woman the benefit of the doubt?* Cherry's murder was a seriously violent crime. It was hard to imagine that a woman of Kim's stature and size—she was not a large woman at 120 pounds—could pull it off. If she did, how could she manage it alone? Cherry was a big woman. How could Kim Cargill move Cherry's body from one place to another as deadweight? Of course, Cherry could have been murdered where she was found. But every forensic analyst and investigator believed she had been killed elsewhere.

Riggle had called for another cop to head over to the Cargill residence. Detective Dan Garrigan's assignment was to stand watch at the house after they left the scene. They were all under the impression that Kim Cargill was unpredictable and volatile, and experience told these intuitive cops that a situation like this one could go any number of ways. As a cop you can never expect anything to go the way it should. Never believe people will do the right thing—because criminals don't think that way. Criminals have one thing on their minds: themselves.

Was Kim Cargill a criminal?

Riggle, Stinecipher and Rathbun stepped out of their vehicles and walked up to Kim's door. One of the cops knocked on it.

Kim answered. At forty-three years old she looked tired. Her blue eyes were hazy and bloodshot. You could tell she'd had a hard time the past week or more. She was running on adrenaline. Kim had always kept up her shape and looks—this was important to her. At one time she had been a gorgeous woman: dark blond hair and fair skin, a welcoming smile, blue/green eyes gleaming underneath plucked eyebrows, pouty and red sensual lips. Men were attracted to Kim; she never had trouble finding dates. On this evening, however, she came across as standoffish, with a nervousness that suggested a woman hiding something. The officers got a clear indication right away that Kim Cargill, despite how long she had known

Cherry, did not want to help the SCSO find Cherry's killer.

Stinecipher explained that they were hoping to conduct a walk-through of the house, with her permission, of course. They were investigating the death of someone Kim knew, and they needed some answers from Kim. They weren't there to arrest her or cause any trouble. They just wanted to come in and have a look around, ask a few basic questions.

"No, cannot do that," Kim said from behind the open front door. "I need to speak with my attorney about this."

Roadblock. Without Kim's consent, the SCSO needed a search warrant. For a search warrant the SCSO needed evidence, circumstantial or forensic, or a judge would never sign off on the warrant.

Riggle, Stinecipher, Rathbun and several other officers left Kim's house—a procession of law enforcement vehicles leaving the residential neighborhood as if escorting the president. If the neighbors weren't talking about Kim already, they surely would be now.

The SCSO couldn't do much else at Kim's residence. She'd told them to leave; she'd had every right to do that. Detective Riggle, the lead in the investigation, decided the next step was to finish writing up a search warrant for the house as quickly as possible. Kim now knew that the SCSO was seriously interested in her. She would be on the move. If there was evidence inside the home, it was a race against the clock for them to get the warrant signed before she was able to hide or destroy it.

Dan Garrigan and another cop were told to remain down the road from Kim's house and keep an eye on her movements. If she so much as walked out of the house to put a bag of garbage into the bin, the team located back at the station house needed to know. The SCSO did not want Kim out of their sights. It would take a day or maybe longer to obtain the warrant. They wanted to know exactly where Kim was at all times until they could walk into her house with the proper paperwork.

The SCSO took a call from Kim's lawyer not long after arriving back at base camp.

"You're not allowed to speak with Kim Cargill," the lawyer warned.

Roadblock number two.

There would be no discussion about the matter. Stay away from her, the lawyer articulated.

Besides Garrigan and another detective, Riggle placed a patrol deputy sheriff, Teresa Smith, in a squad car and full uniform presence in the area just beyond Kim's neighborhood. This was to provide the means by which to pull Kim over, if and when she left the house, and—*ahem*—made a traffic violation, however small an infraction it might be.

Garrigan and his crew sat watch down the street at first, around the corner. They were in an area where Kim would have to pass if she left her house and drove somewhere. From his post inside the vehicle Garrigan could see Kim's house. All Kim had to do was stay put inside. Wait it out. Sooner or later the SCSO would either barge in with a warrant or back off.

Riggle and Rathbun were at the SCSO, along with Assistant District Attorney (ADA) April Sikes and District Attorney (DA) Matt Bingham. They were working on that warrant in the DAO to make sure everything was in order. A lot of what the SCSO had was circumstantial, but as they put it all down on paper, there seemed to be mounting evidence that Kim Cargill was the only person who could have seen Cherry last and been able to pull off the murder—at least out of those whom the SCSO had on radar currently. Anyone else that could have been involved (that they knew of) had been eliminated.

Somewhere near 8:00 P.M., Dan Garrigan moved from where he was parked down the block to almost directly across the street from Kim's house. Not long after that, Kim came out of the house, got into her vehicle and pulled out of her driveway.

Garrigan radioed in that Kim was on the move.

After she backed out of her driveway, Kim stopped, put her car in drive and then pulled up to Garrigan as he sat in his vehicle.

"Is there anything you need?" Kim asked the detective. It was a sarcastic gesture on Kim's part. This was part of her signature style.

"Ma'am?" Garrigan replied, not quite sure what she meant. She must have known who he was—a plainclothes detective in a nondescript car.

"Should I call my lawyer?" Kim said after Garrigan explained that he was a police officer assigned to watch her home.

"I cannot give you that advice, ma'am. It is up to you if you want to do that."

Kim took off.

Patrol officer Teresa Smith was parked down the road.

"Subject has left residence," Garrigan radioed, watching Kim drive toward where Smith was stationed. Garrigan explained what vehicle she was driving, giving Smith the license plate number.

Kim drove around the bend along Waterton Circle,

toward Lakeway Drive, which emptied out onto the 346, or East Main Street. Soon she was out of her neighborhood, motoring along in her 1999 white Mitsubishi Montero, a smaller-size sport-utility vehicle (SUV). Kim lived about six miles from the spot at which Cherry's body had been dumped, a quick ride. Cherry had lived eight miles from the same location.

Deputy Smith took the call and waited for Kim to drive by—so she could pull Kim over and see what she was up to. All Smith needed was a good reason and they could at least stall Kim until the warrant—close to being completed—was signed by a judge.

Kim came up to a stop sign near where Smith was parked. "She failed to come to a complete stop . . . [and] rolled through it," Smith said later.

Smith hit her lights, which would normally turn the dashboard video camera on, but for some reason the camera wasn't working on this night. As Kim drove past Smith, the deputy pulled out and got behind her. Kim pulled over without incident. She rolled her eyes as she pulled to the side of the road.

After getting out and approaching Kim's driver's-side window, Deputy Smith went through the familiar rundown of who she was and what she needed from Kim, telling her to hand over her license and registration, explaining the reason why she had been stopped. Oddly enough, Kim was wearing a long T-shirt and panties, no bra, as though she had been ready for bed but decided to go out, instead.

Was she trying to mess with the SCSO? Taunt the cops?

Kim provided the materials and Smith went back to her patrol car and sat down. Smith needed to give the detectives time to show up at the scene.

Ten minutes later, as detectives arrived, Smith walked over and gave Kim a warning summons for rolling through the sign and not coming to a complete stop. Then Smith told her that the SCSO was taking control of the situation now.

"Please step out of your vehicle, ma'am," Smith told Kim.

Kim grabbed her phone and pocketbook; she did as she was told.

Smith had Kim sit in the backseat of the patrol car. Smith spoke to the detectives, who had arrived and were standing in front of Kim's vehicle.

As they talked, one of the detectives looked over and saw that Kim had pulled out her cell phone and had it up to her ear.

The detective told Smith, "Grab that phone from her."

Smith hurried over. "I need your phone," she said, and then the deputy grabbed it out of Kim's hands.

As the cell phone was being snatched from her grasp, Kim said, "I'm talking to my lawyer!"

None of that mattered now. Patrol officer Teresa Smith told Kim she was bringing her home and the SCSO was impounding her vehicle.

Settle in, because it was going to be a long night.

17

BACK AT THE SCSO, RIGGLE and Rathbun were busy typing up the search warrant for Kim's house. Interestingly enough, some of the information in the warrant added even more validity to the argument that Kim Cargill had a lot more to worry about with regard to Cherry Walker, her testimony against Kim and her care of Timmy.

According to the warrant, before turning to Cherry, Kim had used another babysitter, whom Cherry knew and was prepared to also testify about. This babysitter had taken care of Timmy, even though the woman, the warrant stated, *rarely takes a bath, her house stinks, and there are bees, flies and cockroaches everywhere inside her house—[and] this would be one of the subjects which [Cherry] Walker would be testifying [about].*

In addition, the SCSO had learned that Cherry Walker had been named in a lawsuit "to terminate [Kim's] rights to her son." It wasn't just about losing custody of Timmy for Kim Cargill. Cherry held the keys to a much larger door into Kim's future. If Kim lost in court, she would have to give up all rights to Timmy, possibly never seeing him again. In all likelihood charges would also be brought against Kim for child neglect and other crimes if the judgment didn't go her way—and the one witness that could bury Kim in that courtroom was Cherry Walker.

The SCSO had a witness claiming to have seen: *On Thursday or Friday, June 17 or 18, 2010, two vehicles exit the area on CR 2191 (near the crime scene) that she (the witness) described as a dark-colored truck and a white vehicle.*

Kim Cargill owned a white Montero—the same SUV in which she had been pulled over by Deputy Teresa Smith.

The SCSO's crime scene unit (CSU) had tire imprints from the dump site that they wanted to match up against Kim's vehicle. Since the SCSO had a cast of an imprint, forensic investigators could place the cast on the matching tire and, if it matched, it would fit like a mold. The SCSO needed Kim's vehicle in order to conduct this test. Proving a match would place Kim's vehicle at what investigators believed was the secondary crime scene—that wooded area off CR 2191.

[We] believe a vehicle was used to transport Walker to the location where her body was located based upon crime scene investigation, the warrant claimed. This meant the SCSO had no doubt Cherry had been murdered elsewhere, giving them another crime scene to uncover and investigate. They just needed to find it. A warrant would be a step in that direction.

Within the CR 2191 crime scene, which became a vital piece of evidence for Riggle, Rathbun and the SCSO team: *[There were no] drag marks in the soil, nor foot impressions in areas where such would be expected if an individual had walked with Walker to that location.*

It was clear, at least within the evidence the SCSO

had collected thus far, that nobody had lured Cherry Walker down into that field. She had been driven there, dumped and set on fire.

The warrant went on to speculate what could have happened and how Kim might have been involved, claiming all indications pointed to Kim calling Cherry and telling her she wanted to take her out to dinner on Friday night. Moreover, the SCSO, with help from Rueon and Gethry Walker and other family members, had done a thorough search for two personal possessions of Cherry's that were near and dear to her heart, which she would have never been without: her coin purse and Samsung cell phone. Neither had been located. The SCSO believed that Cherry's killer—Kim Cargill—might have those items in her possession.

Cargill had the opportunity to secrete these items in her home, the warrant noted.

The document next explained why the medical examiner believed Cherry had been murdered by "homicidal violence" and could have died no other way.

The warrant concluded, *[The SCSO] believes that on June 18, 2010, in Smith County, Texas, Kim Cargill did intentionally take the life of Cherry Walker while in the course of committing or attempting to commit robbery of Cherry Walker.* The robbery was believed to be the taking of Cherry's cell phone and purse. The motive the SCSO included in the warrant: *Retaliation . . . on account of [Cherry Walker's] service as a witness or perspective [*Sic: 'prospective' would be accurate*] witness against Kim Cargill.*

The judge sat down, read the document and signed it.

18

A S A GENERAL RULE, WHEN cops enter a home under a search warrant and look for evidence that might help in a homicide investigation, evaluating the premises is first and foremost. As a member of the search team, you're told to look for hiding places: underneath floorboards, carpeting that appears to have been torn up and put back down or recently replaced, inside couches and cushions and pillows, in the back of old-school television sets, false walls, fake drawer bottoms and so on. Cops look for crawl spaces and evidence that interior walls have been compromised in some way—replastered or replaced. Inside fluorescent-light fixtures is another familiar spot where searchers look, additionally behind a pullout medicine cabinet or inside pipes and even J-channel sink drains. There are all sorts of places inside a home where a killer can hide evidence of a murder. It is without a doubt a psychological chess match criminals like to play.

Catch me if you can.

As most cops would agree, however, the pieces of

evidence that ultimately take down the perpetrator are often the ones he or she has no clue have been left behind. Criminals—murderers, especially—like to think that they're smarter than cops, but that is hardly ever the case.

The question that arose as the SCSO team assembled and prepared to enter Kim Cargill's house wouldn't be *what* they would find. Once this team of officers and detectives and CSIs entered Kim's house and began poking around, it would become how *much* incriminating evidence they would find.

From the outside Kim's house came across as a "normal residential" dwelling, one investigator later explained, placed inside a suburban bubble of middle-class bliss. "Light tan in color, trimmed in white with a dark composition roof." Three bedrooms, two baths (one full, one half), a laundry room, sunroom, kitchen, living room: Your typical and quite affordable home for a family of four or five in this part of Texas.

Ten cops showed up to serve the warrant, a major showing. The SCSO was not taking its investigation lightly. The extra eyes and hands were there to make sure they turned over every stone.

Detective Noel Martin, as the SCSO's CSU senior criminalist supervisor and sergeant, with some twenty-five years behind the badge, was in charge of supervising the team, directing officers to accomplish certain tasks, making sure the integrity of the scene and chain of evidence remained unbroken. If anyone had a question about an item, Martin was the man to ask. Martin had a long history of crime scene and search warrant experience and held a master's-level license as a Texas peace officer. He had done just about every job in law enforcement at one time or another. Martin cut a smooth, retro, 1970s-cop-show, law enforcement look: tortoiseshell glasses, dark-colored, thick mustache, bushy black hair, receding just a bit along the forehead line. He'd won awards and certifications for his excellent work throughout the years and had been one of the SCSO's foremost trainers when it came to crime scene and other law enforcement specialty work. Martin had an eye for seeing things others might glance over. He seemed to be able to hone in on a scene and, if evidence existed, find it. A crime scene whisperer, perhaps—a man respected by his colleagues, dedicated to his job and the task at hand.

"We will notify your attorney when we're finished," one of the detectives explained to Kim Cargill, who did not seem at all pleased that nearly a dozen detectives and law enforcement personnel were there to tear her house apart and look through all of her possessions.

Noel Martin addressed his team outside in the driveway before going in, assigning tasks to each individual.

"Discover," Martin explained, "bring to my attention, do not move or pick up or, otherwise, mess with any evidence."

Everyone understood.

Kim asked if someone would drive her to a friend's house.

A patrol officer was summoned. She was driven away.

A second vehicle, a two-door white sedan Kim had also been driving, was confiscated and towed to the SCSO's impound yard "to be stored and processed." Noel Martin would oversee that inspection and evidence collection, as well, when he finished inside the residence.

The clean and affluent exterior image of Kim's house was not a good representation of what the team found after walking inside. Kim's house was dirty and unkempt—to say the least. An absolute pigsty would be more accurate. The woman was an unequivocal slob. A good case for incompetent parenting could be made just for allowing children to live in such squalor. Still, it was the smaller concern of the day. These cops were here for a much bigger purpose.

Toys were everywhere; notebooks and files and other common household papers (billing statements and letters and receipts and unused coupons) spread throughout the living room and kitchen, on the floor, on furniture and all over the place. Above the fireplace in the living area, on the mantel, were a cross, a vase, a smaller crucifix, two porcelain or ceramic figurines (a boy and his dog), as well as other household odds and ends piled up next to a kid's used plastic cup. This area, on a small scale, was a reflection of the entire house: stuff on top of more stuff, piled atop other stuff, which was then tossed on the floor and anywhere else it could land, all surrounded by garbage and bags of rubbish that seemed to be the start of a cleanup that never materialized.

Kim never picked up after herself or her kids—that was clear. Used bags of food, plastic lids, old tins, paper cups, wrappers, empty boxes of food, particles and crumbs of fast food, among many, many other items, were strewn about the house, much of it tossed with no rhyme or reason. It was as if the kids or Kim had eaten whatever was in the package and then had thrown it out or left it where they were at the time.

The sinks in the bathrooms were littered with hair care products, food wrappers and containers, used plates, dishes and cups. Dirty clothes were everywhere. In one of the recreation rooms, where Kim had made use of outdoor furniture, blankets and sheets were strung over the windows for curtains. One of the kids' bedrooms had been painted; the job was left incomplete, paintbrush strokes and missing patches of paint all over the walls. In the half bath off the living room, on the floor around the toilet, one shoe sat on top of what appeared to be used toilet paper; there was what looked to be a squished, small container of cocktail sauce, its contents smeared all over the floor, dried and obviously left in the place it fell. Next to that was a large black plastic bag of garbage—mostly old fast-food bags and bins and wrappers and straws and cups. The toilet was not something anyone would want to use. It had rust around the rim of the water, what appeared to be blood droplets and blood spatter all over the seat and on top of the bowl.

The kids' homework and school projects (some graded and handed back) were spread through the house—on tables, on the floor, on vanities, inside the bathtub in Kim's bedroom, on the couch, atop kitchen counters.

In a chest in the kids' playroom, which was filled with papers and old, used bags, an investigator uncovered a DVD: *A Streetgirl Named Desire,* a soft-porn video by Fat Dog Productions. On its cover a hot brunette held one of her naked breasts as a half-dressed Lorenzo Lamas wannabe groped her body. It fell into the same genre of movie that the SCSO had uncovered inside Cherry Walker's apartment. Cherry had an entire collection of similar videos, along with scores of horror flicks, all from the same production company. A good argument could be made that this DVD belonged to Cherry Walker. Why was it inside the kids' toy chest, of all places?

A detective placed it on the rim of the chest and snapped a photo.

Right away detectives noted the amount of cleaning products Kim had out—spray bottles and bleach containers and paper towels and glass cleaners. It was obvious she wasn't cleaning the house. Or had she perhaps cleaned up only certain areas?

The dining room was no cleaner or messier than any other section of the home. On the floor next to the dining table were a powdery white substance (as if a bottle of talcum powder had exploded), a large box, another box on a dining chair left opened, coloring books and toys on the floor next to a black plastic garbage bag full of household items. The dining table itself became interesting for investigators.

"Over here," one of the searchers pointed out to Noel Martin.

"What's up?"

Next to a spray bottle of cleaner were several packets of sugar with the familiar Burger King logo on the front, a half-dozen or so alcohol prep pads still inside their packages, a set of nail clippers, a candle filled with change (quarters, nickels, dimes, pennies), a roll of paper towels, a half-filled bottle of what looked to be cough syrup or some other type of prescription cold formula, a receipt from a drugstore for the prescription, a pair of pliers, an empty flower vase (clear glass), various pieces of paper (letters and notes and homework), a dustpan (sitting on top of the table itself) filled with a coloring book, a letter from Kim Cargill's lawyer, which sat next to a new tin of black pepper, sugar shaker, pens, a syringe (of all the things a small child could get into!) and other miscellaneous items. In the middle of it all was a Prism MC-80 microcassette tape, the type used in a 1990s answering machine or microcassette tape recorder.

In the living room the end table between the love seat and couch was littered with papers and two self-contained, disposable 35mm cameras sold at any drugstore (with the film loaded already), several Visa statements, fast-food ketchup packets, a box of twenty-eight-gallon, black plastic bags, various pieces of what appeared to be crumpled-up paper or garbage, along with a few stray toys.

A cop placed a placard (Number 2) on top of the end table.

Snapped a photo.

On the couch, next to yet another pile of papers and wrappers and even a used spoon, was a stain that the SCSO wanted tested.

"Mark it," someone said.

Another placard (Number 3) was placed next to the stain, a ruler set down and a photograph taken.

Then something interesting: a coin purse on the couch, black and gray.

Was it Cherry's?

Another placard was placed next to the purse and a photo snapped.

Inside Kim's bedroom, in a soiled, hazardous mess of garbage and used feminine products, old food and food containers and other items, the search took on a much more solemn tone.

"In here," the officer shouted, entering the bedroom.

Noel Martin walked in and looked around.

Both cops stared at one item that seemed familiar. There was, in fact, no one at the Cargill residence search more familiar with the CR 2191 crime scene where Cherry Walker's body had been found than Noel Martin. He had processed that entire scene just five days before. Martin was an expert in crime scene reconstruction and evidence collection. Moreover, he had an impeccable memory for this type of work. Looking down on the floor next to Kim's bed, thinking about the CR 2191 crime scene, Noel Martin knew Kim Cargill was now looking more like a suspect in Cherry Walker's murder than anyone else.

19

AMID PILES OF DIRTY LAUNDRY, empty computer printer boxes, plastic Sears bags filled with old and new clothes, garbage, books, empty Big Gulp and Sonic cups with straws, greasy and empty fast-food bags lying on the floor, old food (rotting and collecting mold), dirt and lint and hangers, underwear and nylons, telephone books and crayons and Magic Markers, empty packets of Burger King sugar (Number 6 and 7, representing where they had been found), Noel Martin knelt down and stared at two plastic Dairy Fresh creamer half-and-half cups identical to the one found between Cherry Walker's legs at the CR 2191 scene.

What were the chances?

Beside the creamer cup were several old French fries and Tater Tots that had either fallen out of her bag of food or dropped off a plate and had never been picked up. It was mind-boggling to think that this was the room where Kim slept every night after caring for patients at whatever hospital she had worked that day.

The obvious thing to do was to test these creamer

cups for DNA against the cup found between Cherry Walker's legs.

After taking photographs of the entire bedroom, including close-ups of the creamer cups, they bagged and tagged the items.

"In here," said another cop.

Inside Kim's bathroom were several additional plastic creamer cups.

A Styrofoam coffee cup's plastic white lid was found inside the master bedroom bathtub. The tub was brimming with garbage, but not just any type of garbage. There were used sanitary napkins and tampons, dried and crusty blood all over them, along with what appeared to be used diapers and several other feminine products.

Noel Martin knew that at the scene, a good distance from Cherry's body, a spongy white Styrofoam coffee cup had been located inside an old tire. It had no lid.

Inside Kim's bathroom, just beyond that revolting bathtub, detectives found a pair of white tennis shoes. One of the detectives, wearing latex gloves, carefully picked up one of the shoes after having a conversation with Noel Martin, who stood nearby and watched. Bingo, there it was: that same black soot they were finding all over the house.

"I saw the same type of material or substance," Detective Rathbun later reported, "that I had seen on the victim's shoes. . . ."

A circumstantial case for murder was beginning to be backed up by forensic evidence.

Rathbun also collected "several fast-food restaurant receipts" from area chain restaurants that Kim apparently had patronized on June 18 and 19. The SCSO would want to have a look at the surveillance footage from those places, if it was still available, and see if Kim could be seen on video with Cherry Walker on the night Cherry went missing.

"Sergeant," one of the searchers, approaching Noel Martin, stated, "we found something in the laundry room."

The Cargill residence laundry room like the rest of the house: absolutely gross and in need of not only a scrubbing, but a major sanitizing. But the lack of cleanliness was not what interested searchers. Inside the washing machine was what cops believed to be a bedsheet. Everyone participating in the search knew the SCSO had been working under the theory that Cherry Walker had been wrapped in some type of linen and taken from the place she was murdered to the 2191 secondary location—the ME had even mentioned that it could have been a sheet. The sheet itself looked to be stained with a dark-colored—maybe even once-red—substance in a particular section, even though it now appeared diluted after being washed.

Why was there just this one item in the machine? Generally, people wash a full load of clothes.

"It's wet," Martin said.

A wet sheet in a washing machine. Not so much evidence of a murder, but another layer piling atop suspicious activity on Kim Cargill's part.

Further bolstering the SCSO's theory that the sheet meant something within the scope of Cherry's murder, the laundry room was full of clothes that needed to be washed. In fact, a basket of dirty laundry sat to the left, in front of the dryer. Yet, inside the dryer cops found only a pair of scrubs, socks and underwear. These were Kim's clothes.

A placard (Number 19) went up on top of the

washing machine, and a photo was snapped. Another placard went up on the dryer, and another photo was taken.

The SCSO had hit the jackpot—or so it seemed on the surface—in Kim Cargill's home. Plenty of forensic work needed to be done in the lab, and plenty of forensic evidence that could be tested against what had been found at the crime scene.

Would all of this be enough to get a judge to sign off on an arrest warrant?

20

KIM'S WHITE SEDAN WAS TOWED to the Smith County Low Risk Jail's impound yard in order to get it out of the elements and into a secure environment. If she had used this vehicle in the transportation of Cherry's body, it should produce some forensic evidence. In addition, the "black soot" and smudges all over the white car were an indication that whoever had driven the car was perhaps covered in the stuff.

Noel Martin snapped on a pair of see-through plastic gloves and, with a few colleagues, went to work on the car to "conduct," as he later put it, a "systematic search for evidence."

First thing Martin did was to make sure the integrity of the vehicle had not been compromised. After a detailed perusal of the paperwork accompanying the car, he was confident that all seemed well in that regard.

Inside the vehicle—which was a horrible mess—Martin uncovered a Burger King hot cup, a roll of silver duct tape and several hairs (African-American).

The hairs were found on the passenger-side headrest, midway up the seat. It was not a stretch to think that Cherry Walker, at some point, had sat inside this vehicle.

Martin swabbed the door handle on the passenger side.

"We were looking for stem cells or epithelial (that thin layer of skin on the outside) DNA," he explained.

If at some point Cherry Walker was inside this vehicle with Kim Cargill, DNA testing would prove it by odds that were too large to argue with.

Along with Martin, the ADA April Sikes was present at the vehicle search. As Martin was going through the car, Sikes pointed to the floorboard: "Look there."

A section of the car's carpet had been pulled back—probably by one of the searchers. There, sitting by itself, underneath where the pulled-up section of carpet would have covered, was "the top portion" of a Dairy Fresh creamer cup; it was the plastic lid piece you tear off so you can pour the creamer into your coffee. It was sitting underneath the carpet on the driver's-side floorboard. By then, detectives had checked and found that Burger King gave those same Dairy Fresh half-and-half coffee creamer cups out with its coffee orders.

With the evidence found at Kim Cargill's home and in her vehicle, it appeared law enforcement had enough for an arrest warrant. The best-case scenario was to get Kim into the station house and shine a light in her face. Get her inside the box and see what she had to say for herself. Would she be able to explain all of this circumstantial and potential forensic evidence away? Or would she plead the Fifth and not say anything at all?

As it would turn out, however, the SCSO would not need to bring Kim in on those charges. Kim Cargill, after all, had other legal problems mounting—which had little to do with Cherry Walker.

PART TWO

"Psychopaths don't change," [Professor of Developmental Psychopathology, at the UCL Faculty of Brain Sciences, Essi Viding said]. "They don't learn from punishment. The best you can hope for is that they'll eventually get too old and lazy to be bothered to offend."

—*The Psychopath Test* by Jon Ronson

21

IT WAS THURSDAY AFTERNOON, June 24, 2010, a hot and humid summer day, when the Whitehouse Police Department served an arrest warrant on Kim Cargill.

The charges?

"Injury to a Child."

Serious accusations stemming from a complaint made by the father of one of her kids regarding an incident on March 17, 2010—though, as time would soon tell, the incident would pale in comparison to other claims made by Kim's kids and ex-husbands.

Brian (pseudonym), one of Kim's sons, did not call his mother "Mom"—which said something about their relationship. Brian called Kim "KC." While sitting on the witness stand, Brian would later describe in horrific detail how growing up in the Cargill household was a chronic abusive experience for all four children. Brian had been savagely and repeatedly abused by KC, he testified, and so had his three brothers. It was not once in a while, or when they acted up and got on KC's nerves, but rather on nearly every day they spent with KC. On a daily basis one or more of the kids was at the receiving end of her volatile, ferocious and violent temper.

Inside the Waterton Circle home that the SCSO had recently searched, Brian had always slept with the family dog, Oreo (until the dog went mysteriously missing one night). Brian would lie in bed and stare at the ceiling, wondering what was going to happen next. For the most part Brian endured what he said were "slaps" in the face from KC on a regular basis. That was a good day. He'd do something she didn't like and— *bang!*—she'd hit him, leaving an imprint of her hand in red on his face.

There were other instances, he explained, when he'd watch as KC "choked" the younger kids. This didn't happen as often as the slapping, but it happened enough to impart fear in the kids. KC generally used her hands, Brian said, when she choked them. But there was one time he could never forget. His brother Blake (pseudonym) had been acting up. KC and Blake got into an argument over something trivial, which caused Kim Cargill to explode in a volcanic rage the children knew meant something bad was going to happen.

Angry and ranting, Kim ran into Blake's bedroom. Brian looked on, worried for his brother, scared to step in for fear of suffering a worse punishment than she was preparing to dish out. Brian watched as Kim grabbed a belt. It was not to whip Blake—that would have been tolerable, in this one instance. Because tonight Kim decided to place the belt around Blake's throat and choke him with it. As she did this, Brian later said, he watched his brother's face turn red as he tried desperately to cry out. Kim kept up pressure until she knew she had to let go or the child was going to pass out and possibly die.

"You little motherfucker" was a common vulgarity Kim screamed at one of the kids. "You will *listen* to me."

Brian wore ortho-k contact lenses. He had trouble sometimes getting one particular lens into his eye. He recalled one time when KC walked over to help him out.

"Stand still," she said with *that look* on her face. Brian didn't want to ask his mother for help to begin with. He knew she had no patience and a low tolerance for anything even remotely aggravating or difficult. It was strange for the boys when they thought of her as an LVN, someone who went to work every night and cared for people.

Brian was "flinching" and "blinking," he explained. He couldn't help it. She was forcing the lens into his eye. It hurt like the dickens.

"Stand. Still. Damn-it-all!" Kim yelled. She liked to grind her teeth when she became angry. Call the kids names: "You stupid son of a bitch, don't move while I do this." Things like that, Brian remembered later. Insults and constant demeaning taunts meant to intimidate and scare.

He continued to squirm and blink as his body recoiled. She used zero finesse or love to place the lens into his eye.

As Brian told her she was hurting him, KC reached in back of her. They were in the bathroom in her bedroom. Stuff everywhere. There was a can of hair spray on the counter. She grabbed it.

"I looked up at her and I just saw her hand rear back and hit me with the edge [of] the bottom of, like, the hair spray can . . . ," Brian recalled.

A severe blow to the head with a metal can left a large welt on Brian's forehead.

There was another instance Brian recalled when KC had chased him down a hallway inside the house. She had an old TV stored in the same hallway near an air conditioner vent. Brian was "backpedaling," walking quickly backward, making sure to stay out of her way, while at the same time keeping his eyes on her.

"I was scared she might do something to me."

The boy knew: Kim Cargill was on a mission to hurt one of her kids and he happened to be the chosen one that night. Simple as that.

Kim chased him down the hallway. She was "looking at [him] with, like, gritted teeth and eyes that were fierce." She waited until he was near the TV, and when Brian reached that section of the hallway, she hurled him over the TV set with the momentum they both had accumulated while walking fast down the hallway. He fell down and over the TV set and scraped up his back pretty badly. Brian knew KC wanted to hurt him. She needed Brian to feel pain.

He felt pain.

When KC would abuse the other children, she would sometimes employ Brian to help out. He said he was far "too scared" *not* to help her.

"[Blake], you get over there," Kim snapped one day.

Blake knew by the sound of her voice that he was in for a solid "spanking," as Brian later called it. Blake walked over. It was such an insignificant thing—not that there is any excuse for abuse in any form—that

Brian later could not recall what it was Blake had done to make her mad.

Brian was nearby. Kim had a hard time giving the "spanking," Brian explained. She couldn't hold the child down. When she was overly angry or in a state of rage, KC had a hard time managing the beatings. "She misses our butt and hits our lower back or hits our thighs," Brian recalled in court. As she had Blake bent over, KC took out the belt and began whacking him, but he grabbed the belt and wouldn't let her have it back.

"Go get me the other belt!" Kim ordered Brian.

"Yes, KC."

Brian retrieved another belt, gave it to his mother. She placed it around the boy's neck and "began choking him," Brian remembered. Brian generally never stuck around to watch what was happening. It was far too painful and scary. There was a screen door, though, and as he walked back "to his room, so I could cry," he said, he happened to look behind and watch as KC placed the belt around Blake's neck.

On another occasion Brian was in his underwear one morning and KC was on the warpath around the house, looking for some reason to scold the kids for another "thing" they had done wrong. Brian was on his way to the bathroom. He had to go really badly.

Blake was doing his chores, but he was speeding through them. "What are you doing?" KC screamed at Blake. "Slow down. Do them right!"

Blake knew that "do them right" also meant *"or else."* So he walked off into another room to get out of KC's way.

She was now immeasurably angry. Turning around, KC saw Brian come out of his room and begin walking down the hallway toward the bathroom.

She needed to release her anger.

"So she turned around and just looked at me," he later recalled. He saw the gaze in her eyes they all knew by then—all of that rage boiling up to the surface, looking for a release. KC needed somehow to get it all out of her. Brian was just there. He hadn't done anything.

"And then she just picked me up by my throat and then set me down."

As she did this, Brian urinated in his underpants, all over himself.

Kim Cargill had a distinctive way in which she placed her hands on the children's throats. It wasn't as though she'd grab them in a rage any way she could. For KC, it was ritualistic; she had a way to inflict the most pain she could.

"She would put her thumbs on my Adam's apple and then caress her fingers around my throat . . . ," Brian recalled. "Her thumbs would just push in and make it to where you couldn't scream or talk or anything."

The belt beatings, chokings, picking the kids up by their necks and lifting them up off the ground, Brian said later, would go on "probably about every day of the week" in some form.

The kids got home from school or from the sitter's house and they never knew which monster was going to be underneath the bed.

KC was fixing Brian a peanut butter sandwich in the

kitchen one afternoon after school. He stood nearby, mumbling to himself. Later he could not recall what had been troubling him. Probably something to do with school, he surmised, or maybe KC getting on him about not feeding the cats the way she demanded. She would blow up about little things, not done specifically the way she had asked.

KC was over near the refrigerator after she had finished making the sandwich. Brian asked for his mother to get him a red Gatorade.

She stopped, stared him down.

Uh-oh.

Kim brought her son a blue Gatorade.

"I don't like blue," Brian said, more to himself than KC. After all, by now he knew better than to sass or question anything KC did.

Not saying anything, KC picked up the knife she had used to make the sandwich and threw it at her son, like a circus performer tossing knives as his assistant stood in front of a board. Then, walking back over to the sandwich on the counter, KC picked it up and shoved it into Brian's face, smearing it all over him.

Even the youngest son, Timmy, the boy Cherry would watch for KC, would make KC mad enough for her to inflict pain and abuse. Brian recalled many times seeing her shove the toddler's bottle deep into his mouth after Timmy made her angry for some stupid reason. Other times, if she got mad at him, she'd wait until Timmy was walking across the driveway or on the hard wooden floor (having just learned to walk) and she'd purposely trip him by kicking out one of his feet.

* * *

Brian said there were times when KC would take the kids out to the "ghetto" part of the city, as he described it, a bad section of Tyler, and leave the kids inside the car while she went somewhere. She'd roll the windows down so they could breathe, but she would leave them there for "four hours" at a time. The kids had no idea where she was, what she was doing or when and if she was ever coming back. She'd pull up somewhere, park the car and get out. No explanation.

As Brian would later tell cops, KC knew what to do to try and hide the abuse. She had a way of making a fist, protruding her middle knuckle out and whacking the kids in the head, so their hair covered up the bruises. When she slapped the kids, she'd use just enough force, Brian maintained, to leave a welt on the side of their faces that lasted just a few hours before going away.

"You're stupid," she'd yell at the kids. "You're all stupid sons of bitches . . . motherfuckers. Little fuckers!"

"Mom!" the kids would respond.

"KC," Brian would answer, "stop saying that."

"You're nothing but a dumb little fucker," she'd snap back. "Get in your room."

KC had a man over one night. He was playing the video game Guitar Hero in the living room. She sat nearby, watching.

Brian walked into the room. "And I smelled this really bad smell," he said later.

"Who farted?" Brian said aloud, laughing.

The guy thought it was funny. "You smelled it, you dealt it," KC's date said to Brian, and they had a good laugh over it. Brian wanted to play the game. He looked over at his mother, though, and knew by the look on her face that he would not be playing games on this night.

"I'll be right back," Kim told her date.

KC grabbed Brian by the arm and walked him to his room down the hallway. Then she knelt down, eye to eye with her son. She put her face right up against Brian's so that they were "head-butting" each other. She gritted her teeth at him and whispered, "You don't say that around people, do you *understand* me?"

"I shouldn't be the one getting into trouble for being in my own house and asking who farted," Brian answered back, realizing maybe he should not have talked back.

Kim hauled off and head-butted him. "Hard," he recalled. But it wasn't just in the head, she made sure she knocked the bridge of his nose, too, so as to inflict as much pain as possible.

"Get your ass in your room, you little fucker."

When KC clenched her teeth, she meant business. On a twelve-year-old's level of thinking, the way Brian described it later, it was akin to when a ballplayer goes up to bat and he's waiting to hit the ball. The ballplayer, focusing, grinds his teeth so he can dredge up enough energy—or "anger"—to smash the ball as hard as he can. When KC ground her teeth, she'd sometimes say, "You don't do that again, or I am going to fucking *kill* you."

Another favorite way of abusing her children was for Kim Cargill to walk by, if they were in the hallway or near a wall, and body slam the kid into the wall for no apparent reason other than she felt like it.

Brian brought home a grade of eighty-nine. He thought it was amazing—and it was, actually.

"One grade away from a ninety," he said, beaming, proud of himself. If it wasn't for that seventy he had gotten on a test, he explained to KC, he would have a ninety average in that class. For a kid whose mother is beating him and ridiculing him, as he claimed, almost on a daily basis, an eighty-nine was remarkable.

"You're a stupid fuck," KC said. Then she slapped and hit Brian in the face, he later recalled.

"What the heck?" he asked.

KC said she wanted the ninety. "It's your fault for not making good grades!"

KC put a lock on the outside of Brian's door, turning his room—a kid's sanctuary, his place away from the world where he can go and be by himself—into a prison.

A cop asked Brian why he thought she did that.

"So she could lock me and [Timmy] in there," Brian said.

"How long?" the cop interviewing him asked.

"Longest would be about four hours, not ever less than one hour."

During one of those times she locked Timmy and Brian in the bedroom, KC said beforehand, "I'm doing this because I am getting your birthday presents ready." She was referring to Brian. He was about to celebrate his tenth birthday. She was trying to make it seem as though it was for his benefit she was locking them up. She didn't want him or Timmy to surprise her and see what she was wrapping in the bathroom nearby, she claimed.

In they went.

KC locked the door.

A few minutes went by and Brian thought he heard something. It was like a car door slamming shut. He got up and looked out his window.

There was KC: driving out of the driveway, taking off.

"So I knew right there she was lying," Brian recalled.

When he was forced to watch Timmy inside the locked room, Brian put on cartoons. This was how he later figured out how long KC had been gone. He would count the episodes of cartoons he watched with Timmy: "four" or "eight" episodes of *SpongeBob SquarePants* meant she was gone for two or four hours.

Timmy was exceptionally antsy one day. He couldn't sit still. He started to jump off the furniture in Brian's room.

"You better stop it," Brian warned his little brother.

Timmy would jump and then fall to the ground, pretending to roll over and play dead.

"Stop it," Brian said. Timmy was jumping higher and higher each time.

Then it happened: Timmy jumped up and his foot turned inward and he landed on his leg and snapped it.

"What happened?" KC asked when she got home.

Brian didn't want to tell because he was scared she'd beat him for not watching the child. All he said was Timmy had hurt his leg somehow. He didn't know how bad the injury was or how he did it.

The kid couldn't walk on it, however.

For the remainder of that day, Brian explained, "He, like, crawled on his butt, like, scooted around."

KC didn't care one way or the other.

A nurse.

She allowed him to crawl around all day with a broken leg. Finally, later that night, the kid was treated.

It didn't matter to KC who it was. If she felt you had wronged her, she'd lash out. One day when Brian's dad, Matt Robinson, lived with Kim and the kids, Matt's mother was over watching the kids while Matt and Kim were at work. The child's grandmother had the kids out back playing on the swings and in the sandbox. Over near the edge of the lawn, by the fence, the grandmother noticed something on the ground. She walked over and had a look.

Photos were spread out all over the place. They had gotten wet from a recent rainstorm. The grandmother picked them up and brought them inside, spread them out on the kitchen table to dry. She figured maybe the kids had gotten hold of them somehow and tossed them, or they might have blown away in the wind. In any event she was looking to help KC and dry them out so KC could put them away.

When KC got home, she found one of the photos—of Matt Robinson—and brought it over to the grandmother and tossed it into her face, saying sharply: "What the *hell* are you doing with photos of my husband?"

Except Kim and Matt aren't married, the grandmother thought right away.

The grandmother didn't know what to say. She was just trying to help. "I picked them up in the yard and was trying to dry them off, Kim."

"You have no business looking at these pictures," Kim snapped. Then she grabbed the grandmother by the arms and twisted them, hurting her. From there

Kim jumped on top of the woman and shook her, twisting her body and arms.

The grandmother kicked KC in the stomach to stop her.

KC fell backward. Then she got up and pushed the old woman.

The grandmother kicked her again.

"I'm pregnant," Kim said. "What are you doing? I thought you knew that."

The grandmother looked at her: "Well, you may not be now."

22

JILL LOWE WAS INFATUATED BY the baby in Kim Cargill's arms. An account executive, Jill worked for a major television network and lived in Tyler. She'd been going to her child's Little League games and seeing one particular woman on the sidelines with what appeared to be a newborn in her arms for some time, so she decided to introduce herself. Their kids played on the same team. Mothers and fathers often begin friendships while their kids play sports.

"I'm Jill," she said.

"He's [two years] old," Kim said. It was 2008, a few years before she started leaving Timmy with Cherry Walker. Apparently, that kick by the grandmother hadn't done anything to KC and she had the baby without a problem. Kim Cargill had two other children with her, beside her fourth child—Brian—out on the ball field. She had just gone through another divorce, her third. Matt Robinson had figured KC out by now and had left her.

Jill had been sitting, watching her boy, admiring

Kim Cargill's baby. As they chatted, Kim seemed kind and friendly. Kim could be charming; she had a side to her that many later described as intelligent and sophisticated. She knew how to carry herself if she wanted to win somebody over.

"Here's my phone number," Jill said. Through conversation they realized they did not live far from each other. Maybe they could get together some day and have lunch.

"That would be great," Kim said. She gave Jill her phone number.

Kim saw a babysitter and a confidante—somebody she could use, control, con, lie to, cheat and steal from.

Jill was the perfect mark.

If their relationship had ended on that day, Jill would have been able to walk away thinking she'd met a nice neighbor. Here was a woman with four kids, her hands full, her days and nights spent changing diapers and making meals. No man around to help out. Here was Kim Cargill, all these kids, wading her way through life, raising the children the best she knew how. That was the façade, the front, the magnificent, martyrlike sense of self she exhibited in public.

Peeling back the layers of Kim Cargill, however, as her relationship with Jill grew to encompass lunches and babysitting and phone conversations, Jill saw a vicious, revolting, crass woman, someone who cared little for her children or anybody else but herself. It was as though KC could not contain herself, or control her emotions. She had to act out. She had that impulsivity most narcissists cannot contain, no matter how hard they try.

"Poor behavioral controls," most psychologists will say.

"If you ever need a babysitter while you're working," Jill told Kim as their friendship carried on into the summer of 2008. This was when Jill was not yet aware of the monster she had invited into her life. At this point Jill felt bad for KC.

"Money is so tight," Kim would complain to Jill. "It is very difficult. I'm never getting enough shift work at the hospitals. Finding babysitters and paying them . . ."

Jill offered to help any way she could, including lending Kim money. Jill would help out, she explained later, by buying "groceries, diapers, get [Kim's] car fixed, maybe pay [the] electric bill or something."

In those early days of knowing KC, Jill thought she and Kim "got along fine." Yet, as she got to know Kim on a more personal level, Jill saw a callous, unempathetic, cunning shell of a human being emerge—one that she had been "warned about."

Most of the uneasy feelings Jill developed as she got to know KC better revolved around what Kim Cargill "could do to other people."

KC called Jill one night. She was livid—entirely pissed off at something involving Jill. "I'm coming over," KC said with vengeance in her voice. It had to do with a deal for a pair of Jet Skis Jill had brokered—acting as the liaison—between a newly divorced friend of Jill's and Kim Cargill's mother. The Jet Skis, according to what KC was telling Jill, were worth $30,000, but Jill's friend was selling them to Kim's mom for $15,000. The deal had been in the works for several months, but here was KC exploding suddenly over it. Jill later learned, "She was irate about it, beyond a normal reaction, because she did not like the person her mother was buying the Jet Skis from. . . ." Mentioning the price meant that KC believed the woman was selling the Jet Skis at a loss of $15,000 just to spite KC.

But it was all in her mind.

KC blamed Jill for the entire mess, which did not seem to be a deal that anybody should be upset over. If anything, KC should have been happy that her mother had gotten such a good price on the Jet Skis. But not KC. To her it was personal. She was mad at Jill for putting her mother in touch with a woman whom KC hated.

The calls started. KC would phone Jill and berate her. "Bitch. Cunt." All the nasty slurs she could muster. She'd scream and yell vulgarities.

After the calls KC stalked Jill.

"I was scared of her by then," Jill explained. "I was looking at her through the peephole, and she was screaming obscenities and threatening me" while in her car or standing on Jill's front porch.

KC would park her car in front of Jill's house. "You *motherfucker.* You *bitch.* I'm going to *destroy* you."

The hate spewing from KC's mouth was intense and very real.

"You're crazy," Jill said, stepping out of her house one time, trying to get KC to calm down. "You do not have nothing on me."

"I will fucking make up lies about you. I'll tell your husband to destroy you. I'll destroy your career." KC was red-faced; she was in a rage and unrecognizable to Jill as that mom she had met at the Little League game.

Jill walked closer to KC's car. Jill could not believe it, but KC had her two youngest sons inside. They were listening to all their mother had to say, learning how

to deal with life's difficulties and disappointments
from a person on a rage-fueled, profanity-laced rant,
stalking one of her former friends.

"Go away! Get off my property!" Jill yelled. "I'll call
the police."

There might have been more to this than Jill setting
KC's mom up with some Jet Skis, Jill soon learned.
One day Jill had noticed some bite marks on Blake.

"What happened?" Jill had asked KC.

"Oh, that . . . he had a fight with his brother," KC
had told Jill. "It's nothing."

Jill was suspicious. It didn't seem as though a child
could cause such a brutal injury, but she took KC at
her word. But then Jill began to think about how "in-
timidated" the children always were when around KC.
They were afraid of her, for certain—all the time. They
seemed to live under a banner of fear, much like an
abused animal would act.

"When she got angry at them," Jill explained in
court later, "you could see the fear on them. . . ." They
were scared of their mother and what she might do.
There had been one instance, Jill recalled, that said a
lot about Kim Cargill as a mother and disciplinarian.

Jill had the youngest child one afternoon and they
were playing ball inside Jill's house. At the time the
child was about three years old. They were bouncing a
tennis ball back and forth. The child missed his target
and the ball accidentally hit a thermometer on the
counter, which subsequently fell and smashed on the
ground. The boy became visibly upset over the accident. He walked over and stared at the broken bits.

"Miss Jill . . . Miss Jill . . . my mama's going to kill me," the child explained. "My mama is going to kill me. I'm going to get a spanking. I'm going to get a spanking." The child took off, running up and down the stairs in a nervous release of energy.

"No, you're not," Jill said, consoling the child, holding him. "I'll say I did it, okay?"

The child bowed his head and nodded.

"Just come and sit down on my couch," Jill told the child. He had started to run up and down the stairs again. "I will clean it up. You're not going to get into trouble. Don't worry."

"My mama is going to spank me. My mama is going to spank me," the child was repeating while continuing to run up and down the stairway.

"No, she's not," Jill kept saying.

One of the older kids came into the house. He looked at what happened and he, too, began to run around inside Jill's house. In fact, he ran so hard and with such force that he purposely ran straight at a sectional, near where Jill had been sitting, and knocked it over. Then "he became so frightened," Jill later remembered, "he ran over to me and grabbed me by the neck."

KC walked in sometime later, saw the remnants of what had gone on and asked, "What happened here?"

"I did it," Jill said, and stood.

"No, you didn't, Jill," Kim said in a low voice, staring at her young boy.

"No, Kim, I threw the ball," Jill tried to explain.

KC stared at her, then at the kids. "I'll help you clean this up."

"No, that's okay," Jill said. "I'll clean it up."

Incidents such as this made Jill take a serious look at her so-called friend and step back, telling herself that there's much more going on than a mother "spanking" a child. Jill could tell by the reactions of the children and Kim's tone with them, plus the threatening looks and stares, that there was serious abuse going on inside KC's house.

Not long after that incident Jill took a call from KC. "Jill, they're going to call you. What are you going to say?" This was right around the time Timmy was being taken away from KC and she was often hiding the child at Cherry's. KC was referring to DFPS calling Jill to ask about the children: Had she ever seen anything? Had the children ever said anything? What was KC's behavior around them?

Jill was going to be honest, though she did not relate this to KC on the phone that day. There were times when Jill had seen KC scream and yell at the top of her lungs at the kids and "jerk" them around— something that had been reported by many sources close to KC. If one of the kids got out of line or was acting up in public, KC would walk over, grab him by the arm and jerk it, hurting the child. It was abuse, no two ways about it.

DFPS called and asked Jill about an incident with Brian. He'd had some injuries his father had reported. KC had been interviewed by the police. She said the incident involved Brian falling and hitting his head on a table or the television set. (It was in reference to the incident in which KC had pushed Brian over the TV set and he scraped his back.) Jill told DFPS she recalled seeing something happen once and watching

Kim jerk Brian backward and he fell into the television set and hurt his head and face pretty badly. (A second altogether different incident!)

All of this was extremely upsetting to Jill to have to witness as it began taking place in front of her and she took a step back from the relationship. It was hard to walk away entirely, Jill said, because of her concerns over the children's safety—but also equally troubling to have to sit and watch. One thing that bothered Jill—for the sole reason that Jill herself had been described as "such a doting mother," still making her eighteen-year-old sandwiches to take to work—was having to sit by and see Timmy (two at the time) be made to fill his own bottles with milk.

"If he cannot pour his own bottle," Kim would say when Jill had a "WTF" look on her face, "he will have to do without!"

Jill was unable to help KC or her kids any longer. The only way she could be of value was to be honest with DFPS.

One of the kids went to Jill and explained that KC had "punched" him in the face. He was frightened. What would she do next?

The same child had his tonsils out. KC brought the child over to Jill's office straight from the hospital after the operation—which Jill found to be strange in and of itself. KC walked in and placed the child on Jill's couch in the reception area and then walked into Jill's office. Jill went over to the child to see how he was feeling. Did he need a glass of water? Some Popsicles? Ice cream? Some motherly TLC? Maybe something to soothe the pain? Why had Kim just dumped him on the couch and walked away as if she could have not cared less about him?

"He was just as white as . . . sick," Jill said later, quite unable to articulate exactly how she felt about the boy and how he looked just out of the hospital.

Brian had a gaze about his face that Jill said she could never forget. He was petrified of whatever was coming next. Jill looked toward her office and then bent down and whispered to Brian, "Do you want to go home?"

He looked at her. He was terrified of something. He said, "Uh-uh."

"Are you scared?" Jill whispered.

The boy nodded yes.

Jill wrote her number down on a small piece of paper and put it in his hand. "You keep this from her . . . and you use it to call me if you need anything."

He said okay.

Any child after an operation might be scared, or feel sick to his stomach. But this was not a look that said, "*I'm sick and scared. When will I feel better?*" It was pure terror, Jill believed. The boy did not want to be alone with his mother.

"It was a look of fear I have never seen before in my life," Jill recalled.

When KC engaged Jill in conversations about her mother, it often brought out a side of KC that Jill rarely saw. Part of it was sad, Jill recalled; the other part, well, quite terrifying. Jill could never understand how much KC "despised" her own mother, Rachel Wilson. She'd rant and rave and degrade her mother anytime her name was bought up in conversation.

"Joan Crawford," KC told Jill one night when they were talking about Rachel. KC was referring to the memoir written by Crawford's daughter, Christina, exposing the antics and abuse perpetrated by the famed actress. (Moviegoers are familiar with the Crawford role played by Faye Dunaway in the 1981 film that took the book's title, *Mommie Dearest*.)

"That bad, Kim?"

"My childhood was a nightmare," KC said.

At the time Jill had not met Rachel Wilson or Kim's stepdad. "I believed everything [KC] was telling me about them. And it broke my heart . . . and when I met her mother and stepfather, I realized that was not the case, as far as I could decipher between the two stories."

Jill soon figured out that everything KC had said, the stories she told—about her childhood, about her ex-husbands, one of whom she claimed had taken off years ago and she had never heard from him again— were all part of a tale of manipulation KC was plying her with. KC was filling her with that "poor me . . . look at my life" rhetoric, hoping to make Jill feel sorry for her. When Jill took a close look at the facts, however, she wondered whether KC was describing herself when she spoke of her Joan Crawford–like mother.

"I couldn't watch them not have groceries or diapers or the lights [being] cut off or the air conditioner in the car not working," Jill said of KC and the way she lived. It all became too much to bear. She had a tough time standing by and not doing anything. Then, when Rachel moved to Texas from Mississippi, and Jill began to discuss the situation with Rachel, "I knew something was very, very wrong up here—and so I just kept trying to distance myself. . . ."

"I cannot do it anymore," Jill told Rachel one day as

they talked about KC. "I cannot watch this [go on, in front of me]."

The behaviors KC was displaying with regard to her ex-husbands, the kids, the way, "in the flash of an eye," Jill said, KC could change from a nice suburban mom to a vengeful maniac made Jill decide enough was enough. Even Jill's own children told her, "There's something wrong with that woman."

Of course, there was the house: the ants, the bugs, the terrible smells in the kids' bedrooms, the mess everywhere. KC was not doing any cleaning up.

"This is the filthiest place I have ever seen," Jill said one day, half jesting, when she and KC had first met. "You could grow plants on the console. There is so much coffee and sticky stuff everywhere."

KC's car was the same.

In addition, there was always some drama playing out in KC's life. Work. The kids' fathers. Other friends. The state. There was always a *thing* KC was involved in, and it was always, of course, somebody else's fault, always directed against her. Poor KC. She could never catch a break. She showed borderline personality disorder, antisocial disorder and pure sociopathic behaviors; she did not care what anybody felt.

If she didn't like something Jill did or said to one of the kids, KC would keep the child from seeing Jill. One child was kept away from Jill for five months. Just over something Jill had said to the child that KC didn't like.

* * *

Jill recalled when KC introduced her to Cherry Walker. "It was, like, fifteen seconds," Jill recalled. Kim had explained she used Cherry to babysit because Cherry was cheap and KC couldn't afford day care. It was not Cherry that Jill objected to. She had no idea that Cherry was mentally challenged. It was where Cherry lived that made Jill realize just how devious and manipulative and downright mean KC could be when she wanted to be.

Jill had gone along with KC on a day when KC dropped off Timmy at Cherry Walker's Citadel apartment. Cherry came running out, grabbed the boy and ran back in. It was as though she was trying to hide him.

"Kim, um, isn't that where [Timmy's dad] lives?" Jill asked. She thought she'd recognized the building.

KC smiled.

"Kim! Does [Timmy's dad] live in the same building?"

It was true: Timmy's father lived right above Cherry. For two years Kim had been bringing the boy to this same building—first to Cherry's neighbor, Marcie Fulton, and then to Cherry—and the dad never knew his son was right there in the same building, underneath his nose—*literally*. What's more: "He hid behind a wall," Jill explained later. "She kept him—made Cherry keep him inside the bricked-in wall." Cherry, in other words, had a hiding place for Timmy whenever things heated up. Jill said if she knew that Cherry was mentally handicapped and watching Timmy, "I would have flipped."

That "bad man," whom KC had told Cherry to be on the lookout for . . . was Timmy's dad.

At times KC would say, "I wish I had your life, Jill.

Your relationship with your parents . . . I wish I could have that with my mother."

Still, that seemingly caring sentiment would turn cold in an instant.

Jill and KC were discussing Rachel once and KC said, "I'd kill her if I could do it and get away with it."

Jill stared at the friend she did not know. The look on KC's face, Jill knew, meant that Kim had not been playing around with words—she was serious. If she could murder her mother and thwart justice for the crime, she would follow through with it.

Jill was out of town when she heard Cherry had been murdered. It was on that Sunday, a day after Cherry's body had been found, when police called Jill and asked: "Did you hear about the murder?"

Jill went down to the SCSO on Monday morning, June 28, and sat down for an interview. The SCSO had acquired Jill's name from the state's child endangerment case against KC—Jill had been subpoenaed to testify.

When she heard about Cherry, Jill later recalled, "I knew." There was no doubt for Jill that it was KC who had murdered Cherry.

How confident was she that KC had murdered Cherry Walker?

For three nights after she got back home, Jill Lowe slept on her couch with a gun beside her.

"I was afraid she was coming for me."

She only moved back upstairs and put the gun away after Kim Cargill had been arrested and taken away.

23

KIM WAS IN JAIL ON a bond of $500,000. One might think that jail would keep KC out of trouble. But that was not to be the case. It was June 26, 2010, two days after her arrest on charges of Injury to a Child. The SCSO knew Kim was not going to be bailed out. So they had her where they wanted as detectives built a case for murder. Considering the potential charges and what had been done to Cherry, the SCSO was looking at a likely capital murder case against Kim Cargill.

As an inmate in Central Jail, KC was a nine on a scale of one to ten—ten being the most difficult inmate—one of Kim's jailers, Adrienne Barnes, later said. Barnes had worked at Central Jail for four years and no one like Kim Cargill had ever come through the doors.

Barnes brought Kim her breakfast tray on Saturday morning, June 26.

"That's not what my doctor ordered," KC snapped at Barnes. Apparently, KC was now allergic to certain foods, had met with the jail's in-house physician and had been put on a special diet. "Take it back."

"Excuse me?" Barnes said.

KC threw the tray back out of her cell through the tiny slit Barnes had sent it through earlier. She yelled, "I'm not eating that!"

This was just one of the many ways in which Kim Cargill decided to rebel against authority. She was "constantly," Barnes later explained, talking about calling her attorneys over everything and anything she didn't like in her surroundings. She would threaten the guards. It was always somebody else's fault for the predicament KC found herself in.

"We're going to sue this place," she would scream from her cell when she didn't like the food, the way she was being treated or something a guard had said or done.

She was "controlling, manipulative and bossy."

Another guard called her "demanding." When they told her no, she "tries to force it upon you to say yes."

One night, following orders from a supervisor to go through all of KC's paperwork, a guard went into her cell to have a look at anything she had in her possession. Inmates weren't allowed to have staples or paper clips in any of their papers. These stationery supplies could be turned into weapons and tattoo needles.

"I need to go through all of your paperwork," the guard said to KC. She handed KC the summons, a piece of paper clearly outlining that she was following protocol and orders from the top. KC was told to hand over any papers she had.

KC became squirrely, walking back and forth inside her cell, pacing. The guard could tell she was "very upset" over having been told what to do, especially regarding her papers—anything she had collected from her case, or anything her lawyers had given her. The guard explained that she was not going to look at any of it. She just wanted to take out all of the staples and paper clips.

"No, you're not doing that," KC sniped.

The guard took it all, anyway, telling KC: "Look, I'm turning all the wording downward so I cannot see any of it." She didn't really care what KC had in her files. She just needed to take out the stationery contraband.

"Miss Cargill, I'm doing this."

"You are not supposed to be doing that," KC said. She was loud and obnoxious.

The guard didn't know what to say.

"I'm not writing you up," KC warned. "I'm telling my lawyer and we're taking you to federal court."

Kim Cargill frequently threatened the guards with lawsuits, but she never followed up. The guard later said that KC "was more manipulative and tried to get under your skin" than anything else. She would do anything she could to undermine authority and see if she could get a rise out of the guards.

Another guard later described dealing with Kim Cargill as something akin to being on a "roller-coaster ride. . . . You get on that ride and you strap yourself in." KC could be nice. She'd ask, "Hi, how are you?" But then once things got going, watch out: "All of a sudden . . . you're in for a bumpy ride."

KC liked to create problems with other inmates. An inmate might ask a guard a question and KC, inside her cell next door, eavesdropping, would yell, "Don't listen to her. She don't know what she's talking about. They're lying to you. I know how things should be done."

Within a week of her stay at Central Jail, KC began
to give away clues about herself and her potential role
in Cherry Walker's murder. KC didn't realize—or
maybe she did and she did not give a damn—that all
jails monitored and recorded outgoing phone calls
that inmates made. With someone as vain and self-
centered as Kim Cargill, it was only a matter of time,
detectives knew, before she opened her mouth—
because Kim Cargill, in the end, could not and would
not shut up.

24

CHECKING HER E-MAIL ONE MORNING during the fall of 2009, Suzanne Jones-Davis sat at her desk and took an immediate interest in an e-mail from Classmates.com. Suzanne's twenty-fifth high-school reunion was coming up and she was being formally invited. Suzanne had been sick, "like a lot of people" in her region that autumn, she later explained. Feeling like maybe the flu was coming on, she did not end up going to the reunion. However, she did manage to reconnect with several fellow high-school peers on Facebook.

A former friend from junior high that became more of an acquaintance in high school, Kim Cargill reached out to Suzanne on Facebook. It had been almost twenty-five years since the two of them had seen or heard from each other. Several alumni were talking on Facebook about how disappointed they were about being sick and unable to make the reunion. One of them suggested: Well, let's just do something else, since none of us got to go.

It sounded like fun to Suzanne: old friends, reliving

memories, reconnecting. Suzanne was married, but she did not have kids. She had a home near the bar where everyone had made plans to meet.

Thus, on February 7, 2010, Suzanne and several others, including Kim Cargill, met and had what Suzanne later called a "happy-hour reunion" at a local pub. KC and Suzanne had been talking offline beforehand and Suzanne made it clear she was glad to open up her home to KC for the night because KC lived so far away.

"I have three kids," KC said.

It was a lie, of course. KC had four. When she later found out, Suzanne never understood why KC had to lie about this simple fact. Apparently, to KC, one of her kids did not matter enough to include him.

KC stayed the night. They went to the reunion and it was a disappointment. Reunions can be one of those ideas that sound better in theory. However, when everyone gets together, they realize how different they all are now and how nobody really knew each other. It can become a disappointment; nostalgia loses.

Suzanne spoke to KC a few more times as the first week of March 2010 approached and then she did not hear from her again.

That is, until June 3, 2010.

Suzanne wasn't home. KC left a voice mail. She was manic, all wound up. She said something along the lines of: "My life is falling apart, Suz. Things are really, really bad. I really need a friend. My life is, like, in the worst place it's *ever* been. I need someone to talk to."

Suzanne picked up the phone and dialed her old schoolmate to see if she could be of any help.

No answer. Just KC's voice mail. Suzanne left a message.

KC called Suzanne a few days later, on June 7. Again she sounded upset, agitated and unable to deal with her life.

"They took my [Timmy], Suz," KC explained.

"They what . . . Who?"

KC explained the state had taken the child out of her home and placed him with his father. "Something happened with my other son back in March," KC added, meaning the incident with Brian that had sparked the entire investigation into Kim Cargill's life and her later incarceration.

This was the first time since Suzanne had reconnected with KC that she had heard about any of the custody issues going on in KC's life. KC had never mentioned anything before this two-hour-plus phone call. By the end of the conversation the two women exchanged work numbers and KC begged her old friend to be there for her when she needed. The next few weeks were going to be rough, KC warned. Things were spiraling out of her control and she needed somebody—like Suzanne—whom she could count on. KC couldn't trust anybody in her life any longer, she said. Everyone had done an about-face on her. She had nobody left.

Over the next several days KC called and e-mailed Suzanne several times a day. Most of it was the same hysterical, frenzied rant Suzanne had heard and felt very bad about—all of which had been, Suzanne would find out months later, manipulative lies. KC knew the state had stepped in, checked out her home, interviewed the boys and had spoken to KC's friends and family. The state had found strong reason for the child to be placed with his father until the family court hearing scheduled for the end of June, in which Cherry and others were to testify. Yet, in Suzanne, KC had found a fresh mind to influence, shape and mold, because Suzanne did not know any of the history, only what KC told her. Suzanne had nothing on which to base what she believed and disbelieved; after all, she had only reconnected with KC recently. Why *wouldn't* she believe her?

In one of the e-mails KC sent to Suzanne, KC railed about the potential detrimental effect it would have on her financially if she was forced to pay "CS (child support) for a second child." She explained that the upcoming hearing with the state was going to decide this, among other issues. Her ex-husband, who was suing her for CS, was a dog. He had lied to get the court to side with him.

Suzanne could not get over what she was hearing. It was awful.

KC generally signed her e-mails with the same salutation: *God bless you—love you and may God be with you.*

Suzanne sat back and looked at everything. KC, she believed, was a God-fearing person being railroaded by exes and the system. Everything KC had told her seemed to suggest that the system was designed to beat Kim Cargill. She had no money for a real lawyer, she claimed, unlike her ex, who was loaded.

Reading further into the e-mails, Suzanne was upset about what was happening to her old friend. KC claimed that her own mother was saying she—KC—was "mentally ill." Everybody was against her and she could really use a friend like Suzanne, not only for support, but to testify on her behalf at the hearing. Suzanne, after all, could vouch for KC's sanity, right?

I'm not mentally ill, KC wrote. *All these people are lying.*

Suzanne suggested in a return e-mail that KC call an old friend of theirs, who knew a great family lawyer. Suzanne even provided KC with the telephone number of the friend.

She's a family lawyer and willing to give you a free consult, Suzanne wrote. *I think you need all the help you can get. Call her tomorrow.* Beyond that, Suzanne added, *My mom wants to start a background investigation on* your mom. *Do you have her Social Security number?* Suzanne went on to explain that her mother was "so mad" she couldn't "see straight." She then asked KC "to come here now."

Suzanne invited KC to stay with her and her husband. She said none of them—Suzanne, her mother, Suzanne's husband—could understand why everyone in KC's life was trying to do this to her. They felt bad. They wanted to help. She signed the e-mail, *Love you, Suz.*

Reading this, KC must have known that she had Suzanne right where she wanted: on puppet strings. She could now take Suzanne and move her anywhere on the stage she wanted and Suzanne would conform— all based on the lies KC had been plying Suzanne with about herself, her children and her life. Suzanne was fully convinced that everyone around KC was trying to destroy her.

The reason Suzanne's mother wanted to jump into investigating KC's mother turned out to be because back on June 7, KC had told Suzanne that the entire root cause of her problems in life and with her kids was her mother. Rachel was to blame for *everything*.

In response to that e-mail about Suzanne finding a lawyer and Suzanne's mother getting involved and wanting to investigate Rachel, KC toned her bombast down, writing to Suzanne that it might be too early "to talk out-of-town attorney." This was merely weeks before that all-important custody hearing. KC added, *Everything out here (where she lived) is so different.* Then, after telling Suzanne she would call her during the upcoming weekend, KC wrote, *I caught a ray of hope today, and the psychologist from a couple of years ago is retesting me . . . so they will stop saying "mental illness."* She referred to this revelation as being "huge."

Furthering the lie, and trying to steer Suzanne away from Rachel, KC explained, *[My mother] doesn't have a criminal record or anything, but I will see if I can figure out her Social Security number.* She wanted Suzanne to know that she was grateful for all "the support" from Suzanne's mother and "especially you, Suz." She talked about a "postponement" that was possible with regard to the hearing—which, in fact, had never been discussed. If that postponement took place, KC said, it would be a "blessing," allowing her additional time to "gather more defense materials."

Did that postponement KC mentioned involve her plans to murder Cherry Walker? Did she mean if one of the witnesses scheduled to testify had been killed before the hearing, it would naturally postpone the proceeding? Was she subconsciously giving away her plans?

KC then asked Suzanne to write a letter on her behalf to her doctor.

Suzanne penned a letter that night.

The idea of this letter to the psychiatric doctor set to evaluate KC before the hearing, and how the content of the letter developed, was significant in so many ways. One, it showed how far KC was willing to take things in order to project an image of being the victim; two, it demonstrated how easily she could convince others to lie for her; three, it illustrated how little she cared about lying to, and trying to manipulate, an expert set to testify in her case. The measures she was willing to employ to get her way were malicious and vindictive and illegal. She was willing to bring unsuspecting, innocent bystanders into her web of lies.

In her first draft, written without any help from KC, Suzanne addressed the letter as "to whom it may concern." She talked about knowing KC since the eighth grade: *We were both the new kids in class, and we lived in the same neighborhood.* (All true.) She said she could recall "sleepovers and many outings together" and how they had a "babysitting club" and how "great" KC was with children: *I've never heard any complaints from the parents.* Further, Suzanne added, she had reconnected with KC over the past several weeks, after not having seen her for twenty-five years. Suzanne said that while KC was at her house, "just this past February," she called Timmy back home "several times to check on him and talk." KC appeared "very nervous" since she had been away from him overnight. Ending the brief letter, perhaps stretching the truth just a bit, Suzanne called KC "the nicest person" she had ever known.

After polishing the letter a few times, Suzanne sent it off to KC.

Click.

KC immediately sent back a detailed critique. She thought the letter needed to be "a lot more flattering, longer." She encouraged Suzanne to "talk about me as an adult"—a person Suzanne did not know—"and be vague about the kids." *Talk about how the kids have come first always, even above education, money,* KC instructed. She wanted Suzanne to "mention" how "cold and unfriendly" Rachel was back when they "were kids," and that Suzanne could never "imagine" Rachel ever being a "better parent" than KC was.

Before sending the e-mail to Suzanne, KC made one final request: *Hurry, please.*

Suzanne had only met KC once as an adult, when the Facebook group met up for the reunion cocktail hour and KC stayed overnight at her house. She didn't *know* her. She had no idea what type of parent KC was, or whether or not she put the kids before herself. She was going strictly by what KC was saying about herself. KC was asking Suzanne to talk about things she had no knowledge of.

Still, Suzanne wanted to help her old friend. She believed what KC was saying. She didn't see any harm in it. So she rewrote the letter, making it more personal and more affecting, what KC had ordered. Suzanne even mentioned in the new draft of the letter that she had two stepchildren. This was important because KC had told her in one conversation that she needed to write about her personal life. She then went on to change her opinion about Rachel, saying

she was "always cold," a word—"always"—that carried
with it the insinuation that Suzanne had known Rachel
and KC forever and had interacted with them.

Suzanne sent KC drafts of her letter and KC edited
and rewrote sections herself, adding her own words,
phrases, paragraphs and descriptions. In one section
Suzanne had written about their childhood together.
KC sent back an entirely new, entirely rewritten paragraph that, in part, read: *Even when Kim was on the drill
team, she lacked love and support from home. She excelled at
school . . . on the student council . . . [had] many friends . . .
and is now being rallied around by old friends from our
alma mater.*

On and on, this new version—totally rewritten by
KC—went, applauding KC for being "Mother of the
Year," sacrificing everything for her boys, being constantly put down by an overbearing and scurrilous
mother. The letter was trying to draw pity from KC's
doctor, hoping he would rush to her side during the
upcoming hearing and argue for her to have custody
of her son and not have to pay child support to her ex.

Had Suzanne known any of the facts surrounding
KC's life—and some of the lies that spewed from KC's
computer keyboard in this new draft—it might have
scared Suzanne into running for the hills. However,
Suzanne had little information about what was truly
going on and zero background data to gauge whether
KC was writing truth or lies. She simply went with it,
trusting KC. In one section of the letter KC wrote (for
Suzanne to sign): *[KC] never buys for herself, but always
makes sure the boys have what they need, and they're happy
kids.* She added how "good grades" were "important"
to KC. In fact, the main reason why KC had moved to
"the small town of Whitehouse" was so her sons "could

have a safe environment." The letter pleaded with the doctor that taking Timmy away from "the only security he has ever known" would be a "travesty" in the boy's life. Carrying on, KC wrote how she would gladly "give her life" for Timmy, and that she wasn't so sure Timmy's grandmother or grandfather would because "they're just doing this for money and selfish reasons." (Rachel and her husband were also named in the suit to obtain custody of Timmy.)

If Suzanne knew anything about KC's personality, she could have seen that it had been interjected throughout the letter. She clearly expressed her hatred for anyone that disagreed with her, anyone that had tried to say she was not a good mother, anyone trying to come between her and her kids.

Rachel is cold and calculating, the letter continued. *I do not believe what [the kids have said about all the abuse]. . . . Kids will say anything to get what they want.*

At 4:08 P.M. on Tuesday, June 15, KC sent Suzanne an e-mail: *Can you get it in the mail today? . . . Thanks a million, Kim.*

Suzanne, who had never met Timmy (or spent any amount of time with any of KC's kids), signed the letter as though she had written it herself.

Then she dropped it in the mailbox.

25

ON FRIDAY, JUNE 18, 2010, KC called Suzanne. "I've got good news and bad news."

"What's going on?" Suzanne asked. By now she had become so deeply involved in her old friend's life, they were speaking every day, several times.

Suzanne was feeling a dash of unease because she hadn't really known KC well enough to have written those things about her in a letter she had signed and sent to an expert slated to testify in court. Was she in some way obstructing justice? Suzanne had an icky feeling about this latest stunt KC had directed.

"I need more help," KC said on that Friday.

"What do you need?"

"Well, there's not a lot of people willing to miss work . . . ," KC explained, meaning that she didn't have a long list of people lined up to testify in court on her behalf. Not because they didn't want to, she gave the impression, but because they didn't want to—or couldn't—get out of work. "Would you consider coming [on] Wednesday?" KC asked.

"If I can, Kim, I'll make it. I do not have a lot of

vacation left. What time is it at? Maybe I can call in sick or something. I will see what my boss says. . . . We . . . have a lot of stuff happening."

Actually, Suzanne did not want to attend the hearing and testify on KC's behalf. Writing a letter was one thing; raising your right hand and going on the record was another. She'd gone too far already. Suzanne was beginning to think enough was enough.

The next day, Saturday, June 19, KC and Suzanne communicated several times. Suzanne told her, "I spoke to my boss and he said I could not go, unless I got subpoenaed. Sorry, Kim."

KC called Suzanne Saturday morning. "Really early," Suzanne later recalled. This would have been the Saturday after Cherry went missing. So early, in fact, that nobody in Suzanne's house was even up yet. When Suzanne got up sometime later, she called KC back and asked her what she was doing.

"Oh, running errands. Washing the car. Going to the cleaners. All those things you normally do on a Saturday. Grocery shopping."

"Oh, okay . . ."

That was it? She called before sunup to say she was heading out to run around doing her Saturday errands?

For some reason, KC then added, "I tried to find my babysitter last night, but I never found her."

Lie: KC had spoken to Cherry. Phone records proved as much.

"Okay . . . ," Suzanne said.

"What are you doing today?" KC asked Suzanne.

"Tomorrow is Father's Day, so we're getting ready for that. We're going to my father-in-law's."

They hung up. Later that afternoon KC called

Suzanne again. "Did I tell you my two babysitters were
subpoenaed?"

"No."

"One is an old lady. . . . The other, my main babysitter, is a young lady whose child has been recently
taken away from her. I'm worried about her."

"What are you worried about?"

"I'm concerned about the old-lady babysitter. She's
dirty and unclean. I am worried the young babysitter
is going to tell [DFPS] about the old-lady babysitter."

Suzanne had a tough time recalling every detail surrounding these conversations because KC had called
so many times. They stayed on the phone for hours
sometimes. A short call, like this one, ran on average
about twenty-five minutes. Yet, during this second call,
Suzanne later remembered, she was certain KC talked
specifically about Cherry Walker (referring to her only
as the "young babysitter," never by name) and mentioned how she had tried to find Cherry the previous
night because she wanted to take her out to dinner
and talk to her. "But I never could find her," KC added,
sharing details with Suzanne for some reason that
Suzanne could not figure out. "I need to take them
both out to dinner and talk to them, but I cannot find
my main babysitter."

During this same conversation KC mentioned that
Timmy's father lived in the same apartment complex
as her "main babysitter." Then, for reasons that would
baffle Suzanne, KC said, "I'm going to call Forrest
(Garner, Timmy's dad) and ask him if he's seen Cherry."
KC mentioned something about Forrest perhaps
"confronting" Cherry.

KC was making a huge deal out of not being able to

locate Cherry and making sure that Suzanne knew all the details surrounding her not being able to find her on that Friday night or Saturday.

Suzanne considered all of what KC had to say—the entire conversation—to be "odd." The idea that she was going to call Timmy's father, for one, who lived in the same complex as Timmy's babysitter, but did not know it—the same guy who was taking her to court to take the child away—seemed bizarre to Suzanne. Things were not adding up anymore. She was beginning to question KC and what she was up to.

KC rarely called Suzanne on Sundays because KC generally worked a full shift on that day. But on Monday, June 21, KC called Suzanne on her cell phone number, which KC had never done. Suzanne was at work. It was just after noon. When KC called, Suzanne said she wanted to take the call outside and sit in her car.

KC sounded different, freaked out about something. Maybe even paranoid, Suzanne considered. "Have you seen the Tyler news?" KC asked Suzanne.

"What?" It was a peculiar question to begin a conversation.

"The Tyler news—have you seen it today?" KC asked again.

Suzanne was sitting in her car in the parking lot where she worked, trying to have her lunch.

"No," Suzanne said. "I don't watch the news that much, Kim."

KC became "agitated more than normal," Suzanne recalled.

"Kim, what's wrong?"

"My babysitter is dead!"

"Which one?"

Suzanne was expecting to hear KC say, "The old-lady babysitter" or "The young babysitter," which was how she had always described both. But KC came out with it: "Cherry Walker," she said, and it was the first time Suzanne had heard that name. "They found my babysitter Cherry."

"Oh, my . . ."

"Yes, on Saturday, they found Cherry."

"How do you know this?"

"It was in the papers."

Suzanne went back to work and Googled the name: *Cherry Walker.*

She scrolled through the results, but found nothing. Not a word about Cherry Walker being found dead. This was weird. She was certain Kim had told her the name and said she'd seen it in the newspapers. Or on television. But there was nothing on the Internet.

Suzanne Googled various words to try and find any story she could about Cherry Walker: a dead babysitter, a dead woman and so on, and finally came up with a news story about a "body being found on Saturday." That was it, though. A body. No name. No details.

Cherry Walker would not be identified publicly until that Wednesday.

When Wednesday, June 23, came, Suzanne received what she later called a "cryptic e-mail" from KC. It was in the morning, at 10:46. KC wrote: *If you don't hear from me by Friday, call [the secretary] at Buck Files' [office] to find me. I'm stranded right now.* She went on to say that the SCSO had taken her "house, purse, phone, car, money." Ending the brief note, she said, *That's all I can say.*

Buck Files was a well-known criminal defense attorney in Tyler.

What in the world is going on with her? Suzanne wondered.

Confused, Suzanne tapped a message back: *Who did? See, you need that power of attorney.*

As she thought about it, Suzanne considered that KC was referring to what had happened back in March with Brian and her potential arrest on those child abuse charges. She assumed that's what all of KC's problems centered on.

Do you need me to come and get you? Suzanne wrote back to KC.

They may get your info from my phone—refer them to my attorney! KC darted right back.

Yes, I will. Or mine, Suzanne responded.

I have nothing in my possession, KC wrote back in an e-mail. She said the SCSO had "seized all." They wouldn't allow her any money. She claimed she'd eaten only "twice since yesterday." She explained that she would know more after meeting with her attorney later that same day.

Suzanne encouraged KC to tell her attorney that she was willing to accept KC into her house: *Unless he's putting you up or getting you back into your house.*

KC said she couldn't remain homeless and was "concerned" the SCSO "would create evidence" against her. There was some urgency in her note here as KC finished by stating, *The worst may have happened. Please don't forget me. . . .*

26

SUZANNE JONES-DAVIS DID NOT HEAR from KC again until June 29. By that time KC had been arrested on Injury to a Child charges and was in jail. Suzanne had no idea KC had even been arrested until a phone call from the prison computer came one night and asked Suzanne to press zero to accept a call from an inmate at Smith County Jail.

After accepting the call, realizing it was KC, Suzanne was aghast. Why was KC in jail? Had things run that far off the rails for her?

KC had a way of leading up to the devilish deeds she wanted people to perform on her behalf. She wasn't one to come out and ask bluntly for a nefarious favor, because she understood those types of demands made people think more deeply about what they were going to do. Instead, she carefully plied one of her minions with that "poor me" persona she had mastered and used time and again. Over the course of a few days, she would make the person believe she was being railroaded, or at least blamed, for something she had not done. Her minion would help her out in that regard;

the request would be met with a bit more warmth and enthusiasm.

"Can you get to my house and get some things out of it for me?" KC asked during a phone call she made to Suzanne from Smith County Jail. It seemed that KC had no one else to lean on, no other friends she could count on or trust.

Suzanne later recalled these items KC requested: "Mementos, photos . . . some specific children's paintings [from a closet] . . . a jersey," which hung on a wall and "said 'Cargill' [on the back], and some clothes. . . ."

It seemed like an innocent, simple, common request. They were personal items. KC wanted to make sure nobody else got them.

On July 1, 2010, guards seized a note from KC as she was being searched before a visit with an old friend, Michael Darwin (pseudonym). The note had been addressed to herself. KC was thinking about making a list of the (additional) items she wanted Suzanne to collect from her house. She reminded herself that she needed to mail the list to Suzanne right away. There was little time left to waste.

The following day, July 2, as Kim Cargill sat in jail (knowing full well that the jail had seized a note from her the previous day), Suzanne Jones-Davis drove from her home in McKinney, Texas, to KC's residence in Whitehouse, a two-and-a-half-hour drive of about 130 miles. KC could have called Suzanne, warned her that the jail had recovered a note that named her, but she did not. She allowed Suzanne to fall deeper into her chaos.

Suzanne walked in and grabbed the items KC had requested. These possessions, KC had explained, held nostalgic and sentimental value and she wanted them out of the house. She gave no reason why she wanted Suzanne to grab the items and hold on to them, however. Suzanne figured KC wanted to make sure no one else took them. Yet, in the scope of her friend's arrest on Injury to a Child charges, why hadn't Suzanne thought a bit more about her mission? Was KC planning on *not* going back to her house? Was she under the impression that the state was going to take the house—or that her ex-husband was going to grab the items himself? It really didn't make sense—except to Kim Cargill, who was working confidently under a carefully constructed plan to lure Suzanne into performing another, more important task.

When they spoke again, KC asked Suzanne if she collected all of the items she'd asked to have.

"I think so," Suzanne said.

"There were some clothes lying near the foot of my bed. Did you happen to get those?" KC asked. She seemed a bit panicky about this. What significance would these clothes have if the trip had been of a sentimental nature? If KC was sending Suzanne to the house to collect items to cover up those Injury to a Child charges (the reason why she was in jail to begin with), or collect sentimental objects, what would those clothes have to do with any of that?

"I did not get the clothes," Suzanne said.

KC told Suzanne during the call that those clothes were the same clothes she had worn on the night of Friday, June 18, 2010. She gave no further explanation as to why they were so important to her. She was apparently just putting that information out there.

The next set of calls KC made to Suzanne took place on July 7 and 8. The new demands KC made were a bit more inclusive. Her main request involved a laptop computer at the house. She didn't have to, but KC added during one of the calls, "The cops seized my desktop computer, but I'm not worried about that."

"Okay" was all Suzanne could manage.

"I need you to go in and change my passwords on my bank accounts and social networks," KC ordered Suzanne, including all of her Yahoo accounts, e-mail and other personal sites. She mentioned Facebook, Twitter and Google. She asked Suzanne to change her nursing licensing address on her computer. Her USAA bank account records portal log in codes/passwords/usernames. All of her passwords and usernames for the Office of the Attorney General CS information records site. She gave Suzanne specific instructions about all of the accounts, what to do, where to go on each site, how to sign in and change all of her e-mail and password/username-protected information.

"I'll mail you a list of my passwords," KC instructed after explaining how to do everything. "You need to do this as soon as you can."

The next day, KC had another visit with Michael Darwin. Guards searched her again and found another note. This one said, *Call Suzanne ASAP [@] wk. . . . Tell her to change all passwords immediately. . . . They listen by phone.*

Suzanne couldn't get to KC's house again until Saturday; she had a job she needed to attend. This latest call had come on a Wednesday. On that Friday before Suzanne took another drive to KC's Whitehouse home, KC called with another request.

"Call my cell phone number."

"But I thought you said the police have it."

"Yes, they do. But I want you to call it, play the voice

mail messages, and then change the password." KC gave Suzanne step-by-step instructions regarding how to do this. She told her what the existing password was, adding, "Change it to something only *you* know, Suz. I will get it from you at the appropriate time. You understand?"

"Yes," Suzanne said.

After listening to this set of phone calls, investigators found it interesting that KC would have had, by then, more than three months (since the Injury to a Child charges had been first lodged back in March) to change or delete any information on her phone or Internet accounts or laptop or anywhere else. But now, while in jail, she was frantic and anxious about getting all those Internet passwords/usernames and her cell phone information changed.

Why?

Cargill had to believe, Detective James Riggle reasoned in the capital felony murder arrest warrant he was drafting at this time, *that something available through her phone was incriminating with regard to the capital murder investigation.*

The same could be said for her laptop and social networking sites.

Suzanne did what she was told. The following day, Saturday, she drove to Whitehouse and changed all of the passwords on KC's accounts so nobody—including the police—could gain access to any of them.

Maybe she did or did not know, but Suzanne Jones-Davis had just committed a felony: tampering with evidence. In her defense Suzanne had no idea KC was being investigated for Cherry Walker's murder. KC had been booked on Injury to a Child charges at this time—she was not publicly a suspect in the murder of

Cherry. As far as Suzanne was concerned, she was helping out a friend who might lose her child and had been jailed on erroneous information that her mother and ex had fabricated about her. Suzanne had no idea she was helping someone cover up a murder.

27

"HOW ARE YOU?" KC ASKED.
Kim knew she had an ally in Suzanne Jones-Davis's mother. She was playing that card now. On July 11, 2010, KC called Suzanne's mother and asked about Suzanne and how things were coming along. KC was becoming increasingly worried that the SCSO would open her accounts, look into her social life on the Internet and maybe see all she had been up to during those days leading up to Cherry's murder.

"I assure you," Suzanne's mother said, "that Suz is working on some things for you as we speak."

"That's good."

"Suzanne got your letter."

"Great. I need Suz to call [Michael] for me."

"Okay, I'll tell her."

"Listen, I need Suz to tell him to get rid of the orange bicycle that is in front of my house—have him take it to his place."

"Okay. . . ."

"I cannot tell you why, but that bike is important to my case."

The implication KC made to Suzanne's mother, once again arranging her puppet strings, was that the bicycle would play a major role in the Injury to a Child charges. The way KC framed it suggested that the child had perhaps fallen off the bike and that's how he had gotten hurt. This bike, in other words, was going to be evidence that could eventually help her prove that she was being railroaded.

It was a smoke screen.

They chatted about menial things, KC plying the woman with her charm and her cover story that *"everyone is against me, but I'm going to beat this nonsense."*

At the end of the conversation KC reminded Suzanne's mother, "Have him go get that bike, *please.*"

As KC worked her "people" on the outside, asking them to take on certain tasks, the SCSO followed along with the narrative. By July 12, Detective Ron Rathbun and a colleague were on their way to an address in Whitehouse where Michael Darwin's girlfriend, Cara (pseudonym), lived. The theory was that Kim Cargill might have had help in murdering and disposing Cherry Walker's body. Since Michael was willing to grab bicycles and help out KC in other ways, effectively taking orders from her during visits to the jail and from third parties, maybe he had helped her dispose of Cherry's body.

Rathbun and his colleague knocked.

The girlfriend opened the door and invited them in.

28

APRIL PITTS AND HER HALF sister, Kim Cargill, did not get along—not after KC's arrest, or even as they grew up in the same household as children.

"We're very different," April said later. "She's very demanding, just *very* controlling. I was more shy."

April explained that for as long as she could remember—even as they attended Berkner High School in Richardson, Texas—she and KC were "estranged." As they grew into adults and each got married, if April had any interaction with her half sister, it was "for the kids," she recalled. She adored her nephews, and worried about them. She would stop by when she could to check on them.

Back in 1992, April needed a place to stay for a few weeks. KC lived close by at the time. She could put up with KC for a few weeks, April decided, and asked her for a favor. After all, what could go wrong in that amount of time? KC lived with her then-husband, Mike West.

From the moment April walked in, the energy in the house was chilly and uncomfortable, April later explained in court. Mike and KC were constantly on the verge of a major blowup. KC was impossible to get along with; she needed to control and manipulate every aspect of life with those around her. April often found herself arguing with her half sister—KC was always the instigator—and April had no idea why they were even fighting. KC would make some sort of crass comment, belittling gesture or remark, or she would try to get April to do things she was uncomfortable with doing. April also saw behaviors in the house that upset her: conditions, hygiene, the way KC treated her husband and kids. All of it was wrong.

One argument turned into a heated battle that placed April at the receiving end of KC's blistering comments.

It was just a few days into her stay. April knew it had been a mistake, but she sucked it up and did what she could to adapt. Still, enough was enough. KC was out of her mind, yelling, screaming, tearing into everyone for no reason.

April announced to KC that she was leaving. She couldn't take it anymore. Sleeping on the street, in a hotel or in her car would be better than another night anywhere near KC. April had no idea how Mike West had put up with his wife for as long as he did. KC and Mike had been married about four years by this time, though the marriage was just about over.

"I was trying . . . to get out of the situation," April explained.

"Trying" was the appropriate word. KC did not want her to leave the house. Not because she loved April and would miss her. No. KC had not *decided* it was time for her to leave. April could go when KC said she could go.

April was in her car, preparing to pull out of the driveway.

"You're not leaving . . . ," KC yelled. She was breast-feeding her child and had him in her arms.

The window was rolled down in April's car. "Yes, I'm leaving," April said. She could not take another moment of KC's volatility and violent tendencies. How does anyone sleep in a house not knowing what a person in the next room will do next, when she will again explode into a vulgar, profanity-laced rant or when she will become violent? It was no way to live.

KC put the child down. (April could not recall where, but she remembered that KC did not have the child in her arms when she approached her.) KC reached in through the car's open window and, thinking she was going to put April's car into the PARK position on the steering column shifter, instead snapped off the directional blinker arm. She didn't realize the gear shifter was on the floor.

"What are you doing?" April said.

April drove away as KC screamed at her.

Later that night April wound up returning. All she needed was some air. Some time alone. Maybe KC was under a lot of pressure? Perhaps her problems with Mike were causing her to act unpredictably? People, in April's view, deserved a second chance.

But things got worse. April came home one night from work, walked in and could not believe what KC had done to April's dog, which she had brought with her for the stay.

"What did you do?" April said as she stared at the dog. KC smiled.

"She had my dog shaved, literally, to the bone," April said later.

Another incident, even more devastating to this concerned aunt, happened between Travis (pseudonym), who was nearly three years old at the time, and KC. KC was yelling at the child for a reason that had been so inconsequential April could not recall what KC was so riled up about. As April looked on, KC angrily began to kick holes in the wall next to where the boy stood. It was as if she was showing the child: *See what I could do to you!*

That was enough. It was time for April to leave and never return.

KC had once spent some time at April's house in Garland, Texas. One moment that April recalled with clarity involved her coming home from work one evening to find KC rifling through her mail—her bills in particular.

"What are you doing?" April asked, startling KC.

"Oh, nothing."

"Why are you going through my bills?"

"I wasn't, April."

April was astounded. She'd caught KC red-handed, and she denied the entire thing.

"Yes, you were!" April said again.

"No, April, you're mistaken."

"You know what, Kim, get out of my house. You are not welcome here any longer."

"I'm not leaving," KC said. Then a look came over her. Anger brewed from a place deep within, preparing to boil over. April knew the look; she'd witnessed it as a child and later as an adult. However, she wasn't backing down.

"You've overstepped your boundaries in my house and you're leaving," April demanded.

"No, I am not!" KC seethed.

KC walked over and stood on the threshold of the sliding glass door inside April's house. She made herself perfectly clear: "I. Don't. Have. To. Leave."

April recalled KC "threatening" her, though she didn't say how.

"I'll call the police," April told her.

KC did not move.

April picked up the phone and dialed her husband, instead. She explained the situation—though, for mostly everyone who knew KC, all you had to do was mention her name and that person knew exactly what you were dealing with.

"I'm on my way," he said.

"My next-door neighbors heard [us arguing] and they've never heard me, in over seventeen years, raise my voice or anything," April recalled.

KC finally left. It was the last time April allowed her into the home.

Why KC reached a point in any social situation where she felt the need to become loud, violent or aggressive, April later explained, was something those who did not know KC could not understand. Yet, there never was a *why* with KC. She became angry, mostly, when she didn't get her way and the people around her failed to submit to her control. KC had not told April she could leave on the day she reached through the open window inside April's vehicle and broke the directional blinker off the steering column. There was no way KC was going to allow April to go off on her own without KC telling her she was no longer welcome.

That's just the way it was in KC's world. You did what she said or you paid a price.

KC's outbursts would happen at bizarre times. She might be laughing and joking, then *boom!* "She could turn on a dime," yelling and screaming and flailing her arms or, in that one instance April witnessed, kicking a wall. April often thought: *If she does this around me, what is she doing when nobody is around?*

There had been spans of time when April had not spoken to KC for as long as six years. Throughout their lives they'd go weeks, months and years without speaking a word.

"It all depended on when she would allow us to see the kids," April recalled.

KC had power and control over that situation and she wielded it.

One day April was driving by KC's apartment, when KC lived in Garland, Texas, not far away from April. They had been "neighbors" for a long time, but April had never seen the apartment or the kids. She decided that maybe she should stop, knock and say hello. They lived so close. The kids needed to see their aunt. April needed to check in on them.

April had no idea which apartment KC lived in. She pulled into the parking lot, parked her vehicle behind several cars and got out. She started walking. Soon she came upon "this big open area," a courtyard. The apartments were situated around an open, grassy area where residents hung out, had a BBQ, tossed a Frisbee, walked a dog, sat and enjoyed a nice day.

As April walked around the courtyard of the apartment complex, where she knew KC lived, she ran into

Blake, who was three years old then. He was outside, alone, in the courtyard playing.

April was appalled by this.

"Where's Mommy?" April asked her nephew.

"In the apartment," Blake said.

"Well, let's go. You need to come with me." April's truck was illegally parked, she realized, and she needed to move it. She took the boy with her and found a different parking space.

After April moved her vehicle, she asked Blake where he lived. "Can you show me where the apartment is?"

"Sure, come on."

When they arrived, April knocked.

No answer.

Strange. Why isn't KC answering her door?

Her son was outside by himself.

Blake assured his aunt that this was the right apartment.

April knocked again—harder.

Nothing.

They made their way back to the courtyard and hung out.

Some time passed and KC showed up.

"She was shocked that I was standing there," April later explained.

April asked where she had been. She explained how she and Blake had knocked on the door, but no one had answered.

"I was in the bathroom," KC said.

April expressed how upset she was that her nephew was outside by himself. KC explained it away, April said later, by saying that she knew where the boy was the entire time and there had been other children outside with him at some point, which made it okay in her mind to leave him and go to the bathroom.

April later talked about KC having a cunning, conning, calculating and scheming way of getting people to do things for her that they wouldn't normally do. She could convince anyone to do anything; it didn't matter if it was law enforcement, DFPS, the children, anyone. And if you didn't do it the exact way KC had wanted, then watch out.

KC had once asked April to feed the kids and then call the airport. April called the airport and fed the kids. KC snapped. She screamed at April for not doing the two tasks in the order she had demanded.

When KC became angry (which happened often), she became another person, April acknowledged. She would shout at the top of her lungs; her eyes would gloss over and tighten into slits, her face red. KC became somebody else—and to April Pitts, KC's own flesh and blood, she later explained who she thought that "other" person was.

"It's like seeing the Devil."

29

MICHAEL DARWIN'S GIRLFRIEND ANSWERED the door and allowed two SCSO detectives, one of whom was Ron Rathbun, to enter her home. The SCSO had a few questions for Michael and his girlfriend. Most important, could they account for their whereabouts between the night Cherry Walker went missing and the day her body had been found?

Michael worked for the town of Whitehouse. He'd met KC in 2004 while he and several coworkers were working on a water line in front of KC's Waterton Circle home. She came out to chat with the workers, and Michael and KC struck up a friendship. He felt bad for her—all those kids, no man around the house, the chores not being done, KC working all the time. Or, at least, that's the story he got out of KC.

"We were on a talk-every-now-and-then basis," Michael explained later. KC had needed a man's help around the house after her recent split with her husband, and Michael filled that role. He started doing handyman work for her: plumbing, landscaping, lawn mowing. She'd take him out to eat sometimes or would pay him at others.

"There was no romantic relationship," he insisted. What's more, his girlfriend knew about the friendship and had even befriended KC herself.

During the early spring of 2010, Michael later said, he was receiving between "five and maybe eight texts a day from" KC. There weren't many phone calls during that particular period, he said. KC liked to text. That was how they mostly communicated.

He was mowing KC's lawn regularly by then, but she had trouble paying him. He didn't really mind. He felt he was helping out a friend. When they'd chat after he was finished with the lawn, KC would explain how financially strapped she was.

"I'm behind on my property taxes," KC said in early June. "I'm working a lot of overtime, but it's all going to the damn taxes."

He understood. "Don't worry about paying me for mowing the yard, Kim. I have other work. Money ain't no big thing. You're a single mom, I get it."

Michael and his girlfriend became close with KC. In fact, she felt so comfortable around them that she came out one day and asked if they would mind undergoing a DFPS background check in order for them to become supervisors for her visits with Timmy. If they passed, he or his girlfriend would be sort of a chaperone for KC and Timmy. Either one would be present when the child was dropped off and picked up and during the entire visit.

Once again KC was manipulating the system—placing allies in a responsible role that she would, obviously, later exploit in some fashion. Michael and his girlfriend didn't know it, but they, too, were becoming pawns in KC's narcissistic game of conning and tricking Timmy's father.

Michael and his girl had rarely heard the name Cherry Walker from KC. She'd only mention Cherry in passing, saying that Cherry was someone who watched Timmy. Her comments would generally be accompanied by a remark about Cherry's "issues" or state of mind.

"There's this woman who watches [Timmy]," KC said once in early June, "and she's a little slow."

KC also mentioned how "afraid" she was of losing custody of Timmy. She made it clear to Michael on several occasions that the reason why she was so afraid of losing Timmy was because of "this Cherry lady, who was slow." Cherry was all set to testify against her, KC indicated.

As he got to know KC more intimately, he realized that maybe there was more to her story. Perhaps it was a good thing, he began to think, that she didn't keep the child.

One day Michael went with KC on a ride to her mother's house to pick up Timmy, who had been visiting his grandmother. They were in KC's car. She drove. Being one of her confirmed DFPS supervisors now, Michael had to be there.

When getting into KC's car, he later explained, you had to move all sorts of trash out of your way in order to get comfortable and make room for your feet on the floorboards. It was littered with piles of garbage: fast-food bags, coffee cups, plain old trash of all types piled as high as the seats! It smelled. It was disgusting. But this was how KC lived.

"Most of it was Burger King and McDonald's," he later recalled. On top of that, he said, you couldn't miss seeing all of the little Dairy Fresh coffee creamer cups—they were everywhere inside her car.

During this trip to KC's mother's, Michael and KC were laughing, joking around, talking about normal, everyday things. KC seemed loose, in a good mood. But then he said something that KC, apparently, wasn't prepared to hear.

"Hey, just wanted to let you know that I am not going to be able to spend the whole day with you and [Timmy] today." KC knew that without Michael around as a supervisor, she couldn't have Timmy. It had been the first time during many visits he'd supervised that he had done this to her—cut the visit short. It wasn't planned. But something in his life had come up and he had to make an early dash. He wanted KC to realize this before they got the child.

First, KC got "loud," Michael said. Then she began to beat herself in the leg with a blunt object. Hard. After that, she placed her hands over her face and screamed into them. She was having a fit—all while driving the car.

"What are you doing?" he asked. He was terrified. It was as if she wanted to crash the vehicle to teach him a lesson. "Drive the car," Michael said. Her behavior, he later related, scared him. She had shifted her demeanor entirely from happy to angry to self-destructive, while he sat, helpless, next to her.

KC went back to hitting herself in the leg before slapping herself across the face. It was beyond bizarre, he felt. She had no one around to unload her anger on, so she was taking it out on herself. He'd never seen such a thing.

"You cannot fucking do this to me, not right now!" KC raged. "You cannot do this to me. You *cannot* do this to me." *Slap, slap, slap.* "Not now. Please." *Slap.*

"What are you doing? Stop it."

Michael later said he would have gotten out of the vehicle if possible, but she was traveling too fast.

30

MICHAEL'S GIRLFRIEND SAT DOWN WITH
SCSO detectives and said she would help any
way she could.

"We went to Jacksonville, [Texas], on Saturday
night," his girlfriend, Cara, explained after Detective
Rathbun asked where she and Michael had been over
the weekend of June 18 through June 20. "We played
pool."

On Friday nights, Michael Darwin would later explain to police, he and his girl went down to Jacksonville to a certain pool hall and spent the night playing
pool with friends. It was a routine of theirs. Jacksonville is about a twenty-five-minute ride due south of
Whitehouse. It was the only pool hall around that allowed children. Michael and Cara liked it because they
both had kids and they liked to bring them.

"Can you tell us about Friday night?" Rathbun asked.

That would have been June 18, the night Cherry
went missing.

As Michael would later recall (and as his girlfriend
and several others verified during their interviews with

the SCSO), "We had a cookout at my girl's house. After the cookout, we all got into about three vehicles and we drove down to Jacksonville to the pool hall, and we shot pool."

Still, Michael needed to explain a few things. For one, KC had texted him on June 18, 2010, at 6:33 A.M. It would be the first of many texts throughout that June weekend: **Call me when you can or stop by about 8:30 P.M.**

Then, at 9:43 A.M., on that same Friday, KC texted him again: **Text me a time I can call you today.**

At 2:13 P.M., KC sent another text to him: **Please call me ASAP. I'm on break.**

Michael was at work inside the town garage, loading things into his work truck at the time that "ASAP" message of urgency came to him. He looked down, read the text and, at first, wanted to ignore it. But as he thought about it, he couldn't shake off the resolve KC had used, as if there was something wrong and she needed to speak with him. KC had never texted him with "call me ASAP" before. He figured something was going on.

Michael stepped away from his colleagues and called KC. He had a break at 2:20 P.M. and used it to make the call.

KC was livid about something, he recalled. He realized this as soon as he got her on the line. She was not her normal self.

The gist of the call—Michael did not remember specifics when later asked about it—centered on, he "thought," Cherry Walker testifying against KC in court that coming week, on June 23. KC was ranting that Cherry was going to destroy any chance she had to regain custody of Timmy. This hearing was going to be the final nail and she would lose custody for good. KC was certain of this.

They talked for about twenty minutes and he said he needed to get back to work.

On that Friday night, Michael, his girl and their children all played pool for "about four hours" after arriving at the Jacksonville pool hall, near nine o'clock. They also brought along a friend of his soon-to-be daughter-in-law. The pool hall staff and other friends would all verify his and his girlfriend's account. Receipts from that night would further prove where they were.

The next day, Saturday, after spending the night at Cara's house, Michael, Cara and and the kids went to a nearby lake. They loaded the grill and a cooler and some supplies into Mike's truck and took off for the day, with the intention of having an old-fashioned family picnic.

They stayed at the lake on Saturday until dark. When they got home, he said, the kids, exhausted, sat in front of the TV, lazed around, texted friends. He and his girl got themselves "cleaned up," he explained to police, and got ready to go out to "do our thing that we normally do on Saturday night"—hang out at the local VFW bar, have some innocent fun with friends.

The kids, however, wanted to eat.

"Burger King?" Michael asked.

Yes!

He and Cara went off to the local Whitehouse Burger King to grab some food. As they were entering, he turned and looked toward the drive-thru window.

"Hey, look," he said to his girl.

It was KC. She was at the window.

Michael got her attention and waved to her.

After KC left the drive-thru, she pulled over in the parking lot. He and his girl walked up and stood on the passenger side of KC's car. She rolled the window down.

"Hey, guys, what's going on?" KC asked.

The first thing he noticed as he leaned in through the rolled-down window, his head nearly inside KC's vehicle, was how clean KC's car was. It seemed as if she'd spent all day scrubbing and shampooing and polishing. Not only the inside of the vehicle, but the outside, too. Even the tires, he noticed, were "shiny" and the outside of the car had a brilliant glow to it. The dashboard, the console, the rugs—everything was spotless.

"Wow!" he said through the open window. "Your car is so clean. You finally got some time to have it cleaned. I almost don't recognize the car." He was serious. The change was that remarkable.

KC laughed.

"She was in a good mood," Michael remembered. Quite a bit different from the woman he had spoken to the previous day on the phone. That person was extremely agitated and upset and manic and freaking out, he later said—all because of Cherry Walker testifying against her. Now, suddenly, KC didn't seem to have a care in the world. To boot, she'd gone and cleaned her vehicle as though she was going to be displaying it at a car show.

* * *

The SCSO was interested in what Michael and Cara had done that Sunday. Had they seen KC? Had he spoken to her? Had she texted him?

Michael had plans for that Sunday, June 20, to drive out to Red Oak and spend some time with family, as they normally would do on Father's Day. Red Oak is directly west of Whitehouse, about a two-hour drive, 121 miles on the 20. It's a little town of about ten thousand that is considered part of the Dallas-Fort Worth metroplex. Michael also had planned on seeing KC on Sunday. He had texted with her and promised he'd mow her lawn. What sparked that conversation was a rather strange text, or, at least, it seemed so when he looked at it later in context of that entire weekend. KC had texted: You didn't stop by Friday night after 8:30 or Saturday morning. Just wanted to say thanks again for everything and say Happy Father's Day in person. Hope that means you and [Cara] have special plans.

He read the text and found it rather odd that KC would mention Friday night, his not stopping by, or a specific time, eight-thirty. Why so much detail about Friday? Hadn't he just run into KC the previous night, Saturday, at the Burger King? Why wouldn't she have said anything then?

"I thought it was kind of weird," he commented later.

He responded to the text by telling KC he was coming out to cut her lawn and then going out to Red Oak to spend the day with his girls. They were planning on grilling.

Before he arrived at KC's to mow her lawn later that morning, she sent him a text to the effect of You are a sweetheart. The yard is bad, but I don't want you to do it on Father's Day.

KC then restated in a responding text, now for a

second time, that she had not seen Michael on Friday or Saturday.

He looked at his phone and thought, again, how strange it was for her to keep mentioning those days.

Why is she doing this?

Even odder to him was that after he had gotten that "come ASAP" text and called her while he was on break, she had not once asked about him coming over at 8:30 P.M. or on Saturday morning. It was as if that eight-thirty comment only mattered in the context of her texting him.

During that same text conversation on Sunday morning, KC also mentioned that she had set off several "foggers" inside her home and had been away because the house was being bombed with poison. She'd had a terrible roach problem inside the house because of all the garbage and she was trying to fix it.

Later, just after noon on that Sunday: **Quick question: Does that fogger stuff work? . . . Can't afford an exterminator.**

Michael texted back, saying he believed the foggers worked as long as you followed the instructions.

The more Michael thought about it, the more he understood, and explained to SCSO detectives that the texts KC had sent him implied that she was at home on Friday evening and Saturday morning, waiting for him to call or come over. KC had noted that fact in several additional texts she had sent to him throughout that weekend. In addition, having foggers placed in her house had allowed her to tell him that she was out for at least six hours on Sunday. KC was, in effect, using him to create a timeline of her whereabouts.

The SCSO detectives believed Kim Cargill was trying

to provide herself with an alibi, using Michael to lay the groundwork for where she was at all times throughout that weekend. She had never, in the four years he had known her by then, texted him so many times, with as much detail, as she had during that one weekend in June when Cherry Walker went missing and was murdered.

Interestingly, when the SCSO would later go into KC's phone records and have a look at all of her texts, many of the text messages she sent and received from Michael Darwin during that weekend had been saved. Meanwhile, others pertaining to matters that would not indicate where she was or what she was doing, or at what time, had been deleted. Even more compelling as evidence against KC were texts she shared with him throughout that weekend that had been systematically deleted. She'd saved one at 4:14 P.M., for example, but then had deleted one at 11:45 A.M. and another at 1:05 P.M., leaving just the one at four-fourteen. If you took all the texts from that weekend and laid them out in a narrative, it would tell a story of Kim Cargill asking her friend to come over, giving him specific times, noting that she was waiting at home or doing other chores; then, when he failed to show up, there she was asking him why he hadn't come over, leaving the impression to anyone reading these texts that she was at home the entire time.

Kimberly Cargill thought she was smarter than the detectives investigating her for capital felony murder.

31

ON JULY 12, 2010, WITH KC in jail, the SCSO believed they had enough on Suzanne Jones-Davis to make an arrest on charges of tampering with physical evidence. The main reason why the SCSO wanted to get Suzanne into the interview suite—beyond the fact she had broken the law—was to see how much more she knew about her friend Kim Cargill and her whereabouts and actions during those days leading up to and after Cherry Walker's murder. Maybe Suzanne held the final piece of the puzzle Detective James Riggle needed to prepare an arrest warrant for KC on charges of capital murder.

Riggle, Rathbun, a third detective and Sergeant Mike Stinecipher drove to the McKinney, Texas, residence that Suzanne shared with her husband. They knocked on the door with an arrest warrant and search warrant in hand.

It was just before midnight—a good time, cops knew, to shake people up by rustling them awake. The time alone puts people off their game. The charges against Suzanne were serious. She could see jail time for her crimes.

Rathbun announced both warrants when Suzanne's husband answered the door. He was shocked and amazed at what was happening. When Suzanne came down to see what was going on, Rathbun read Suzanne her Miranda rights.

Her days of helping KC cover up a crime were over.

The major crime Suzanne had committed, perhaps without knowing, was when she went into KC's cell phone and changed the passwords. That phone, at the time, was in the custody of the SCSO. Suzanne had gone into a piece of physical evidence the SCSO had confiscated and tampered with it. It was no different than if she had walked into the police station, stealthily made her way into the evidence collection room, found a piece of evidence in a plastic bag and changed it in some way.

While detectives searched Suzanne's home, Ron Rathbun sat down with her and asked if she wanted to talk to the SCSO. It would be in Suzanne's best interest to tell everything she knew at this point, he said. Suzanne had long, flowing, somewhat curly brown hair with reddish-blond highlights. She was stocky, with trusting eyes and fair skin. To Rathbun, this wife and stepmother seemed defeated. They sat in her dining room, while the search went on around them. Suzanne's husband, Marty (pseudonym), stood nearby. He had a look of disbelief on his face, along with a hectoring, smug tone to his voice whenever he spoke.

"Can you tell me what's going on?"[1] Rathbun began.

---

[1] This interview was recorded, but the conversation here is written using Detective Rathbun's report, which might be slightly different (he summarized the interview) from the recordings, which I did not have access to.

"I did help her," Suzanne admitted.

Suzanne explained that she went into KC's house in Whitehouse to retrieve "some belongings" and "some paintings" and "some clothing."

"Do you have any of that stuff here?" Rathbun wanted to know.

"I do. Yes, in boxes upstairs . . ."

Suzanne said that she had gone to KC's house for the first time back on July 2 and returned to her home in McKinney at about ten o'clock on that same night.

"The reason for this arrest warrant," Rathbun explained, "is because of you trying to change some of Miss Cargill's passwords."

"I didn't know it was illegal to help a friend."

"I warned her," Marty said at one point. "I told her not to get involved in all of this. I told her not to go to . . . Whitehouse."

"Are you aware of what's going on?" Rathbun asked Suzanne. He wanted to make sure she understood the gravity of the situation.

"I am very aware of the murder investigation going on in Smith County," Suzanne said. This had to be a surprise for the SCSO. The SCSO was under the impression, perhaps giving Suzanne the benefit of the doubt, that she only knew about the child custody matter. Apparently, KC had told her about the murder investigation.

Suzanne was going to be handcuffed and taken into custody and booked downtown. Her mug shot would be taken, and her story part of KC's legacy forever. The local media would soon latch onto Suzanne's involvement and run with it, posting her mug shot on the nightly news and in the newspapers, branding her an alleged felon and co-conspirator in helping a friend hide evidence in a potential murder case.

Upstairs, amid those items Suzanne had described without hesitation, searchers found a "spiral notebook," which contained notes "about information on Cargill's accounts, i.e., cell phone, bank, Facebook, etc." They also uncovered a letter KC had written to Suzanne, detailing the list of things she wanted Suzanne to do.

A McKinney police officer needed to make the official arrest, and he did. Soon, though, Suzanne was transferred to Smith County Jail, the same place where her "friend" was just about a permanent resident. She was put in a cell until she could be arraigned, but she was unable to post bond.

As investigators wrapped up their work at Suzanne's house, word arrived for Rathbun and Riggle that Orchid Cellmark, the company responsible for the forensics on those items found at the crime scene and at KC's house, had some results to share.

Perfect timing.

The main piece of information that the SCSO was interested in on Cellmark's report: *Kimberly Cargill could not be excluded as a contributor on the creamer package which was found near the deceased Cherry Walker.* The findings, expressed as overwhelming odds, were not in KC's favor. To a high degree of certainty she had touched that creamer package found in between Cherry's legs at the crime scene. The SCSO had definitive DNA evidence to prove KC was possibly at the scene where Cherry Walker's body had been found.

For Rathbun, Riggle and the rest of the team, that information—so impartial and scientific—was enough to finish off the arrest warrant on charges of capital murder for Kim Cargill. They presented it to a judge for his signature.

On July 14, 2010, the judge signed the arrest warrant for Kim Cargill. KC would be arrested on charges of capital murder, which meant her case was going to be eligible for a death penalty status.

The warrant contained three separate counts. One asserted: *[Kim] had intentionally or knowingly caused the death of Cherry Walker while in the course of committing or attempting to commit a robbery of Cherry Walker [phone and purse];* second: *[she] intentionally and knowingly caused the death of Cherry Walker while committing the offense of Retaliation . . . on account of Cherry Walker's service as a witness;* thirdly: Kim Cargill wanted to "prevent or delay the service" of Cherry as a witness.

The narrative, which was spelled out in the seven-page, single-spaced warrant, detailed how KC could have been responsible for Cherry Walker's abduction and murder and also how she had "conspired," with "three individuals," to cover it up. The warrant claimed the medical examiner had concluded Cherry Walker's death was the result of "homicidal violence"; though no means concerning how she was murdered were outlined.

Thus, the mystery remained: How had Kim Cargill, if guilty, killed Cherry Walker? And how had she transported her body alone?

Several additional pieces of evidence came in as the warrant was served, one being a stack of cell phone records previously unavailable. As they sat down and studied these records, Riggle and the team discovered some compelling, interesting information: They noted how many times KC had called Cherry Walker during the days leading up to June 18, 2010, and how many times she actually spoke to Cherry (or Cherry's cell phone number, at least) on that Friday. But then, after that Friday, suddenly no more calls to Cherry Walker's phone from KC's phone. She had stopped calling Cherry altogether. The SCSO theorized that the reason she had stopped calling was because Kim Cargill knew Cherry was dead. There was no reason to call.

It's the subtle clues killers leave behind that catch them.

The warrant said a lot about the legalities surrounding Kim Cargill's then-alleged crimes. It detailed the lead-up to a brutal, vicious murder. It provided plenty of circumstantial and forensic evidence linking Kimberly Cargill to the abduction and murder of Cherry Walker, along with evidence that KC also poured an accelerant over Cherry and lit her on fire.

Amid all of the allegations, there was nothing in the warrant to explain who Kim Cargill was, where she came from or how and why her life had spiraled into a chaotic mess.

That was an entirely different story—one of violence and psychotic behaviors, purported abuse and medical afflictions, which began, if you believe Kimberly Dianne Cargill, during her childhood in Mississippi.

PART THREE

The lamp of the body is the eye. If your eye is sound, your whole body will be filled with light; but if your eye is bad, your whole body will be in darkness. And if the light in you is darkness, how great will the darkness be.

—Matthew 6: 22–23

32

MISSISSIPPI IS ONE OF THOSE charming states wherein you speak with a local and there's no mistaking he or she has been born and raised in this magnificent place. There is a sense of honor and community in the way Mississippians talk about their homes, the land, the people they call their neighbors. How they brag—quite humbly—about the mighty river that bears their state's name, or the soul food, the size of the catfish, the deltas, the cotton fields or the kindness most everyone you meet greets you with. They say *"gree-its"* for "grits," and *"hey-a"* for "here," an accent state residents are especially proud of displaying.

Rachel Wilson, the only girl born to a family of boys, grew up in a "strict" Mississippi household, where her father was said to be "domineering" and "often spoke to Rachel's mother as though she was his child." It was a tough way to meander through life as a kid in the 1960s, Rachel later explained in court and in accompanying documents. What's more, going to high school and falling in love with your sweetheart, you were under the impression that life was going to be nothing but the dreamy bliss of a fairy tale. For Rachel, that fantasy boy was Charlie Snyder (pseudonym), a kid who was said to have "worshipped" the ground Rachel walked on—at least in those early days of courting.

A loner, Rachel was a girl some later said was "hard to get along with." Beautiful and elegant and the complete Southern belle, Rachel did not keep many close friends besides Charlie.

Rachel enjoyed being the center of attention, but wanted things done her way, said a report detailing Rachel's adolescence and early life.[2]

Feeling pressured, or perhaps feeling the pressure of that rebellious teenage noose tightening, Rachel and Charlie decided to elope during their senior year of high school, ditching the education system in favor of the puppy love they shared. Rachel was seventeen years old, still a child, really. Some would look at this later, even Rachel herself, and conclude that she had married Charlie at such a young age in order to "escape her father's house" and get away from a dad with whom she did not get along.

---

[2] The "report" cited/quoted here (and used throughout this biographical section of the book and in other sections) is titled *Initial Application for Writ of Habeas Corpus*. It was filed on August 19, 2014, with the 241st Judicial District Court in Smith County, Texas, on behalf of Kimberly Cargill, by her appellate attorneys, Brad Levenson, Janet Gilger-VanderZanden and Derek VerHagen. This 193-page document provides intimate details surrounding the life and times of Kimberly Cargill and her parents. Rachel Wilson also testified extensively in court about her and her daughter Kim Cargill's life, as did Kim Cargill and other family members. Moreover, this *Initial Application* document was discussed at length during Kimberly Cargill's appellate hearing and in the judge's ruling of that appeal, which can be accessed here: http://law.justia.com/cases/texas/court-of-criminal-appeals/2014/ap-76-819.html

Charlie had been raised by a foster family since he was five years old. His biological parents, according to that same *Initial Application for Writ of Habeas Corpus* document, had issues with substances. He rarely saw them.

The year 1966 defined the civil rights movements across the South with marches and protests seemingly taking place every day. In June of that year, James Meredith, the first African-American student at the University of Mississippi, was shot and wounded by a sniper just after he started what was called the "March Against Fear." (After he healed and was released from the hospital, he was able to join the other marchers before they reached Jackson, Mississippi, and completed the trek.) It was a volatile time in America, especially for anyone living in the South. Rachel and Charlie found a trailer home that Charlie's foster parents helped him pay for and decided to start a family, merely five months after getting married. When they looked back, the couple realized it probably wasn't the best time to begin having babies. After all, Charlie wasn't working. Rachel, pregnant and not yet a legal adult in many states, had a job at the local phone company.

Kimberly Dianne was born to Rachel and Charlie on November 30, 1966. From the first moments of her life, it was clear to Charlie and Rachel that their child was going to struggle. According to the *Initial Application* source, Kim suffered from projectile vomiting. She was allergic to baby formula. Rachel had suffered from anemia and other ailments for the entire nine months she carried Kim. It was a tough pregnancy for this young mother.

If that wasn't bad enough, Rachel had not taken maternity leave from her job (in fear of losing it) after giving birth to Kim. She went back to work as soon as she felt physically up to it. Charlie, a young, immature kid, just out of high school, decided on a career in the military and joined the National Guard as Kim turned one month old, leaving Rachel to take care of the child by herself, while trying to maintain a full-time job. The only solution Rachel could muster was switching to second-shift work, from three o'clock to eleven at night, making it easier for her to find someone to babysit.

Kim's teenage aunt—Charlie's sister—picked up the slack while Charlie was gone and took over parental duties during Rachel's shift on most working nights. But soon, that companionship itch began and Rachel found herself going out after work, instead of heading directly home to her baby girl. During one of those nights out and about, Rachel ran into Charlie's best friend, Calvin Dorsett (pseudonym), a boy Rachel herself had known from school. Cal was tall and handsome and strong. He was just like Charlie in so many ways and filled the role of companion, lover and friend. The major difference between the two was that Cal was there and Charlie was not.

Rachel often stayed out late at night with [Cal] after her work shift ended, the *Initial Application* report claimed.

This, of course, did not sit well with Charlie upon his return from basic training. Seeing the two of them together—his best friend and his wife—was "very difficult," as one might imagine. It seemed everywhere Rachel's now-estranged husband went, once he was back on the local scene, there the two were, in his face,

Despite being diagnosed as mentally challenged, thirty-nine-year-old Cherry Walker moved out of her parents' house and into a studio apartment in Tyler, Texas, to carve out a life on her own.

The gravel road leading to the dirt path where
the body of a woman was found on June 19, 2010.
(Photo courtesy of Smith County Sheriff's Office)

Just off County Road 2191 in Whitehouse, Texas,
a pizza delivery man made a gruesome discovery.
(Photo courtesy of Smith County Sheriff's Office)

A section of rolled-up carpet and other items were recovered near the body. *(Photo courtesy of Smith County Sheriff's Office)*

Detectives found the charred remains of personal items that, like the victim's body, had been lit on fire using an accelerant. *(Photo courtesy of Smith County Sheriff's Office)*

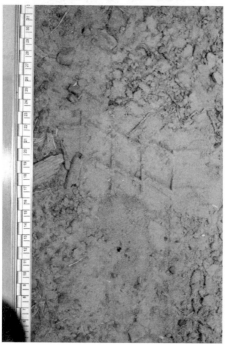

Tire tracks left in the hard red clay and soft dirt proved vital in identifying the last known person to have been with the victim. *(Photos courtesy of Smith County Sheriff's Office)*

An empty and recently used plastic creamer cup, found between the victim's legs, was another key piece of evidence.
(Photo courtesy of Smith County Sheriff's Office)

On the same path nearby, inside an old car tire, a Styrofoam coffee cup was found, and a scenario began to take shape for investigators.
(Photo courtesy of Smith County Sheriff's Office)

After Cherry Walker was reported missing, detectives entered her apartment in search of clues as to what might have happened to her.
(Photo courtesy of Smith County Sheriff's Office)

Things seem undisturbed inside Cherry Walker's home, just as she might have left them. No signs were found of a struggle or a crime having taken place there.
(Photo courtesy of Smith County Sheriff's Office)

Cherry Walker liked to keep her apartment neat and clean. She took great satisfaction in doing routine chores like ironing her clothes and making her bed. *(Photo courtesy of Smith County Sheriff's Office)*

Cherry's calendar indicated plans to babysit on the day before (and one week after) she was found murdered. *(Photo courtesy of Smith County Sheriff's Office)*

A stack of DVDs next to Cherry's TV
showed her interest in popular films.
(Photos courtesy of Smith County Sheriff's Office)

Forty-three-year-old Kim Cargill, a mother of four and licensed vocational nurse, often used Cherry Walker as a babysitter for her young son.
(Photo courtesy of Smith County Sheriff's Office)

Kim Cargill's Whitehouse, Texas, home was located about six miles from the site where Cherry Walker's body was found.
(Photos courtesy of Smith County Sheriff's Office)

Smith County Sheriff's Office investigators obtained a search warrant to examine Kim Cargill's home. All over her white car, and especially on the door handle, they found extensive black soot — which was also found on the bottom of Cherry Walker's tennis shoes. *(Photos courtesy of Smith County Sheriff's Office)*

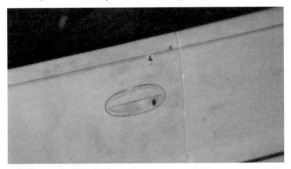

The tire treads on Kim Cargill's vehicle matched the imprinted tracks left in the red clay near Cherry Walker's charred remains. *(Photo courtesy of Smith County Sheriff's Office)*

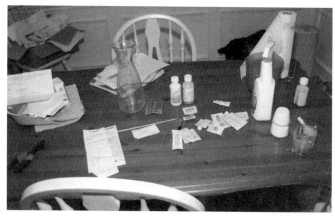

The kitchen table inside Kim Cargill's home told investigators
a lot about her lifestyle in general — and about the moments after
Cherry Walker went missing. The presence of various cleaning supplies
and products was of particular interest.
(Photo courtesy of Smith County Sheriff's Office)

Kim Cargill's bedroom, like the rest of her house, was a mess.
In her bathroom, the tub seemed to serve as a Dumpster.
(Photo courtesy of Smith County Sheriff's Office)

Among the debris, investigators found a plastic coffee creamer cup identical to the one discovered with Cherry Walker's body. *(Photos courtesy of Smith County Sheriff's Office)*

In Cargill's laundry room detectives found a sheet — still wet — inside the washing machine. They believed it had been used to transport Cherry Walker's body from the place she was killed to the dirt road where she was found.
(Photos courtesy of Smith County Sheriff's Office)

This cellphone was one of Cherry Walker's two most prized possessions. She would never go anywhere without it. *(Photos courtesy of Smith County Sheriff's Office)*

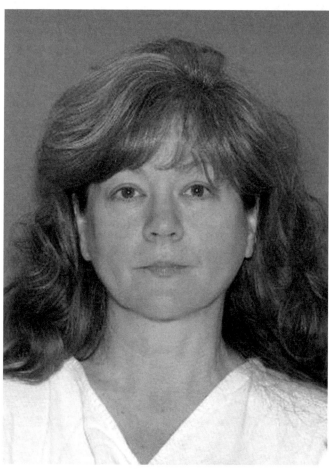

Kim Cargill was found guilty for the murder of Cherry Walker
and the desecration of her body by fire.
Cargill was sentenced to the death penalty.
(Photo courtesy of Smith County Sheriff's Office)

flaunting the relationship. The first time they ran into each other, Charlie swung at his former friend, hit him and wound up spending a night in the local clinker.

Rachel later claimed Charlie "drank and was abusive" toward her after he returned from military training, so she filed for divorce. The dissolution of their brief marriage was not to be a harmonious legal proceeding, however. Charlie was unhappy dissolving a marriage that, in all fairness, should have never taken place. Charlie fought Rachel on just about every issue, while little Kim sat on the sidelines, pulled from one courthouse and visitation to the next, her developing mind absorbing all of the emotional and verbal attacks, the screaming and fighting. It was, some might contend, a pivotal point of time in Kim's life, when she was soaking up everything her parents were doing to one another, learning how to live her own life later on and parent her future children. Others would argue that Kim was just a few years old, far too young to understand or grasp the animosity between her parents.

After rounds of their sparring in court, Rachel came up with a solution to resolve the spiteful conflict between her and Charlie. She knew Charlie did not want to pay child support—it was one of the more contentious issues he had been fighting.

"I'll drop the child support claim, [Charlie]," Rachel told her soon-to-be ex-husband one day during a lull when they were speaking civilly, "if you relinquish rights to Kimberly and allow [Cal] to adopt her." Rachel explained further that as soon as Charlie signed off on their divorce, she was heading to the altar with Cal. There was nothing Charlie could do or say to stop the new union. Their life together was over. A new chapter in Rachel's young life was beginning.

What Charlie did next would shock everyone involved.

33

RACHEL GAVE CHARLIE A CHOICE: Allow her to live her new life—the way she wanted with Calvin—and not pay her child support. Or he could give her a hassle and be expected to hand over part of his paycheck for the next sixteen years. (Kim was two years old by now.)

"Okay," Charlie agreed. "Go ahead."

He cut his losses in love and moved on.

Rachel and Cal married; Cal adopted Kim, just as he promised he would. The *Initial Application* report contended that Charlie lost touch with his daughter. Charlie's mother stayed in contact with Rachel's mother and even taught Kim's Sunday-school class; however, Kim never knew who the woman was. It was the beginning, some would later point out, of a series of detachments Kim would experience regarding those closest to her.

Rachel and Cal had their own child before Kim turned three (April, Kim's half sister). Growing up together, Kim and her new sibling never really connected. Around this time, or shortly thereafter (if we are to accept the statements in the *Initial Application* report, a document that is based on affidavits from some of those—not all parties—involved), Rachel made Kim feel as though she did not approve of her or anything she did. Through that, Kim claimed, she "never felt good enough." As kids, according to Kim, she and her half sister were treated differently by their parents.

When Kim was nine years old, she approached her mother. She had only recalled seeing Cal around the house. She called him her dad.

"Why don't I look like [Cal]?" Kim asked her mom.

According to Kim, Rachel explained to her "in a casual manner" that Cal had adopted her. It was a "revelation," Kim argued later in that document, which affected her "significantly."

Rachel would see things differently. She said Kim had a "normal" life up until the time KC was about twelve. "She was a good student and very outgoing, very personable, and played sports . . . a little cheerleader!" As for Kim's relationship with Cal, Rachel added, "It was great. They were close."

There were conflicting versions of her upbringing and childhood: one that Kim later described in that *Initial Application* document (backed up by selected sources) and another that her mother, Rachel Wilson, testified to in a court of law.

As a child Kim felt unwanted within the family "because of their biological differences," claimed the *Initial Application*.

A gulf between Kim and Rachel grew as each year passed. In that same document Kim's lawyers submitted to the court (in 2014) on her behalf, Kim would accuse her mother of being "physically abusive."

"She hits me," Kim would tell friends. Some of them submitted signed affidavits of support on her behalf, detailing the alleged abuse.

In that report Kim explained how she showed one particular friend a bruise one day, making the claim that her mother had given it to her with a belt buckle.

[Her friend] saw the imprint of the round metal part from a belt on Kimberly's body and head, said the report.

One late afternoon, when Kim and her friend were at Kim's house, with her friend upstairs, waiting for Kim inside Kim's bedroom, something happened. As she sat on Kim's bed, the friend "heard Rachel choking and smacking" KC "in the next room."

The sounds were so horrifying that Kim's friend covered her ears, afraid to do anything.

When Kim walked into the room, she was crying.

There was another time with another friend when Rachel and Kim started fighting. "You did not mop the floor correctly," the friend heard Rachel scream at Kim. According to the friend's later recollection in an affidavit accompanying the *Initial Application,* Rachel was "hitting" KC with a "hairbrush."

As her home life spiraled out of control, Kim's personal health crashed. When Kim was twelve, about the time the family moved from Mississippi to the Dallas area to Richardson, Texas, Rachel took a call one afternoon from Kim's softball coach. She needed to come right away.

"She's . . . not feeling well. She's feverish, clammy and vomiting."

Rachel went and got her.

Kim had come down with meningitis (according to the *Initial Application* report). She was rushed to the local emergency room and the ER doctors performed a spinal tap. They quarantined Kim and she spent "several weeks" in the hospital.

You'd think a hospital would be a safe place to get well. Not for Kim. According to that same report (though it was not supported by any medical documents I could locate), she contracted the mumps while there, which turned into tinnitus, a constant ringing in the ears. From that, Kim lost the hearing in one of her ears. It took her a full year before she felt normal again, or accepted what had now become her *new* normal.

Her health crises weren't over. A year or so after she recuperated from the meningitis and tinnitus, she lost the feeling in her "lower extremities" and found herself back at the ER. Doctors had no idea what had happened. The cause was undetermined. The only result was that Kim now had trouble sitting down because of a pain in her tailbone.

One note about this time period that Kim's mother later made in court was that Rachel had never noticed any "temper" or irrational behavior on Kim's part as a child or even into her early high-school years. That explosive temper that Kim had later in life, which she seemed to take out on her own children, did not arrive until Kim became a young adult.

In high school Kim took to the social scene, where friends recalled her as "popular" and "well-liked." She didn't seem to exhibit any major social flaws or psychiatric episodes at this point. Still, it seemed Kim could not escape a shadow of hardship that followed her.

One night a "group of male classmates" approached her, and, according to Kim, "a traumatic event," involving "something sexual" (she never elaborated), took place afterward at a boy's home. Kim told her parents about it and they threatened, according to "rumors" working their way through the high-school hallways, to press charges, but nothing was done.

Ultimately, Kimberly's parents refused to acknowledge that an assault had been committed against [her], claimed the *Initial Application.* Rachel Wilson never commented on this episode of Kim's life.

With her head spinning from all that had happened before she was old enough to move out on her own, Kim decided one day that she needed to do something about her life or, rather, her history. She sought out her mother, Rachel, to inquire about something that had been on her mind lately.

"I want to meet my father," Kim supposedly said.

Kim went off to Mississippi to meet Charlie and his new wife. All agreed that Kim should spend some time there, so Charlie filed for legal guardianship so that Kim could stay permanently. Kim was about the same age as her mother when she and Charlie had eloped and had Kim.

Kim could not get over the fact that she had been adopted by Calvin and that no one had told her until she asked. It was as though they had all conspired to hide her identity from her. (This was another contention that Rachel Wilson never agreed or disagreed with.) This put a tremendous strain on Kim's heart and the feelings she had for Charlie. Why hadn't he fought for her? Why had he not tried to contact her? Why had he left? She couldn't get over it. Soon it drove a wedge between her and Charlie. They could not get along the way Kim had envisioned when she set out to start a relationship with the father she had never known. There was no connection. She had wanted to stay in Mississippi and get to know her father, but it wasn't going to be in the cards. She left "much earlier than expected" and went back home to Texas—to Rachel and Calvin and her half sister, April.

As she graduated from high school and entered college, Kim's life took on another significant change—one, she would soon learn, that was perhaps far worse than anything that had happened before.

34

IT WAS SAID TO HAVE started in high school for Kim, a routine display of "unstable and irrational" behavior—though Rachel Wilson later disagreed, claiming that Kim's temper and her being "easily provoked" began later, when she left college and entered adulthood. Regardless of the exact timeline, all of those emotions Kim was said to have been bottling up since childhood were now stewing, just waiting for the opportunity to explode into rage.

Soon after she started community college classes—"RN prerequisites and general studies" were Kim's focus—she began to blow off classes, sleeping late and spending her days in bed, a sure (and classic) sign of depression. It wasn't as if she were a lazy teenager, looking to sleep in and hitting the snooze button one too many times. Kim was spending days in bed, with shades drawn, door locked, withdrawn from the world. Antisocialism was now a core part of her personality.

When Cal found that Kim had skipped classes once again in favor of sleep, he blew a gasket. It wasn't going to be this way for Kim if she wanted to live in the

family house and go to school. She was an adult now.
She needed to start acting like one. Sleeping all day,
walking around as though the world was about to end,
developing a chip on her shoulder, it all had to stop.
Kim needed to grow up and get a life.

Leaving community college, Kim took a secretarial
position at a local law firm. It was a job she had viewed
back then as nothing more than passing her time. This
wasn't what she *wanted* to do—but, more or less, what
she *had* to do.

Through that first job out of college, Kim met Mike
West, a young man Kim's mother, Rachel, viewed as
"polished and well-educated." Kim worked at the same
law firm Mike's father used and the two were introduced. The relationship moved fast. Kim was so fond
of Mike, who was obviously smitten by her, that they
took off and got married in Hawaii.

Mike seemed to be that all-around perfect guy.
Raised from good stock, good-looking, he had a solid
disposition regarding work and family, and he had
been successful in his own right.

According to friends, Kim thought "if she married
Mike, she could prove to her mother that she had
value as a person and was worthy of being loved." She
believed that if she married a man with money, a good
family and a prosperous future, maybe Rachel Wilson
would see that her daughter was a valuable human
being.

They got married in June 1988. Kim was twenty-
one, Mike not much older. They argued all the time,
according to various statements and reports. It was
tumultuous, volatile and even violent right from the

start. Both were young and immature and full of angst. They agreed later that when they argued, they both became "mutually physical"; the police were called on a number of occasions.

Mike once threw Kimberly into a wall and left the imprint of her body in the sheetrock, said an affidavit Kim filed with the court—though Mike was never charged or convicted of any crime in relation to this matter.

What's important about that accusation is what was left out. Mike later testified in court about tossing Kim into the wall, adding how she had first violently hit him with a can of hairspray and cut him open. He described Kim's temper as "volatile," even during those first few months of knowing her. "In my experience," Mike explained, "you could never judge how she might react."

Kim tried to get pregnant immediately, but she had issues with fertility. Then, after some treatment, Kim took a look at a pregnancy test one morning and saw that she was going to have a baby. Within a marriage that had, only two years in, seen extreme lows and not many highs, Kim thought maybe this would calm the storm, remove the anxiety and lift the resentful dynamic between them. She was "ecstatic" after Travis was born on July 16, 1990. She believed the newborn would "fix the problems in her marriage." Even those who had close contact with Kim saw a sudden change in the right direction. She seemed happy and "in heaven" as she finished school and began her life as a nurse and raised a young child, still very much in love with Mike.

Kimberly was finally where she wanted to be in life, said the *Initial Application.*

Mike saw a different person emerge as their marriage hit a new stride and a child was part of their daily existence. Kim became explosive and would often get angry at minor things that Mike did. Her behavior, he said, got "progressively worse." It appeared that those issues that had been between them in the beginning had not gone away at all, but they might have just simmered after Kim had the child.

"She was quick to anger and had a volatile temper," Mike later said. Kim began to throw things at Mike: "Glasses, knives, whatever she could find."

One day Kim got extremely mad at Mike for something he said. It was so insignificant he could not recall what it had been. After she finished screaming and yelling at him, she hopped into the car.

He followed.

"What are you doing?" Mike asked as Kim started the car. It was parked in the garage. She revved the engine.

"Kim?"

She then drove the vehicle and rammed it into his workbench. "[It] was attached to [the] wall and shifted the wall about three or four inches," he later stated. This incident showed what Kim was capable of.

When later asked about his childhood, Travis could recall only vague parts of it. When asked in court about his "mother," Travis said he could not call Kim his mother. He could only call her Kimberly. And he did not consider her to be his mother. Asked to describe Kimberly in just one sentence, Travis responded: "Scary and abusive." Moreover, Travis said his dad, Mike West, was never abusive at all, but that Kimberly had choked him routinely.

Kim sought help from a psychiatrist. The marriage

seemed to be doomed. Mike sat down with the clinician and explained what was happening inside the house.

It appeared that Kim seemed "attracted to danger" and precarious situations "without fear of the consequences," said two individuals who later prosecuted Kim. She did not care what people thought, especially Mike or her children. More than that, she had a low tolerance for frustration, a short fuse that Kim's mother described as ever-present.

A psychiatrist's report submitted to the court by a doctor that Kim had seen reads like a page out of an abuser's handbook, with the emotional bottom falling out on Kim seemingly the moment she entered into this relationship with Mike. In October 1992, as her marriage to Mike crumbled into bits and pieces, Kim was diagnosed with a "not otherwise specified" (NOS) anxiety disorder, major depression and intermittent explosive disorder. These are serious mind disorders. Kim had been severely depressed and acting irrationally near this time. She was admitted into a psychiatric hospital and there was a question of whether she could care for her child any longer. Her doctors, during the hospitalization period, saw a mild "improvement in her functioning." When Kim was discharged, she was diagnosed with yet another condition, this one even more severe and dangerous to those around her: borderline personality disorder (BPD). Her doctors diagnosed Kim's BPD as "indicative of chronic and severe maladjustment in interpersonal functioning."

She was a mess. She couldn't get along with anyone. She had to have things her way all the time. If she didn't get her way, Kim would explode in a fit of unchecked rage, screaming vulgarities and cussing and threatening and hitting. The idea that her child could someday be removed from under her care and taken away infuriated Kim.

From reading her psych report, it's clear that Kim Cargill was unfit not only to be a wife, but also a mother. Her doctors were greatly concerned for the welfare of Travis.

"I have always been [Travis's] primary caretaker, and as his mother I should have primary custody," Kim told her doctors. Travis was two years old. He needed mothering and solid parental supervision at such a pivotal time in his development. He needed stability, especially where a mother and father were concerned, Kim argued.

"Michael is worse off than me," Kim tried convincing her doctors, meaning his emotional state. Why? "Because he has *not* sought treatment."

The blame game. Kim used this tactic routinely. She thought she could win any argument, legal or otherwise, by simply placing the onus of a situation on the opposing party.

Her doctors asked Kim if she would acknowledge some of her past behaviors, which had gotten her to this place she was now in—the past being a good indication of future behavior, where emotional instability is the matter at hand. If she was going to blame others, her doctors seemed to suggest with their questions, where in that scenario did she see herself?

Kim reluctantly admitted, "I [am] damaged property . . . but I have not hurt anyone. And I would never harm [Travis]."

Travis would beg to differ. One day, while Kim was getting him ready for his school pictures, she was combing the kid's hair with a large hairbrush, the type with the bristles and hard-plastic handle. Travis was fidgeting and wasn't interested in his mother making sure his hair was spit-shine perfect. Kim kept telling him to sit still, but Travis kept moving around. So Kim hauled off and "hit me over the head with the hairbrush a few times," Travis later recalled—something that happened to Kim, if she is to be believed, when she was a child. Then, after he still wouldn't sit still and allow her to comb his hair, Kim placed her hands around Travis's small, fragile neck and choked him, leaving a red mark.

Another time, Travis later explained, Kim hit him with a baseball bat.

Travis smiled in the photo taken on that day at school, but his expression was fake. He was twisted up inside and scared to death of what his mother might do next.

In a letter Travis later wrote as a seven-year-old detailing one of the incidents, he revealed, *I was at . . . home. One day my mom choked me. It felt like an alligator bit me on the neck.*

Mike told the doctors he had never seen her hurt their child. However, one of her doctors noted, "They disagree on whether she has hurt Mike."

"Five times," Kim told her doctors, "Mike has hurt me." She provided reports from the local police department to "prove" her allegations.

Her doctors went through the reports, which told a different story. One report turned out to be "inconclusive," because it failed to contain any statements from Mike, who was gone by the time the police arrived, so Kim was able to make up any accusations she wanted. What's more, that same report did not have any "visual confirmation" as evidence by any of the on-scene police officers indicating Kim had been injured. It was her word alone.

In all of the other reports where Kim had complained of being injured, there were "conflicting accounts" of how the "various (relatively) minor injuries" occurred, both Mike and Kim blaming each other, "justifying their own behavior as accidental or in self-defense." No charges were ever filed against Mike. He had, in fact, reported an injury on his arm, a gash deep enough for him to need stitches—and the police officers involved concurred. The only clear conclusion one could draw from all of the documentation was that when these two argued, they went at it. Sometimes each of them got hurt, but Mike always worse than Kim.

As Kim's psychiatrists interviewed Mike and evaluated the situation, it became obvious that the two of them could not agree about who was at fault. Each blamed one another, charging that the other was a bad parenting example for Travis. Mike and Kim were headed to divorce court. There was no way this relationship could withstand such a barrage of insults, accusations, abuse and emotional uncertainty. If they stayed together, an already-volatile situation would get progressively worse and might have dire and long-lasting implications on the child, if it hadn't already. Someone, sooner or later, was going to get badly hurt.

Later, after being asked as a twenty-two-year-old man how he had dealt with everything that had happened back in his early life, Travis said, "A lot . . . of therapy."

Within the report later filed by Kim's psychiatrists, a budding sociopath rose to the surface as clear and present as a slow-moving, dangerous fog rolling in from the sea. Her doctors said Kim not only lacked "empathy and is extremely self-absorbed," but she displayed an "overly authoritative" nature and became extremely "vindictive" and controlling whenever somebody challenged her. You look at the list of character defects these doctors checked off as Kim was closing in on twenty-six and you see a dangerous person materialize. The question became not would Kim ever act out on her abusive, unpredictable nature again, but *when?*

In individual sessions Kimberly West presented as an intense and anxious woman, who felt victimized in all of her significant relationships (especially by her husband and his extended family and by her first family), wrote one doctor.

Kim felt the entire world was against her. She blamed everyone but herself for the problems she faced in her life, and showed no real desire to seek treatment to make herself a better human being for her child. Whether she lost custody or not, didn't Kim want to be a better mother for Travis?

The psychiatrists Kim saw decided the next thing to do was to observe the child in each environment before making any firm recommendations. Their decision as to whether or not she kept her child was going to determine the outcome of many lives—either way, everyone involved knew.

35

TRAVIS WAS OUTSIDE PLAYING. IT was cold and wet, not the best day to be out of the house. An observer had shown up to watch and report how Kim interacted with her child. This was not by surprise; Kim had been given notice. She knew people would be watching her. Every move she made would be judged. Her chances of keeping her child were going to be based on her behavior.

The ongoing battle between Kim and Mike was vicious, each saying the other was unfit to raise the child as sole conservator. The court had decided the only way to understand the situation was to investigate. Apparently, the reports Kim's psychiatrists had handed in were not enough to convince a judge that she was unfit and unstable, even though the results stated, *Her psychological testing . . . indicates a number of significant issues which can be expected to significantly interfere with parenting.*

The observer on this cold, wet day noticed that Travis's nose was running, and Kim was not doing anything about it. Also, Travis had no jacket on. It was freezing cold—certainly not the type of weather to be wearing only a T-shirt outside.

It got to the point where the observer could not allow the child to continue playing without a jacket. "Isn't it too cold for him *not* to have a jacket?" the observer asked Kim. Travis was two years old.

"I am warm-blooded, and so is [he]," she snapped back in the abrasive tone she used when addressing anyone who had authority over her or questioned her or did not comply with her suggestions and requests.

She never did provide the child with a jacket and "was observed to wipe his nose only once" during the entire visit.

Kim believed that her truth was the only truth; she felt she could control the evaluation simply with words spewing from her mouth. Yet, she seemed to have no idea she was losing this battle. She would challenge the observers and doctors when it was "unnecessary" and speak to them as if they were below her, and acted as if what they had to say did not matter in the grand scheme of her life.

There were times during her sessions with Dr. Sandra Craig, the clinical psychologist in charge of Kim's final evaluation, when she'd admit she had issues. "My own bad temper has been a big cause of my troubles," Kim told Dr. Craig one day. But then she was back to her normal, everyday routine of making demands and being unwilling to admit her faults and try to fix them. Her doctors had even given Kim the benefit of the doubt and some positive reinforcement to build upon.

Kim . . . clearly loves her child, her psych report noted. *In raising certain issues like child care, she sounds knowledgeable and competent.* The doctor went on to say that she believed Kim would "promote" her son's "safety from external dangers." She added that Kim had "enthusiasm for athletics" and "concern for his medical treatment." She "would promote his development of gross motor skills." Still, in that same section of the report, the doctor went on to note that even within all the love Kim might have had for her child, her "narcissistic personality disorder" with its "histrionic features" would win out if she didn't continue ongoing psychiatric treatment.

As a profile of Kim's emotional turmoil came into focus during that 1992 psychological evaluation, it was clear who was the best parent for Travis. Kim was seen as a person who gravitated toward "risk-taking excitement." She tended to be "attracted," Dr. Craig summarized in her final assessment, "to danger without regard for the consequences."

Kim brushed off such comments as if she had gotten mad one time, had an episode and was being judged on that alone.

Perhaps the most dangerous of her emotional instabilities with regard to Travis was her "self-dramatizing style." Kim exhibited an "extremely low tolerance for frustration." She had a "tendency to think differently than others." This was at the core of Kim's psychosis, Craig wrote: *Kimberly can be expected to explode or act out her feelings onto the environment.*

There was that word: "explode."

It would become a perfect description that followed Kim all of her life.

Kim's doctor ultimately determined that her behavior was "consistent" with what Mike had claimed from the beginning: *She initiated and provoked their physical interactions.*

Her doctors worried that Kim would hurt Travis if she were put in a perilous or difficult situation and unable to figure out the best way to handle it. Of serious concern were Kim's "angry impulses." There was no telling what she would do when faced with a situation in which she disagreed with someone and perhaps felt she had been wronged.

Another of Kim's behavioral problems was described as a "long-standing, maladaptive personality style." This was characterized by "narcissistic and histrionic features." Kim was viewed as an "overly self-absorbed" person who lacked empathy for anyone around her and behaved as if she "has no awareness of the problems her behavior creates for others."

Kim was perceived as a tried-and-true sociopath, someone that could easily turn violent—and become a vicious psychopath.

Dr. Craig explained that meeting Travis's needs would be "extra-ordinarily difficult" for Kim as time went on because she was "extremely needy emotionally herself." The report even went so far as to project how Kim would react during a situation, sketching it out in a way that Kim would absolutely "challenge" the child while in the role of being Travis's caretaker: *In ways such as the flip "I hate you"* . . . In other words, if Travis became upset and told his mother he hated her, as some kids might be prone to do, Kim would respond to it in kind, instead of taking control as the parent.

Kim had been feeling ill in the final months of her marriage to Mike West while she and Mike had still lived together. According to the *Initial Application* affidavit,

Kim claimed it was about "two weeks after she was released from the hospital." She had gone in with stomach pain and digestive issues and had been diagnosed with Crohn's disease. This was occurring while Mike filed for divorce, ready to fight for full custody of Travis.

Mike had, in fact, taken Kim to court and sued her for custody because he felt she was unfit to parent the child. The summary portion of the recommendation by Dr. Sandra Craig recommended: *[Mike] West be named sole managing conservator of [Travis].* After assessing the situation and interviewing Kim and Mike, Kim's doctor believed: *[Mike's] psychological profile suggests he has the capacity to meet his son's needs and that his capacity to do so is significantly greater than Kimberly West's.* Furthermore, in what must have been a devastating blow to Kim, on page eight of the evaluation, in a concluding paragraph, the doctor wrote, *The profile generated in the evaluation . . . supports Mike West's account of his concerns about her.*

Kim later complained that bringing in her mother, Rachel Wilson, to testify on her husband's behalf allowed Mike the opportunity to convince the judge that Kim was unfit. She also made an allegation that her husband had "money and legal resources at his disposal" and she "did not."

In reality, however, Kim had nobody to blame but herself.

Losing her child sent Kim spiraling into a "deep depression," she later said. Not long after the decision came down, she checked herself into an outpatient mental health program, the *Initial Application* claimed. *Kimberly did not want the marriage to end,* said the *Initial*

Application, and was overwhelmed by what was happening to her.

Her present profile, Dr. Craig's assessment concluded, *indicates that she would have very great difficulty handling . . . challenges.*

This would become the understatement of Kim's entire life.

In her point of view Kim maintained that everyone was against her. As time went forward, and she learned to live without Travis and Mike, things would only get worse for those in Kim's unpredictable, violent path of destruction.

36

MIKE WEST MET A WOMAN, Sonja. She moved into the house Kim had been forced to leave. By this time Kim had met James Cargill, a strong, good-looking chap. Still, in Kim's eyes, Mike had kicked her out, replaced her and had gotten to keep their child to boot.

She was beyond livid.

By 1993, with their divorce finalized, Mike West knew he could not turn his back for one minute on Kim.

"In my experience," Mike said, "you never could judge how she might react."

Mike had been with Kim and she would, for no reason, pick up things "within an arm's reach" and throw them as hard as she could at him, hoping to inflict as much pain and injury as possible. It was in her nature to destroy those who hurt her—or, rather, those she believed had hurt her. A favorite had been drinking glasses, the hard and heavy kind. He'd seen her just go off the handle for no apparent reason, scream vulgar, hard-core obscenities, then find a heavy glass and toss it. Her anger, Mike added, "was progressive." As she got mad, her anger expanded like a water balloon.

Years after the divorce Mike sat one day and studied Travis's class photo. The child was eight at the time. There was something strange about the picture. Something *off*. Travis looked like a ghost.

Mike recalled that Kim had had the boy on the day Travis had his photo taken.

With a closer look Mike finally figured out what he was looking at. His son looked scared.

He called Travis into the room and asked him what had happened on the day the photo had been taken.

Travis told the story about the hairbrush.

Mike wondered about the red marks, visible in the school photo, on Travis's neck. Where in the hell did those red marks come from?

Travis told his father that his mother had also choked him that morning before school.

During divorce proceedings the court agreed to a visitation arrangement between Mike and Kim regarding Travis. Mike had sole custody. Kim could see the child on every "first, third and fifth weekend."

"I want you to write down everything you can remember about your visit with your mom," Mike told Travis. He was referring to the day of the hairbrush and choking incident.

Kim and Mike fought constantly. Mike's new wife, Sonja, had a child who lived with them, too. By June 1994, Kim was hot and heavy with James Cargill and they got married. On November 16, 1994, Kim gave birth to her second child, another boy, Blake Cargill.

When Kim was allowed only supervised visitation with Travis, the visits often took place at a neutral facility/location, and Kim had to pay any court costs or other expenses associated with the visits. Mike, Sonja or both were always there when the child was handed over to Kim and she was then allowed to take them.

Kim fumed inside, every time she had to abide by Mike's "rules" and was not allowed to do as she wanted.

It was impossible for [Travis] to be natural, Kim's later *Initial Application* claimed, *and have a good time with Kimberly when someone was watching everything [they] said or did.* Because of the so-called "fees" associated with "court costs for each visit," Kim wound up seeing her eldest son "less and less."

Thus, according to Kim's later assessment in her *Initial Application,* the reason why she did not see her boy as often as she might have wanted to became Mike West's fault. Every problem of Kim's life—from the time she had been a teenager causing her parents problems to her adult years, to when she would later fight Timmy's dad for custody and blame losing that child on Cherry Walker's potential testimony—was somebody else's fault. Never was any of it a result of her own doing. Kim consistently blamed others for her own behaviors and failures and faults.

Within the *Initial Application* account Kim made many accusations that were not supported (at the time the *Application* was filed) or backed up by under-oath, courtroom testimony. Among the charges Kim made in her report, she claimed Sonja and Mike conspired after they "created a new family together." She alleged that they tried "to get their exes out of their lives." While she involved herself in their lives, Kim contended in the *Application* that Sonja had lied about her ex regarding something having to do with the daughter Sonja brought into the marriage with Mike. The connection among Kim, Sonja and Mike was as fragile as a cobweb as this new family dynamic carried on throughout the next few years and Travis and Blake grew.

During that time Kim, apparently adopting the rule of war that encouraged keeping your enemies close, became friendly with Sonja's ex-husband, Roy (pseudonym). It was clear within this relationship with Sonja's ex that Kim had a premeditated plan.

Kim stayed married to James Cargill for a little over a year before James decided to end the marriage. He had experienced the same turmoil and disquiet and conflict and violence that Mike West had endured before him—and any man stepping into Kim's life would encounter in the future. It was December 19, 1995, when the divorce became finalized. Kim wound up with "joint managing custody" of Blake. If the past was even a half-accurate crystal ball, it was an arrangement James Cargill was going to live to regret.

37

KIM WAS AT HOME AND stewing about her ex and his second wife, Sonja. Though some years had passed, Kim had not let up with the constant bickering and insults against them. There was never a time when Mike or Sonja West could say that Kim was *okay*. With Kim Cargill, there was always a drama, always a reason to fight and spit venom at her exes. In her view she had been replaced—she would never look at it any other way. Mike had tossed her to the curb, found someone else, and they were raising *her* child.

Rockwall Police Department (RPD) officer Brad Merritt was answering phones on July 25, 1997. Kim had been divorced from Mike West for about four years. Mike and Sonja lived in Rockwall, a Dallas area suburb within Rockwall County. It's a quaint little town where people raise families in fine homes and send them to decent schools. According to the official Rockwall website, *[It's] the third wealthiest county in . . . Texas.*

Officer Merritt answered a call from an unknown female (whose identity, it would later be determined, was Kim Cargill).

"Have any threats been made this morning?" the caller asked.

"Well, ma'am, I'm not sure what you mean," Merritt responded. He was thinking, *Threats? What is this woman talking about?*

"Threats!" she said, losing a bit of patience. "Has anyone called in to claim any *threats* of any kind that have been made to them?"

"Well, what kind of threats?"

Odd, here was a caller phoning the RPD, trying to pump information out of a cop about something that may or may not have taken place.

After being prompted to explain herself further, the caller said, "I told my ex-husband that I was going to find his . . . wife in an alley somewhere and I was going to twist her head off!"

Merritt was perplexed. The way the caller had said it, she was admitting to making a threat herself.

"Look, ma'am, that in and of itself is a threat and you could be held responsible for it," Merritt advised.

The caller hung up without saying anything more.

38

ON AUGUST 1, 1997, SONJA'S ex-husband, Roy, contacted Kim—the two were apparently close friends now—and asked her to pick up his daughter when she went over to Mike and Sonja's to collect Travis for a scheduled visit. By now Kim had worked herself up to picking the child up and dropping him off without supervision.

Sonja was home with the two kids, Travis and her daughter. Mike was at work. Sonja's ex-husband was at work also. Sonja had been at work, too, and the nanny was there, watching the kids. However, as Sonja told the story nearly two decades later in court (still married to Mike West, by the way), "We (Mike and I) *never* let these pickups and drop-offs happen without one of us being there."

Who knew what Miss Unpredictable would do next?

"Kim is picking up [our daughter] for me," Sonja's ex-husband told Sonja during a phone call before Kim arrived.

Sonja thought it strange, but she agreed to it.

Kim showed up. Mike did not allow Kim into their

home. Although she sometimes burst in, barging through the door, announcing her arrival, yelling about something, on this day Kim knocked and waited outside. (There was one report claiming she walked into the house uninvited and used the bathroom before this event took place.)

Travis walked out the door and up the few flights of stairs leading into the driveway. He later said he dreaded visiting his mother. He understood that building a relationship with KC was—or could be—a good thing, had she wanted to participate, but the idea of her coming to fetch him for a visit always caused him great anxiety.

Sonja's daughter, six years old at the time, stood by her mother and said good-bye as they stood near the door. Kim, growing a bit agitated and nervous, making it clear that it was taking too long, watched them. In fact, while Sonja said good-bye to her daughter, Kim got fed up with waiting, walked over, grabbed the small child by the arm and, in one of her signature abusive moves, yanked the kid toward her. She jerked the little girl hard and walked away, with the child's tiny feet dangling off the ground.

"Come on, let's go!" Kim said through clenched teeth as she walked away.

Sonja was amazed by the sheer gall of Kim.

The child began to "scream" and "cry."

Travis was waiting to leave. He turned and saw what was happening, Sonja recalled. Travis could not believe what his mother was doing to his young stepsister.

Sonja ran toward her child—"This happened all so fast," she later explained—and tried to pick her up so she wasn't hanging from Kim's grasp. The little girl's legs were off the ground and, undoubtedly, her arm socket was in terrible pain.

Kim let go. Not because she wanted to, Sonja later said, but for the sole purpose of confronting Sonja. The child was in her way, an obstruction.

"What do you think you're doing?" Sonja said. She could tell Kim was "enraged at that point." Everyone who knew KC described her angry look in a similar fashion: the eyes narrowed to slits, the grimace, the red face and the clenched fists.

Kim, without warning, kicked Sonja in the stomach as hard as she could. Then she took one of Sonja's arms, a hand specifically, and "we had a brick wall, and she threw it against the brick wall." Then Kim kneed Sonja in the stomach and began "flailing about."

Here was Kim Cargill in one of her violent rages, overwhelmed with an overpowering need to inflict pain. The kids had experienced it; so had Mike West and James Cargill. Kim's mother, cops and social workers had witnessed and felt it. Now Sonja was experiencing it; Kim was going ballistic.

Travis stood by, watching it all, feeling helpless. He took the blue duffel bag he was carrying (his weekend clothes) and swung it at his mother, hoping she would withdraw from beating Sonja.

"Stop it! Stop it!" the boy shouted.

When he realized he couldn't do much, though, Travis took off running.

The little girl stood behind her mother, scared. She had a hand in her mouth and was flinching. Sonja was shielding the child from Kim's fury.

Travis stood by a fence near the property line, scared to be anywhere near a woman he knew could hurt and cause injury when she wanted. When Kim finished beating on Sonja, screaming obscenities, she took off toward Travis and grabbed him.

The boy was crying.

Kim picked him up off the ground and placed him over her shoulder like a sack of potatoes. While Travis kicked and screamed ("Let me go. . . . Let me go. . . .") and pounded on her back, she shoved him into the car through an open window. She treated Travis as though he were a package—her possession, her property.

Inside the car, watching all of this, was young Blake, about three years old at the time.

Mike and Sonja's nanny stood inside the house and looked on. She was scared to walk outside and get in the way of this crazy woman on a rampage. Everyone in the West household had had run-ins with Kim and knew she was dangerous.

The nanny picked up the phone and dialed 911.

In her *Initial Application* the appellate lawyers for Kim Cargill described this scene on her behalf in one sentence: *Kimberly and Sonja had a physical altercation on a day when [Sonja's ex] asked Kimberly to pick up [his child] from Sonja's house.*

After tossing Travis through the open window, Kim jumped into her car and took off, not giving the boy a chance to say he didn't want to go with her. She left Sonja's child there—not that Sonja would have allowed her to take the girl, anyway.

Standing in the driveway, watching Kim speed away, Sonja looked down and saw that Kim had manhandled Travis with so much force that as she tossed him in through the open window, one of his shoes had fallen off. This was now the only sign of what had just tran-spired, besides the physical wounds on Sonja's body

and the emotional confusion the children would take
with them for life.

Sonja ran to the phone and the nanny handed it
over. Sonja wanted to make sure Kim did not get out
of Rockwall County.

As Kim approached a nearby 7-Eleven, an RPD
police officer pulled her over.

"Can you come down to the police station with me,
ma'am?" the officer asked Kim after the usual dialogue about license and registration.

Kim said she did not want to talk about anything.

"Just please stay right here," the officer explained.

He went back to his vehicle and ran a check on her
name and license number. There it was: Kim had several outstanding warrants for traffic violations and
unpaid tickets.

While Kim was at the RPD being booked and asked
about the confrontation she'd had with Sonja, another
cop stood nearby, listening. At some point, while Kim
was rambling on, she said, "If I ever find that woman
(Sonja) in a dark alley, I am going to twist her head off."

Brad Merritt, the officer standing by, stopped her,
realizing that the comment had a familiar ring to it.
Merritt was the same officer who had taken a call the
previous week from a woman who had failed to identify
herself, but had used those same words while asking if
a threat had been called into the RPD. The cop put two
and two together.

Merritt walked over to Kim. "Hey, wait a minute," he
said. "That's verbatim, exactly what I . . . I got a call
back on July twenty-fifth. . . ." Merritt paused. He
looked at the other cop, then at Kim.

"We need to advise you, ma'am, of your rights. You
have the right to remain silent . . . ," Merritt said, fully

Mirandizing KC, who was now under arrest on a variety of charges. None of the allegations included the assault she had just committed. That charge would come later.

It appeared that Kim might need to see an emergency medical technician (EMT). She had some injuries—superficial as they were. Both cops asked her several times if she needed medical attention.

She said no.

They had her sign a release, which indicated they had asked and she had refused.

Kim signed it.

Sometime later, Kim posted a cash bond and was released.

About fifteen minutes later, Kim walked back in and asked for the same two cops she had been dealing with.

"She was very irate," one of the officers later described. "She was uncooperative. She was upset."

"I am going to sue all of you!" Kim raged. She had that look: squinted eyes, red face, clenched teeth and tensed fists.

The officers looked at each other. *What is she doing back?*

"Ma'am, please . . ."

"I am suing everybody!"

"What is the problem?" an officer asked.

"You did not provide me with medical care," Kim claimed. Kim was now saying she asked for medical treatment and was denied.

This was ridiculous. Both cops that had arrested Kim that day later testified that they had asked her if she wanted to see an EMT and she declined. Kim had signed a release, saying she refused medical treatment.

What was she talking about? Why was she even back? Did she want to be arrested again?

"I want to file charges against my ex-husband's wife," Kim said, changing the subject.

"Ma'am, you'll want to make sure you clear your particular cases before you pursue charges against Mrs. West."

Kim left the RPD, seething.

Kim was ultimately convicted of assault. (She pleaded out her case.) She was sentenced to twelve months deferred adjudication probation. While she was on probation, she attacked Matt Robinson's grandmother, twisting her arm and tossing her out of her chair in the backyard. In her *Initial Application*, then, Kim talked about this arrest and later conviction as though it was some sort of misunderstanding she wound up taking the fall for: *Kimberly could not risk a felony on her record because she was trying to get her nursing license, so she had to plead guilty to a lesser charge.*

Kimberly *had* to do that!

For Travis, Kim and her incidents of acting out in her violent outbursts were becoming all too much. Granted, he was referring only to those incidents he was willing to talk about later, not everything that had gone on inside the house. Travis indicated to his dad that he did not feel safe around his mother. Seeing her attack Sonja showed Travis who his mother was and what she was capable of doing.

Travis's father encouraged the boy to tell her.

Thus, there came a time when Travis sat down with his mother within a Family Connection session and explained the decision he had reached: "I'll talk to you from now on when *I* want to."

When later asked what he recalled most from that time when he was living with his mother and would visit her after the divorce, Travis had a very simple, sobering explanation: "That I always wanted to run away." It was also quite clear that although a requirement was for Kim to have someone supervise the visits, she was able to manipulate the situation to where she could get the children alone.

"I don't want to see her anymore," Travis told his dad after that meeting with his mother.

"Okay."

That meeting with Kim was the last time Travis ever saw his mother.

39

IN 1997, KIM CARGILL WAS able to get her licensed vocational nurse certification, also called licensed practical nurse—LPN—in some states, from North Texas Professional Career Institute (NTPCI). Kim had her college and apartment paid for (while going to school and after) and received "just about anything she asked for, materialwise," one of Kim's doctors later reported. KC's mother and stepfather, trying to show love, spoiled her, giving her what she needed to make a life for herself.

LVNs choose this field, particularly, because it is, as a vocation, a rewarding experience. The hands-on approach to nursing is focused on people of all ages. You're a frontline provider. A close bond is often fused between patient and LVN because of the intimate, prolonged contact they have on a daily basis. Did the job description fit Kim Cargill in any way? Was her chosen vocation a good match for her character/personality/temperament? Was she the type of person to give tender, loving care to the patients she would spend copious amounts of time with?

Could Kim hit her child, lock him in his room, scream obscenities and insults at him, bully him, fight with her ex-husband's new wife, and then head off to a job that required her to be a loving, caring, all-purpose medical professional, caring for sick and needy people for eight, ten or twelve hours at a time?

Apparently, the board at NTPCI, which gave her that LVN license, thought so.

While she was in nursing school, Kim met Tammy (pseudonym) and charmed her to the point that she asked if Kim was interested in meeting her brother, Matt Robinson.

"Sure," Kim said. She didn't have a boyfriend at the time. And if there is one aspect of human life that stimulates the borderline personality/narcissistic sociopath's mind, it's being involved in a romantic relationship. Where borderline people are concerned, a romantic relationship presents the opportunity to fill their emptiness; it is a chance to replenish the emotional well they will often claim to be dry since early childhood. The relationship provides a stable, readily available place to release their aggressive and violent emotion. So when the chance presented itself for Kim to have a man in her life, she rarely resisted. And, as would be the case with Matt Robinson, she often dove in headfirst.

Matt lived with Kim for the first eight months they were together. But as time went on, Matt became aware of the true person Kim Cargill was and decided he did not want to stay. She was far too needy and unbalanced. When he came home from a hard day's work, the last thing Matt wanted was to walk into his home and not know what he would be facing, what type of person he would be dealing with or how the night would progress. There was always a drama brewing with Kim.

Those eight months for Matt, as he got to know Kim and realize how angry and erratic she was, were longer than Matt planned to stay after he realized he had moved in with a monster. Matt later explained, "I tried to stay there as long as I could, because I knew [Blake] wasn't safe—I should have left a long time [before I did]."

Blake was around three years old during the time Matt lived with the child and Kim. Matt saw what he later called a "whole lot of crazy stuff" Kim did to the child. Matt protected Blake in many instances, but he couldn't be there all the time.

"I want to go to your sister's," Kim said to Matt one day. This was near the end of the eight months Matt lived with her.

"Why, Kim?"

Kim wanted Matt to "start a fight" with Tammy "because she was mad about something." Kim worked with Tammy at times. She could have been angry for any number of (silly, inconsequential) reasons, Matt later explained. Her perception of the world was different from anybody else's. Everyday conflicts had become almost impossible for Kim to handle without becoming hostile. The way Kim experienced her own emotions was vastly different from that of the average person.

Matt decided to oblige her, though he had no intention of starting a fight with Tammy. They took off in Matt's car—Kim, Matt and Blake—and drove out to Matt's sister's house.

When Matt refused to start a fight at his sister's, Kim became so upset she stormed out to the car, sat down in the front seat and put Blake on her lap. She was stewing, probably thinking of a way to get back at Matt for disobeying her.

Matt took this as a sign that it was time to leave. He said good-bye to his sister with a roll of his eyes; then he collected their belongings and walked outside to the car. It was pitch-dark, about ten or eleven at night.

Matt sat down in the driver's seat. The car was parked over a concrete sidewalk. Kim had her door open, with little Blake still on her lap.

"Why didn't you start a fight with her?" Kim asked in her best calm-before-the-storm voice—it was a scornful, scathing tone that Kim could always muster without any effort at all. Matt knew it well by this point. She meant business. Kim was leading up to something when she used that irritated inflection.

"Kim—" Matt tried to explain, but she cut him off.

"I told you to pick a fight."

"Kim, I am not—"

Before Matt could finish what he was about to say, Kim tossed Blake "out of the car, onto the sidewalk," Matt explained later. It was as though Blake needed to pay for the anger she felt toward Matt. By doing this, she would teach Matt not to *ever* disobey her again. Kim knew Blake was a child Matt cared for and that hurting him would cause Matt pain. For Kim there was always a price to pay—whether by one of her kids, Matt or somebody else—for not doing what she told them to do.

Yet Kim was not finished.

Before Matt could react to the child being thrown

out of the car, Kim punched Matt in his eye socket. A solid shot.

Pow!

Even though Matt had seen Kim choking Blake and "throwing him around like a rag doll," he could not believe what Kim had just done to Blake. He was a helpless, tender, innocent, lovely child. She could have cracked his skull open. Blake could have wound up in intensive care, his brain swelling. Kim's utter lack of concern for her child's welfare was startling to Matt.

He thought he'd seen it all. Apparently not.

Kim jumped out of the car. Blake was on the concrete ground, crying. He'd gotten pretty banged up. Kim walked over and fumed, "Get up! Get the hell up off the ground!" She grabbed Blake by the arm and jerked him up and started walking. Matt followed, holding his eye, wondering what in the hell was going on.

She must have taken off running, however. The darkness of the night swallowed Kim and Blake up and Matt couldn't see them.

Matt went back to the car and drove slowly around the neighborhood. He searched carefully, thinking Kim had gone off into a tizzy and would calm down sooner or later, hop back into the car and maybe even say she was sorry.

About "three or four streets over" from where Matt's sister lived, he saw Kim with Blake, thumping her way down the road.

There would be no apologies from KC this night.

Matt pulled up alongside. "Come on, get in." He was terrified of what she might do to Blake once she got him home, in private, or if she took off and spent the night with Blake somewhere other than home.

Matt needed to get the child into the car, get him somewhere away from her so she could get control of herself and Matt could keep an eye on him.

"Please, Kim, please, I'm begging you here. . . . Get. In. The. Car." Matt stared at Blake. The child had a look of absolute terror on his face. "Like he always did," Matt commented later, adding, "I wasn't really worried about her. I was trying to get [Blake] home."

Kim's *Initial Application* document, which was said to outline her entire life of so-called trauma and ill treatment by those in her life, contained no mention of this incident. In fact, in a section titled, "Despite Assertions to the Contrary, There Was a Positive and Compassionate Side to Kimberly Cargill," one quote made the claim: *All Kimberly ever wanted was a "normal life," as wife and mother.* Further, it stated that she "loved" being a mom and "took good care" of her children. She was "fun to be around" and had a "sweet personality." Kim "got along well with others." Another quote made the erroneous, even laughable assertion that her children "enjoyed" being around their mother and that she "loved [them] very much" and they were "physically affectionate."

These comments, supported by personal affidavits submitted to the court, came from "friends" of Kim's— old high-school mates and former coworkers and people she had (supposedly) known throughout her life. All of it, however, fundamentally contradicted later courtroom testimony by those—including her own children—who lived with Kim and knew firsthand what she was capable of and what she had done.

This incident was the final straw for Matt Robinson. Matt was horrified by the visions of what she might do to Blake in his absence, but he could do little about it. He could not be a part of Kim's world any longer.

So Matt left.

About three weeks after Matt walked out on her, Kim called.

"What is it, Kim?" He wanted nothing to do with her anymore. There was nothing she could do or say to change his mind. The woman was toxic. Absolute poison.

"I'm pregnant," Kim said. There was almost an *"I win"* tone in her voice. (*"Aha! You bastard—you thought you could walk out on me?"*)

"Yeah, sure," Matt responded. "Nice try, Kim." He wasn't so much doubting that Kim was going to have a baby more than the notion that he was the father.

"She had this friend that she was always hanging out with," Matt commented later. "And she would leave and go do stuff with him." Matt assumed Kim was sleeping with the guy on the side and he was the father. She had been spiteful in every other way; why should Matt believe that she was faithful? If Matt was the father, it meant he would now be tied to her for the rest of his life, or at least the next eighteen years. The thought made Matt ill.

Matt couldn't accept it. They weren't a couple when she called. They had not been living together and he had rarely spoken to KC since walking out. This call was just another of her attempts to be the center of attention, another manifestation of her inherent narcissistic nature, and her desire to always do things *her* way.

Kim had told Matt from the first occasion they started sleeping together that she *couldn't* get pregnant. She had lied to him about something that would make him feel at ease when they had intercourse. She'd tricked him. She'd manipulated the situation.

Kim would later deny all this, of course. She would play, once again, her woe-is-me card—from a seemingly endless deck she kept in her pocketbook. She was great at using the everyone-is-against-me role of being the victim in any situation that did not favor her, especially with people whom she had just met. Yet, every aspect of her romantic and parental life proved that Kim Cargill was what many doctors over the years treating her had claimed she was: an absolute, nonconforming sociopath, to which one could add "pathological liar" at this point.

"An individual with antisocial traits has difficulty following the rules and will engage in behavior that subjects them to arrest," one of Kim's doctors said. "There is deceit, manipulation, lying and impulsivity. . . ."

Kim felt perpetually entitled. She had grandiose opinions of herself and impossible fantasies about what her life should be. Kim Cargill's behavior displayed textbook antisocial personality disorder. A person like Kim "exploits others for personal gain," a doctor analyzing her had testified.

Kim gave birth to her third child in 1999, each of her children now fathered by a different man. Matt Robinson was not there for the birth of Brian because, Matt later explained, he didn't know it was his child at the time. Later, after the proof came in that Matt was, indeed, Brian's father, he stepped up—which was when the real trouble for Matt Robinson began.

40

IF MATT ROBINSON THOUGHT DEALING with Kim Cargill was a nightmare while he was living with her, as this new phase of his life began, Matt was about to learn that she was, at her core, evil. The woman spewed venomous hatred the same way others showed love.

As the first few years of his son Brian's life passed, Matt lived under a constant and unremitting fear that Kim would severely harm the boy. Matt had seen what Kim could do to her own flesh and blood with Blake. As Matt put it later in court, "I found out a lot of information that was going on [with Kim], which I knew he was being abused."

Some of the mistreatment Matt uncovered included a report that Brian, in diapers, was wandering aimlessly "out on the street . . . walking down the road" by himself one night. What's more, Matt heard Kim was being evicted from where she was living. Matt feared his son would not have a roof over his head, not to mention three square meals, medical care and the attention he needed during his formative years. There was no telling what Kim would do if she were tossed out on the street. Someone would have to pay for that failure, for sure—and Matt knew from experience that it was not going to be Kim. If she had no man around to beat up, the kids were next in her line of fire. Matt had to do something for the sake of his child.

In the *Initial Application* document Kim brought in an old friend who was "around Kimberly from 1996 to 1998," a tumultuous time in her life, to say that she was a "normal" and "friendly" person, whose behavior during "custody situations" was never "out of the realm of a normal level of intensity." This same "friend" signed an affidavit to the effect that he knew Kimberly took "good care of her second son, [Blake]," and he did not see "any kind of abuse or neglect."

Contrary to the fairy tale Kim later scripted about her life (and managed to get others to not only believe, but even back up with signed affidavits to the court), Matt felt he could do nothing to protect his son but take desperate measures and deal with the fallout later on. Matt decided to pick the child up one day for a visit and not return him. There was no way Kim would allow Matt to take the child for an extended period of time, or even in the interim while she found new housing and worked out the specifics of her disordered, chaotic life. To do so would mean she had to admit defeat, admit failure and admit that she could not handle being a single mother.

"I made a decision to keep him and take her to court," Matt explained later.

Of course, this did not sit well with Kim. She had Matt arrested and charged with kidnapping. Matt was brought up on those charges, a serious felony with major time in prison if convicted. He had to hire a lawyer (spending $27,000 in total) and fight the charges in court, but he was able to eventually get the entire case dismissed.

It felt like a win. However, it wasn't.

Kim got to keep her child.

If there was a silver lining for Matt in all of this, it was that he had not married Kim. At an arm's length, he could monitor the situation, talk to Brian and gauge how the child was managing. He could find out how Kim was treating Brian and Blake, then decide the right course of action to take against Kim as each situation presented itself.

What would Kim do next? Anything was possible, if you ask those who *truly* knew her and interacted with her during this period of her life (early 2000s). Kim's first and foremost goal, however, was to find another man. Kim needed to have a whipping boy, someone to soak up the negative energy she discharged. This was important to her neurosis—and, actually, probably a good thing for the children. Without a man in her life Kim's entire focus would be on the kids, and history already had proven that was dangerous.

41

HE WAS SHOOTING POOL AND having a few laughs. He was a good ol' boy enjoying some country fun. Forrest Garner had gone to Clicks Pool Hall near his mother's house to enjoy a night out. It was a quiet evening in September 2004, calm and cool, the dry wind blowing in from the east with a mellow hint of humid, late-summer air hanging on behind it. It was the kind of night, with the stars as bright and far as the eye can see, with the sky a perfect dome, that Texans like to brag about.

Forrest took a break from his pool game and did a lighthouse look around the bar, to see what kind of crowd was hanging out. A few times before, he had seen the woman with the long, flowing blond hair and wayward smile, who stood by the bar. There was something about her. She drew attention to herself. Forrest Garner decided to approach her, say hello and introduce himself.

"Kimberly," she said. "Kimberly Cargill."

"Forrest Garner—nice to meet you, Kimberly."

Forrest was impressed. He was a big guy, who favored ten-gallon cowboy hats to go with his black goatee. Kim was good-looking and had a nice shape. She seemed cordial, charming and articulate. Kim seemed to be someone who, like him, wasn't afraid to laugh and tell things the way they were.

They talked. There was chemistry.

"You want to play a game of pool?" Forrest asked. As time would tell, he might as well have asked: *"You want a bite of this apple?"* Kim beat Forrest in pool that night and this Texan thought, *Well, this is mighty embarrassing, doggone it—but in a good way.* Forrest wasn't about to let this one slip out of his hands.

They started dating.

Throughout the past few years Kim had gone through a long list of men, many of whom had seen her violent and alarming ways and had run as far away as they could. She was a woman with three kids, two failed marriages behind her (and a host of additional relationships, both long and short), though that's not what she always said while out "man shopping." Yet, none of this, Kim would later insist, had anything to do with the person she was or could be for the right man.

If you took Kim Cargill at her word, her marriage to Mike West had poisoned her way of thinking, feeling and her future romantic, emotional well-being. Mike was the person to blame for the way she was; he was the bad guy who started it all. Kim called that marriage "tumultuous." She said it was consistently combative and unsustainable. She claimed that the divorce from Mike was "acrimonious," and the "subsequent loss of custody of her first son" sent her into a "deep depression and further undermined her sense of security and self-worth." All of it was Mike's fault. All those years in which she sparred with Mike over their child, Travis, set her up for future failures. Mike was an easy target.

Later, though, Kim would blame "sexual abuse" by an extended family member for sending her down a path of discontentment and violence. However, that purported sexual abuse existed only as a "self-report," one of her doctors later testified in court. Therefore, it should be taken with a "grain of salt." Why? Because the doctor was "factoring in that [Kim Cargill] is deceitful, lies, manipulates."

With no outside or second-/third-party corroboration—medical reports, police reports, charges, an admission by the alleged perpetrator—supporting Kim's claim, it was hard to believe *anything* she said, especially since the allegations were coming thirty-plus years after the event.

"The only credibility I put in it," said that doctor while testifying about the alleged sexual abuse, "is that it's consistent with individuals with borderline personality disorder. I don't know whether it happened or didn't happen."

Kim described the abuse as having taken place when she was "eleven or twelve years old." She said she was staying at someone's house one night. She was asleep. She woke up to him "touching her breasts and her vagina." She said she "pretended to be asleep and he went away." It never happened again. Yet, she said, that one instance of alleged sexual abuse set her up for a lifetime's worth of emotional pain.

* * *

As Kim and Forrest dated, Kim shared her life story, telling Forrest she had *two* sons. Forrest had no idea during the first few months of the courtship that Travis existed.

As Brian grew and went to school, according to one of his classmates' mothers, Kim was the perfect suburban parent whenever the classmate's mother ran into her. Kim could be "warm and open to others," said an affidavit written by Kim's friend and filed with the *Initial Application*. This particular parent claimed she had often seen Kim when she was with Brian and her other child and she "was not rough with them." The document purported: *In fact, [Kim] was the opposite of rough. . . . There was not ever anything amiss and . . . Kimberly [was] responsible and conscientious.*

Kim could certainly lay on the charm and put on a mask of a loving parental custodian when she needed to impress—as she was now doing with Forrest. It was an act. Kim knew how to display her best self to anyone around her; she worked hard at it. A mere eight months into their relationship, whatever Kool-Aid Kim Cargill was serving to Forrest Garner, he liked the taste of it: Kim had herself her third husband fewer than four months before the year anniversary of meeting and dating him. Forrest and Kim were married on April 30, 2005. Even though Forrest said later that the relationship was only good for the first three months, he went ahead, anyway, with the nuptials. Kim's mother, Rachel, wasn't on hand for the wedding. Kim and Rachael had been "estranged" since 2001, a fallout between them that would last six years.

No sooner were they living together (Forrest said later he did not live with Kim until after they married), did Kim begin to tear down her former marriages and the fathers of her children. Whenever she and Forrest got to talking about previous relationships, Matt Robinson being the most recent, Kim went after him: "He's an asshole!"

"Come on, Kim."

"He's a bad father and a bad influence on [Brian]."

For anyone that spent any amount of time with Kim, when they went back and looked at this comment later, it was beyond laughable. The idea that Kim could call anyone a bad influence on her children showed the sheer arrogance of this woman.

"Kim . . . ," Forrest said. "Come on. . . ." Forrest was not the type to fall for Kim's nonsense just because it came out of her mouth.

"I want you to kick his ass for me, Forrest. First chance you get."

"No, Kim." (Later, Matt and Forrest—along with James Cargill—would become acquaintances.)

"He's a very good guy," Forrest said of Matt Robinson. In fact, all of Kim's children got together once when Rachel Wilson, Kim's mother, hosted a Fourth of July cookout and invited the dads with their kids. All the dads talked while the boys, having not all been together at once since who knows when, "were in heaven," Forrest later explained.

As they got to know each other while dating, Forrest later recalled, he asked Kim about her mother. He wanted to know why Kim never mentioned Rachel, or never asked him to take her to see her.

It would have been easy for Kim to explain that they

did not get along, saw the world differently and hadn't talked for years. But Kim felt the need to lie, instead. "She's dead," Kim told Forrest.

Forrest had only met Blake and Brian. He queried Kim one day about a possible third child. It seemed she had another child, but she hardly even mentioned him. Forrest wanted to know why.

"He's dead," Kim said.

"I'm so sorry, Kim."

The worst-possible thing ever: a mother losing a child. Forrest was overcome with empathy and sympathy for his girlfriend. She had gone through what no parent wanted to think about. Forrest was under the impression the child died at a young age—that is, until they were moving one day and Forrest was preparing some boxes to load from the apartment into his truck.

As he grabbed an overstuffed box overflowing with various personal items, some photos fell out and onto the floor.

He picked up a photo of Blake with another boy— a much older kid. Didn't make sense. If her youngest boy had died, who was this older child in the photo?

"Who is this?" Forrest asked Kim. He pointed to the older boy.

Kim walked over and grabbed the photo from Forrest's hand. "Give. Me. That." She then "flipped" out, Forrest said.

While she yelled obscenities at him, she picked up the items in the living room, pictures in frames, knick-knacks, whatever was in reaching distance, and hurled them at Forrest. It was your typical Kim Cargill rant. She had turned into the beast she would become whenever someone questioned her and one of her many, many lies was exposed.

Forrest wasn't putting up with it. He walked out of the house and did not call her.

Kim called three days later. "Listen, I need to tell you about [Travis.]" He wasn't dead, after all, Kim explained. "His father is rich. He paid off a judge and turned [Travis] against me. So that is why I said he was dead to me."

When Forrest realized Kim was lying about the child (assuming she was probably lying about her mother, too), he wanted to know why. Regarding the time they dated, Forrest said later, "It wasn't bad. It was just basically a normal . . . ," but he stopped himself there. "You know, like I said, we really didn't live together, so it was more of like a dating relationship," he amended.

"Why would you tell me your mother is dead?" Forrest wanted to know. Relationships, from where Forrest came from, were based on trust, acceptance and honesty.

"She was such a bad mother, Forrest, she's dead to me," Kim explained.

This incident when he found out about Travis took place before Forrest and Kim were married. For some it might have been the last red flag in a field of them, though Forrest said later, "Love is blind . . . I guess. I don't know." He decided to give Kim the benefit of the doubt. People lost their tempers. He had opened a touchy subject and she had snapped. The lies about her mom and Travis, well, she was expressing her desire not to talk about subjects that upset her. When it comes to love, denial is part of the territory.

"I cannot get pregnant," Kim assured Forrest time and again.

Seven months into the relationship: "I'm pregnant."

In April 2005, pregnant and now married, Kim moved in with Forrest. He rented an apartment behind a Home Depot store. The fact that she became pregnant, Forrest later said, was a big deal for him. He wasn't about to let a woman, pregnant with his child, fend for herself. That was not how Forrest Garner had been raised.

From the day they met, life for Forrest Garner would never be the same. It started with the phone calls.

"Are you mad at me?" Kim would call and ask.

"No."

A half hour later, "Are you sure you're not mad at me?"

"Kim, come on."

Forrest would be at work. "And the phone calls," he explained, "just started really, *really* getting excessive and excessive."

Obsessive might be more like it. She called and called and called—about the silliest, most inconsequential things. Her insecurity became a disease growing out of control.

I cannot do this anymore, Forrest would think after hanging up for the fifth time in a day. Kim would ask (repeatedly): *"Do you love me? Do you hate me? Are you mad at me? Why are you mad? You seemed mad when you left this morning—are you?"*

"I need to break up with you," Forrest told Kim at

one point. He'd agonized over the decision. "This is not working out."

She said no.

"No?"

"Not happening."

Forrest went home to the apartment they shared. "You need to leave," he told Kim. This was about two weeks before she announced she was pregnant. She must have known she was pregnant then, but she wasn't sharing the fact with him. Kim was holding on to her trump card. Knowing Forrest was a man's man, a guy who had morals and integrity and would take care of his child, she was waiting for just the right moment to unload this big news, and use it to her advantage.

"You need to get out," Forrest said. He tried to "physically get her out" of the apartment, but couldn't. She would not listen. She could not take rejection. Forrest didn't want to hurt Kim; he just wanted her out of his apartment.

"Kim, you need to leave."

At that point Kim clamped herself to Forrest like a child to her mother's leg. She would not let go.

"I was trying to get her out and she had, like, this grip on me . . . ," he recalled. "I couldn't get her off of me."

Human Velcro.

Forrest had a son, Martin (pseudonym), who was five at the time. He lived there with them and had been with Forrest since the boy could walk. After breaking free of Kim, Forrest took his child and went to his mother's house, telling Kim she needed to be gone when he came back the following day. It was over. If she could not leave right then, Forrest made clear, he would stay at his mother's until Kim got the message and moved out.

Before sunup the next morning, Forrest was awoken by his stepfather. "Hey, Forrest . . . get up. You need to get up." It was too early to go anywhere or do the lawn or help the old man around the house.

Something was going on.

Something important.

Something tragic.

"What's wrong?" Forrest asked.

42

FORREST LOOKED AT HIS STEPFATHER.
"What's going on?"

"It's the phone," he said. "Forrest, get up—it's for you."

"Hello?" Forrest said.

It was the fire marshal telling Forrest his apartment "had been burned up." Forrest was still half asleep. He wasn't able to comprehend what was being explained to him.

"What?"

"Your apartment caught fire and burned up."

Kim. She was the last one inside the apartment. Though it was never proven that she lit the fire, it seemed obvious to everyone that she was getting Forrest back for running out on her and wanting to end the relationship.

After getting dressed and rushing over to the apartment, Forrest called Kim.

"What happened at your apartment?" Kim asked right away.

"What do you mean? Why are you asking me that?"

How could she know? Did she sit and watch it burn from the parking lot?

"Well [the fire marshal] told me," Kim said.

"She had dated the city marshal," Forrest explained later, "[and he] lived right across the parking lot from where my apartment was."

Continuing, Kim added, "He called me and told me that something had happened in your apartment, Forrest."

In the end Forrest had his "doubts," he said, about Kim. The fire marshal told him that the door into his apartment was locked. However, Kim had a key. Nothing had been cooking; no candles burning; there was no apparent reason for the fire. Moreover, Kim had none of her belongings inside Forrest's apartment at the time of the fire. On top of that, where the fire started was suspicious.

The fire originated in the bedroom (where they had been arguing when Forrest walked out). Apparently, Forrest's mattress spontaneously combusted, because the mattress caught fire and was put out after smoke was reported and the fire department arrived. Still, everything inside the apartment was trashed because of the black soot caused by all the smoke damage.

Forrest had kept a photograph of him, his boy and his nephews in his room. They were smiling and having fun at the zoo. It was a picture dear to his heart—Kim knew this. When he went back to salvage what he could out of the apartment, he noticed that when he picked up anything in the room, there was a clean space underneath. All around, the item had been covered in black soot from the smoke; but when you picked the item up, it left an outline of the soot, or imprint of the item's outline. Forrest couldn't find that favorite photo at first. Then he walked over into the corner of the room and there it was: on the floor, facedown. He determined that the firemen could not have put it there because after picking it up, he saw an outline of the picture in black soot. So it had to have been placed facedown before the fire started. He remembered, specifically, before leaving during that argument with Kim, that the picture was where he had always kept it. There could be only one explanation, Forrest knew, for the scenario.

Forrest did not have insurance for fire damage. He lost all of his clothes and his large collection of cowboy hats. Anything made of fabric had to be tossed. Many photos of his son had melted and were gone forever. The TV was a blob of plastic on the stand, as was anything else in the room made out of material that would melt.

"You know, Kim, I left there mad," Forrest said when things calmed down and he spoke to her, "the next thing I know, my apartment is on fire?"

"Listen, Forrest, I would never, ever do anything like that to you. I love you."

Her sincerity felt real, honest, Forrest later said. "She was *so* convincing," Forrest added. "If it would have happened after we got married, there would have been no question in my mind." Meaning, he would have known Kim torched the place, because after they married, Kim revealed her true, horrible colors to him.

This was that superficial charm all sociopaths exhibit—when at the top of their game, most could talk the Devil out of hell.

Forrest thought about it. *There's no way that people do that kind of stuff to other people,* he considered. It was unbelievable to him that a woman he loved, a woman who seemed genuine at times and even lovable at others, could love him and burn his apartment down.

Kim worked hard at gaining his trust and his love back. She pulled out all the stops. She put on her best behavior.

Forrest bought Kim an engagement ring from a pawnshop. He was proud of the purchase. It was a nice ring. He'd "saved a lot" for it. The apartment complex gave Forrest a new apartment, the same layout, and he moved all of his stuff into it. Kim began staying with him again. They'd worked things out. They still argued and fought, but in the end Forrest always went back to believing in love.

"What is this?" Kim said, staring at the ring.

"Let's get married," Forrest said.

Kim took the ring, looked up at Forrest, who thought she might throw her arms around him and jump for joy. Instead, Kim walked over to the sliding glass door leading out to the balcony, stepped out onto the deck and tossed the ring over the railing.

The ring landed in the parking lot below.

Forrest couldn't believe it. How could she hurt him so profoundly, so impulsively? How could things go from a moment of great joy and celebration to absolute darkness?

He ran downstairs and searched for the ring, locating it sometime later. If Kim wanted to get married, she'd have to accept the ring.

Forrest Garner was not offering to buy another one.

43

FORREST WAS DRIVING, KIM SITTING shotgun. They were on their way to a clinic on Houston Street. Kim was in her third trimester. She was pushing forty, so they needed to run some tests on the fetus to see how things were going.

At the clinic, the doctor explained that Kim would have to go to Baylor, a bit of a drive, so she could get an amniocentesis, an amniotic fluid test to determine if there are any fetal abnormalities. Usually, doctors insert a large needle in through the belly and extract a sample of the fluid.

"I'll take the day off," Forrest said, "and drive you up there."

Kim said that would be fine.

When the day came, they got into Forrest's truck and headed out. It was early morning. Before getting on Gentry Parkway 69, Forrest had stopped, as he generally did, at the Starbucks down the block from the apartment to pick up hot coffees.

As they drank their coffee and drove toward the test, Kim "started talking about" Forrest's mother. Kim thought it was silly that Forrest's mother had been upset that he had lived with her when they weren't married. Kim would always encourage Forrest to stop talking to his mother. She wanted him to become estranged from his mother, just as she had done with her own.

"Look," he said, "I'm going to take you to [Baylor] and do all that stuff. Don't bring up my mother's name again today."

Kim looked at Forrest and, obviously, didn't like what he said; she stripped the lid off her coffee and tossed the hot beverage all over his face and body.

Forrest was overwhelmed with pain. He pulled over.

After cleaning himself off, he got back into the truck, turned it around and headed back home.

He got dressed when they returned, sat down in the living room and didn't say anything.

Hours went by, and Kim acted like nothing had happened.

"[We] got back in the [truck], and I drove her," Forrest recalled.

Kim gave birth to Timmy on November 11, 2005, seven months after they were married. Not four months later, Kim and Forrest were talking divorce. At the time Kim's third husband was driving back and forth from where they lived outside Tyler to San Antonio for a company he worked for. The gig was three times a week. Forrest worked every other day, so he was around the apartment a lot, especially when the boys came home from school. On one of those days he was off, Forrest decided to make them all some sandwiches and have some chips and soda ready for them when they got out of school and walked through the door. A nice bonding experience. They'd appreciate it, Forrest knew. Kim was out. They could have some quiet father-son time together.

The boys came home and were ecstatic. Forrest had made them this great early supper and there they were, sitting at the table, eating and talking and enjoying one another's company, much like a normal family. On top of that, Forrest had taken the stress out of dinner for Kim, who had her hands full with a newborn baby. She didn't have to worry about feeding those hungry mouths. She could come home from wherever she had gone off to and take it easy the rest of the night.

When Kim walked in through the front door, Forrest was in another room doing something. Blake was in the kitchen, sitting, smiling and eating out of a bag of chips. He was a boy doing what boys do.

"What in the hell do you think *you're* doing?" Kim screamed at the kid after walking into the kitchen. "Why are you eating chips?" She was livid. When Kim screamed, the walls shook, glass panes vibrated and the neighbors knew.

Forrest heard her shouting at Blake and came running into the kitchen. "What's going on? What's wrong, Kim?"

"He's eating these chips!"

"I told him he could have them, Kim. Calm down."

Forrest moved into the living room, away from Blake. He knew this was going to be a meltdown. He knew that look on Kim's face. She meant business. She was in the mood to go at it.

"She started hitting me in the face, like all over," Forrest later explained. "I mean, just like hitting a punching bag—in the face, chest, everything." With Kim, Forrest explained, there was never any slapping; she used her fists when she hit her men or the kids. These were not girl punches, either. Kim could throw a jab like a man.

The kids walked into the living room to see what was happening. Kim was going crazy on Forrest as the kids looked on in horror. Blake was in one doorway, scared, yelling at his mother to stop.

Forrest's son, Martin, couldn't take watching it. He ran toward his father and soon stood in between them. "Stop it! Stop it!" Martin told Kim.

Kim cocked her arm back and swung a fist at Forrest's son as hard as she could. "She hit him in the face and knocked him all the way across the living room," Forrest said.

The boy was five years old.

This made Forrest turn into somebody he was not. She had hit the boy as hard as anyone would hit an adult in a fight. The kid was on the ground, crying, holding his face, a red welt swelling into a shiner.

Without thinking about it, Forrest picked Kim up off the ground and shoved her across the room and into the fireplace. He'd had enough. This was the last time she would hurt a child in front of him.

Forrest walked over and grabbed Martin, picked him up gently, patting the child on the back, then walked outside and away from Kim.

Pacing outside, Forrest called his mother. He didn't know what else to do.

"And she called 911," Forrest said later, meaning his mother.

Kim ran out of the apartment and left.

The cops showed up. Forrest filed a report. His son's

face was swollen as though he'd been stung by a swarm of bees. His little eyelids were closing into slits.

After the police left, Kim called.

"You bastard," she seethed. Of course, it was all Forrest's fault. He'd instigated the trouble. If he could have just shut his mouth and not said anything about her disciplining her child, the entire incident could have been avoided. "I'm in the emergency room," Kim continued. "You hit me and broke my jaw in two places."

"Whatever, Kim." Forrest knew she was lying. If he had actually hit her, with his catcher's-mitt-size hands, he would have knocked her unconscious and probably would have broken all the bones in her face.

Before this incident Kim had had Forrest arrested on several occasions for what turned out to be one felony and two misdemeanors. She'd go off on a rant, throw stuff or try to get violent with Forrest or the kids; he would be forced to defend himself or the kids, and she would call the cops and say he hit her. This was a pattern with Kim. She was the aggressor—always. Yet, she turned it around anytime she involved the police. In the end it wound up costing Forrest close to $30,000, just about the same as Matt Robinson before him, to defend himself against the chaos and character assassination and lies and violence that made up Kim Cargill.

Forrest Garner was able to plead down the felony and admit guilt on the two misdemeanors. He cut his losses and settled for two years' probation.

After Kim struck his son in the face, there was no coming back for Forrest. He moved in with his mother. Kim called three days later—right on schedule—but no one at Forrest's mother's house answered when she called. Kim was relentless. "Over and over and over and over," Forrest said. "And we never answered the phone."

Kim would leave messages in a voice that was disturbing and eerie—a menacing, creepy whisper: "If you do not talk to me, something bad is going to happen." They had heard that threat numerous times.

And Kim had meant it, Forrest would soon learn.

Sometime after Forrest began divorce proceedings, his older son's mother showed up for a scheduled visit with the child. She seemed different, though. Something was wrong. Forrest's ex-wife asked the child to pack his things.

Forrest wanted an explanation. "What in the name of . . . ?"

She handed Forrest a subpoena. The ex-wife now had custody of their child.

It was devastating. No warning. Just *bang!* She had been granted custody. Whatever the ex had proven to a judge must be disturbing enough to warrant immediate custody.

She left with the boy, on her way to Dallas, and Forrest stewed back at his mother's, trying to figure out what was happening. *Is this real? Did she just take my child from me?* Forrest needed to know what was going on.

"I'll tell you what's going on," the boy's mother said over the phone after Forrest pleaded with her. "I know everything about you, Forrest! Kim called me. She told me everything. You're a drug addict. You're an alcoholic. You're *never* going to see your child again."

Click.

Forrest hired an attorney. Kim had stopped calling

during this period, but once he hired the lawyer, she started "calling and calling and calling." In one message she said, "Listen to me. If you'll do . . . If you listen to me and do what I say, you know, and not press charges on me hitting [your son] in the face, I'll get [the boy] back for you."

The master manipulator at work.

The con artist.

The spiteful deviant working her twisted way of thinking.

The sociopath, unconcerned for anyone but her own needs.

Forrest's lawyer advised him to go get a drug and alcohol test. He did. Everything came back negative. He spoke to his ex-wife, convincing her that Kim was a lunatic and she'd made it all up. Somewhat hesitant, the ex slowly began to understand what was going on. Then Forrest started a dialogue with Kim, turning the tables.

He was now playing her.

"Well," Kim said after Forrest spent some time charming her, "I'll go to your lawyer's office and sign an affidavit and say I lied about everything."

Could it be true? Or was this another one of Kim's controlling lies?

To his utter shock and amazement Kim did as she said she would.

"I'm sorry," Forrest's ex told him after it was all done. "I know what you're dealing with now, as far as Kim is concerned." She brought the boy back to his father. Forrest had had the boy since he was one. The ex was crying. "I'm so sorry for taking him away."

The police did not want to press charges against Kim, Forrest later said, for what she did to his child.

He had called them. "They never called me back . . . ," Forrest insisted.

For Forrest, the problem with leaving Kim was with her boys. He hated to see them subjected to her torment and violent tendencies with nobody around to protect and stick up for them. Above that, his son missed his stepbrothers. Forrest, however, knew the only way he could survive, and raise his son away from Kim's emotional and physical abuse, was to remove himself and the boy from the situation. Kim was on a fast track of imploding somewhere down the line, Forrest knew. Sooner or later her anger was going to get the best of her and she was going to do something she could not come back from.

Timmy, his son with Kim, was growing and Forrest was scared for his well-being—but there would come a time, sooner rather than later, when Forrest saw an opening, had the means available and could take Kim to court to get Timmy out of that horrible situation. Until then, he'd have to do what Matt Robinson was doing: monitor the child from afar and keep an eye on what was going on in Kim's world. The problems with Kim weren't over for Forrest—and, in many ways, were just beginning.

44

FORREST COULD NOT AFFORD A high-end apartment. Still, he wanted to be as close to his boy Timmy as he possibly could be. There would come a day when Forrest set out to fight Kim for custody. She was not going to be raising Timmy. First, though, Forrest needed to get himself and his son from his previous marriage settled into a new apartment. Then he needed to somehow convince Kim to give him back his belongings—which she had been holding on to and was unwilling to return since he walked out on her and began divorce proceedings.

Since the split Forrest had watched the kids for Kim once at her house. She'd called and asked. He said okay, realizing the alternative—Kim leaving them home alone—was a situation he wanted to avoid.

Before she left, Kim stopped and visually scanned the house, saying, "Forrest, listen to me. I know where everything that's yours is in this house. If when I come back I find out you took *one* thing of yours, just one, I'll burn your mother and your son up in that house where you are staying. You understand me?" She turned, did not wait for a response and walked out.

"I knew not to touch anything," Forrest said later. She had taught him already that when he wasn't around, things he owned caught fire and burned.

"I'm going to start being nice to you," Kim told Forrest sometime later.

He rolled his eyes.

"Really," she insisted. "I promise."

Forrest knew there had to be something in it for Kim, but he went along with her new attitude.

At this time Forrest was still driving back and forth to San Antonio for his job as much as he could, so he had limited time to search for an apartment. There were only so many options available in and around Tyler that he could afford.

"I'll find you an apartment," Kim suggested.

Forrest was reluctant: "But I thought, well, if she's going to be nice enough to help me look for a place . . ." He figured, why not?

As a manipulative sociopath, Kim could zero in on a man's weaknesses and use them to her advantage, to control him, to maintain that balance of power she so much preferred. She knew Forrest was a forgiving man. He would always err on the side of caution, but once she was able to charm him, he would come around and believe what she said. She broke him down, using her influence to create a situation that was ultimately designed to benefit her.

Kim found several apartment complexes. Among them was the Citadel, where Cherry Walker would, in the years to come, move into the studio apartment directly below Forrest (without him ever knowing she was watching Timmy).

"It was real inexpensive," Forrest explained, "and so I decided on that place."

It was also not far from the house Kim lived in.

After settling in, Forrest approached Kim about his belongings. He needed his things in order to build a home with his son. He didn't have the money to go out and buy a whole new wardrobe. Why was Kim keeping them?

"If you allow me and [Timmy] to come over and visit you, I'll give you your belongings back."

One of Kim's many ultimatums.

Yet, Kim meant not all at once. With each visit she would bring over certain items. If Forrest played nice, then sooner or later he would have everything back.

Forrest said okay. (What else could he do?) Kim would show up with a pair of jeans and a shirt, walk in, get herself comfortable and sometimes demand to stay the night.

"She would piecemeal it all to me."

There was no gray area with Kim Cargill, Forrest knew. During one trip he took to San Antonio, Kim called him 180 times. He was not even gone an entire day. He was asked years later if that was an exaggerated number.

Check my phone bill, Forrest responded.

Forrest didn't want to deal with Kim that night. When he returned home from work, he turned off the lights in his car and crept into the parking lot. If by chance Kim was waiting for him to come home, he wouldn't be seen. After driving into the lot without seeing her, he got out of his car, slipped into his apartment, got into bed, rolled over and tried falling asleep.

It was as though Kim had watched his every move. No sooner had Forrest gotten comfy in bed than Kim started banging on the door.

"Let me in, damn it! Let me in!"

I'm not answering it . . . I'm not dealing with her.

Forrest ignored the banging. He wanted to slip under the covers and disappear. Kim was like a persistent ulcer, constantly causing pain and discomfort.

It got quiet. Then he heard a key slip into the lock, the lock unlatch and the door pop open.

"I had made it a point not to give her a key," Forrest later recalled. "She must have had a key made when she was looking for those apartments for me."

Perhaps one of the reasons why she was so eager to help him?

Forrest had often wondered how Kim had known so much about his new life away from her. When she called and left crazy messages, she would mention his mail, things he was involved in, stuff inside his apartment that she could not have seen or known about without snooping around.

"I could never figure out how she would know stuff like that. . . ."

Forrest realized that whenever he went away to San Antonio, Kim would slip into his apartment, search through the place, then slip out before he got home.

By this point he was "scared" of Kim and what she was capable of. He'd never had a feeling like this about anyone else, he said.

Forrest couldn't just go over to where Kim lived and

get his stuff one day while she was out, or the kids were left alone. You'd think perhaps he could work his way into the house while the kids were alone, collect his belongings and then be on his way. But with Kim, nothing was ever that simple.

"She had put locks all over—like big, huge master locks on garages and everything," Forrest said. Plus, he stayed away from that house where Kim lived as much as possible. Showing up at Kim's without calling would only mean friction and arguing.

One night, having not been to Kim's in quite a while, Forrest was passing by and decided to stop in, unannounced. He felt perhaps he and Kim could chat, and maybe he might be able to talk her into handing over some more of his belongings. It seemed good, too, to let Kim know that he could pop in anytime, regardless of how she felt about it. He brought Martin with him. They parked, approached the front door.

Standing on the porch, however, Forrest hesitated before knocking. He could hear what he later described as sounding like a "barroom brawl" going on inside the house. Kim was screaming and yelling, as usual. All of it, Forrest overheard, was directed toward the kids.

"All you could hear was 'sons of bitches' and 'motherfuckers,' and I mean it was bad."

Forrest looked at Martin. "You get into the van and wait for Daddy there."

Martin did as he was told.

Forrest banged on the door. He needed to make sure Kim wasn't beating the kids. Timmy was also there, just months old. Forrest felt he had a right to be curious about what was going on.

Kim opened the door in a rage. "Don't you *ever* fucking come to *my* house without letting me know you're on your way!"

Forrest took one look at her face and knew she was a breath away from stepping out onto the porch and taking a swing.

It was the last time he ever went over there, and the last time he would ever put his boy in a position to be close to her.

About five months into the process of Forrest getting his belongings back a piece at a time, Forrest and Martin were at home watching television. He'd cut Kim off nearly entirely, keeping contact with her to a minimum. She had been too argumentative and loud and obnoxious, not to mention violent. It was too much. Forrest had, in a way, given Kim a second chance to make amends and try to have a normal relationship, only because they had made a child together. But she couldn't do it. Kim couldn't contain her anger, her outbursts, her controlling methods of threatening and her acting out.

On this night, however, Kim decided she was visiting Forrest. Nothing was going to stop her. Nobody was going to tell Kim Cargill she could not walk into Forrest's apartment.

As Forrest and Martin sat and watched television, they were startled by a crashing, loud noise.

Ka-boom!

Kim had kicked the door in, right off the hinges, as Forrest and Martin were in the living room nearby.

She had placed Timmy on the ground in the hallway, out of the way, backed up and had kicked Forrest's apartment door as hard as she could. The strength of this woman in a fury was undeniably barbaric, as though she was in a steroid-induced rage.

"She actually broke the door in half," Forrest later said.

The dead bolt fell off and onto the floor. Splinters scattered everywhere. The noise shook the entire wall, knocking things down inside Forrest's apartment.

Forrest was able to get Kim out of the apartment building after calming her down.

"I had to call the police on multiple occasions," he said.

After their divorce was final, Kim seemed to accept it was over and calmed down—somewhat. She must have known by then that they were completely through and her way of raising a white flag was to contain her rage. She'd stop by unannounced (apparently, this was okay for Kim) and want to chat about Matt Robinson, Mike West, James Cargill or any one of her old boyfriends. It was beyond bizarre, Forrest thought, but he felt like he had to listen—or else. Their divorce, in some strange way, allowed Kim to open up to Forrest, asking him his opinion about certain "problems" in her life.

"I wish you would have beaten his ass," she said one night, referring to Matt.

I wish, I wish, I wish"—it was a favorite phrase of Kim's.

It was around this same time that Matt had begun proceedings to take his son, Brian, out of the situation he was living in with Kim. Matt was photographing the bruises and wounds he'd witness on his child whenever Brian visited. He was building a solid case, with evidence, for getting custody.

The walls were closing in on Kim and she was feeling stressed by the pressure.

After Kim would bring up an old boyfriend, she'd tell Forrest, "I wish you would kill him." Forrest never asked her sick reasoning behind such wicked drivel.

Then, one day, as they sat and talked, Kim said, "Forrest, would you think I was a bad person if I had Matt murdered?"

Forrest thought that perhaps she was saying this same thing about him to others. Or was she saying this about Matt to scare Forrest?

As the winter of 2006 merged with summer and fall, the intimidating calls to Forrest started up again: "If you don't call me back, something bad is going to happen." Over and over, she'd call and make threats, even though he wouldn't answer.

Cops showed up one night at Forrest's apartment. He had no clue they were looking for him.

They had handcuffs. An arrest warrant.

"For what?" Forrest asked.

"Kim Cargill, your ex-wife, claims you beat her up."

Forrest was taken to jail. Locked up. No questions asked.

Turned out Kim had gotten into a car accident in front of the kids' school, got a little bit banged up and used those injuries to claim Forrest had beaten her.

Forrest bonded himself out.

A week later cops were at his door again.

"Wait a minute, what's happening?" Forrest pleaded. They had another arrest warrant on another felony charge.

"Wait, though," Forrest said, thinking the police were confusing his cases, "I just bonded out on that charge a week ago. . . ."

"Oh, Mr. Garner, no, sorry, but this is for an incident that happened months ago!"

Months ago? How could it be?

The police explained that this latest arrest was on a felony charge: "You hit your ex-wife while she was holding your son."

The incident Kim had told the cops about had supposedly happened many months back. It was an argument. At the time, she said, they were working on their marriage, had gotten into a fight and Forrest hit her while she was holding Timmy. She did not want to file charges, back then, predivorce. But postdivorce, of course, things had changed.

"Now I want to file charges," she had told cops after going back to the police station and demanding they arrest Forrest.

He fought it and worked it all out, but it cost him money he did not have. All for something he had *never* done to begin with.

Forrest was washing his laundry one afternoon down the block near Houston and Vine. It was a little place near Citadel that many local renters went to. Cherry would also use this same Laundromat when she later moved into the building. Forrest could not recollect the exact date, but he recalled Timmy being in a "car carrier" and several months old, so it was during that turbulent period in 2006 when he was dealing with Kim's craziness almost daily.

While loading the washer, Forrest looked up and there was Kim, stomping in through the front door. She was in a rage.

"There were so many arguments," Forrest said later, "you never knew what set the argument off."

Kim Cargill didn't need a reason—just a target.

On this day Forrest recalled that Kim was yelling about him not being home to watch Timmy when he said he would. She had an appointment and she was going to miss it, and it was all Forrest's fault. He was going to pay and she was not putting up with this nonsense.

Kim "threw" Timmy "up on a washer," next to where Forrest was doing his clothes. She said nothing more and stormed out of the Laundromat.

Forrest stared at his boy, the angelic child with his fist balled up in his mouth, eyes looking all around. He was so innocent and caught in the madness of a mother constantly going off the rails, not knowing what in the world was happening.

A few minutes later, however, as Forrest was playing with the boy inside the Laundromat, Kim came back—with a vengeance. Here she was again, ripping and roaring her way through the dryers toward Forrest.

Without a word Kim grabbed the child from Forrest, turned around and walked back out. Forrest was scared she was going to hurt the boy so he—and just about everyone else inside the Laundromat looking on—followed. Kim hurried out to her car and (what everyone believed was purposely because she knew Forrest was following) banged the car seat carrier with Timmy inside against her bumper, startling the poor little baby. Then she opened the back door of her car and actually hurled the child, while in his car seat, into the back and slammed the door shut, without buckling him up. She jumped into the driver's seat and screeched out of the parking lot, the car's tires spitting up bits of gravel and sand.

A maniac on a mission.

Forrest wanted to call the police, but he had second thoughts, adding, "It had gotten to the point where they wouldn't even, you know . . . What are they going to do? They wouldn't do anything. That's the way I felt."

He hadn't said this without speaking from experience. A cop had come over to the apartment one day. Forrest and his sister stood on the balcony with the officer. Forrest had called the police on Kim because she had been in the hallway of his apartment, yelling, screaming, ranting and raving. It was not long after he had first been arrested. Forrest felt trapped. If he pressed charges, nothing would be done and she'd retaliate. It would just continue along this mess of a maze where there seemed to be no way out of.

"What do I do?" Forrest pleaded with the cop. "What. Do. I. Do."

The cop looked down at an extension cord Forrest had on his balcony. "I guess if I was you, I'd take that extension cord there and wrap it around my neck and jump, because there ain't nothing you *can* do, sir."

Forrest would file a report. Nothing would be done. He'd even had cops at his house when Kim phoned and threatened him, or kicked at the door, yelled and flailed. Still, nothing was ever done about it. On the other hand, it seemed to Forrest that all Kim had to do was go running down to the police station and complain of him hitting her and he was in cuffs, owing his lawyer several thousand dollars more.

45

ON SEPTEMBER 22, 2006, James Cargill was granted a temporary restraining order against his ex-wife. James's greatest concern was for his child, Blake. He knew that Blake was being treated like a captive, beaten and abused and screamed at and locked inside his room. James had been secretly gathering evidence to take Kim to court and sue her for full custody. None of the boys' fathers, for that matter, had ever given up on their children.

It was hard to get a court to listen to a father—judges tended to want to see children stay with their mothers. James was not lying down, however. He started photographing Blake and his injuries. The photos are shocking, alarming, disturbing and painfully sad. Despite what she would later dispute about her involvement in Cherry Walker's death, these photos depict Kim's handiwork, showing what she was capable of when she made the choice to abuse her children.

Still, a temporary restraining order and custody were two very different matters. James was in for the fight of his life. What would Kim do once she realized James was not backing down?

Asked to "characterize" that eighteen-month period he had been married to Kim, James Cargill later said, "It was the worst time of my life."

It was a sentiment many other men in Kim's life would ultimately agree with.

James, an architect by trade, kept a detailed account of the calls he and Blake received from Kim. The phone was one of Kim's weapons. The relentless, threatening nature of her voice would send shivers down the spine of whoever was on the receiving end. Just her number on the caller ID screen was enough to cause anxiety.

James and Kim had dated three months. Kim told James she couldn't get pregnant. Then, all of a sudden, Kim was carrying a child and James was set on doing the right thing for the kid by marrying her. Kim would get loud, hurl things at James, cuss out and bully the kids in front of him. James had kids from a previous marriage. He had not planned to marry again.

"Dishes, vases, whatever was just near," James explained, looking back through the time he spent married to Kim Cargill. These were items Kim would choose to throw at him. One night, James said, she took a hammer and flung it at his head. He ducked and the hammer, luckily, whizzed by and lodged itself into the wall.

James took photos of the damage.

Asked what had brought Kim to a point of rage whereby she felt tossing a hammer at her husband was justified, James explained, "I don't know. They (the incidents) kind of just all run together." Kim went from "zero to a hundred miles an hour for unpredictable reasons."

Kim would later complain of suffering from Crohn's disease, an intestinal disorder that slows people down, immobilizes them and affects their entire daily life. Kim, though, never seemed the least bit hampered by it. In fact, one of the things that usually set Kim off was not complications of the Crohn's but "her appearance," James remarked. Kim was obsessively "concerned" about the way she looked. She needed everything to be perfect. And if she thought for a second that some-one was looking at her strangely, judging her, sizing her up, she'd go off on a tear.

"She was extremely sensitive to criticism," James added.

James had taken blows to the jaw from Kim's closed fist more than once or twice, he later said. She hit "pretty hard," repeating what others had always said: Kim "hit like a man."

One Christmas, James was required by their divorce decree to bring Blake back on the twenty-sixth, or the day *after* the holiday. Blake "was maybe three at the time," James remembered. The boy was tired from the holiday. James cradled the boy in his arms as he walked up to Kim's door and rang her bell. James had his arms and hands full. The child was sound asleep.

Kim came to the door. She must have realized that James was defenseless, so she decided to take a shot while he wasn't able to protect himself. Without any warning sign she cocked her fist back and hit him square in the face, grabbed the child out of his arms, took Blake inside and slammed the door shut.

Merry Christmas!

Blake was a one-year-old when they divorced. James had unsupervised visitation. In 2006 (James could not recall an exact date), he picked Blake up for a visit. The boy seemed to be favoring one side of his arm as though in terrible pain.

James asked what was going on.

Blake lifted his shirtsleeve up.

Bite marks. Blake explained that his mother had bit him. The boy was beyond upset. He didn't know what to do anymore. She was constantly, Blake felt, treating the other kids better than him, hitting and biting him more and more. He was always the one to take the weight of Kim's anger. The boy was torn. In some ways Blake felt he needed to protect the other kids by making himself available in this way. A martyr, if you will.

The bite marks were enough to send James to a lawyer to begin his quest for permanent custody. It was Blake's only chance. Blake was bound to wind up in the hospital, and James wouldn't be able to live with himself, had he not tried. So he filed an affidavit. He explained the situation and included those photos of the bruises and bite marks and other injuries. The evidence was all there. James made sure to keep detailed records of all that had happened between him and Kim. He was building a case.

One Friday in September (2006), Kim called James ten times. Generally, it was for nothing—just more of her spiteful and angry virulence. James would not answer all the calls, but whenever he picked up the phone, all she did was rant about whatever wrong thing Blake, or the other kids, had done to her.

"Look, if he wants to go and live with you, okay!" Kim raged at one point. "He can live with you." Yet, as the conversation went on, Kim rethought her position and felt the need to berate James, call him names, threaten him and spew off-the-wall comments, which, at one point, forced James to hang up on her.

She called back—several times.

The next day Blake had a doctor's appointment. James took him. While they were gone, Kim called incessantly, both to James's cell and home phones. When they got back home, James allowed Blake to speak with Kim. When the boy got off the phone, he was upset about something she had said.

"What's wrong?" James asked his son.

"It's okay. I'm fine." The kid was tough. He could take a lot.

Kim called back several times. Finally, after a call at 7:15 P.M., where she left one of her typical threatening, scathing voice messages, James called her back. He wanted to discuss "something the doctor had said [at Blake's] checkup." He thought Kim should know about it. Kim changed the subject—apparently uninterested in the child's health. She broke into a soliloquy about an "order" James had filed of late, with which she had just been served. Kim claimed it was "invalid," before getting down to the business of why she was really pissed off, adding, "He should not be enrolled in school."

James was planning on keeping the boy as soon as

the judge signed off on his petition. Sensing the court would side with him, he had gone ahead and enrolled Blake in the school system.

Kim was livid. This was a direct violation of her order. She hadn't okayed this.

Over the next several days she called and called and called: "You cannot enroll him in school." She swore and insulted James and Blake. She might have thought that if she stated it one hundred times or more, that it would somehow become a fact—because that's all James heard for the next week.

"You cannot enroll him in school!"

Click.

"You cannot enroll him in school!"

Over and over and over.

On October 3, 2006, James was at work. Kim called.

"Don't call me here," he said. She knew this.

"You do not have the right to enroll him in school."

"Do not call here. This, I consider, to be harassment, Kim. Stop it."

"Fuck you. You do not have the right to enroll him in school."

"You can contact my attorney if you wish to address any matters before the court."

James hung up. He gripped his forehead. A headache—no, a *migraine*—was on its way, knocking on his skull somewhere in the back of his head.

That same night James took Blake out to dinner at a local Chili's. They met James's sister, brother-in-law and mother. Blake was around people who loved him and treated him with kindness, respect and sincerity. It should have been a normal night.

James's cell rang several times as they sat and ordered and ate. James would pick up his cell, turn it over, stare at the screen, shake his head and put it face-down.

It was Kim.

"Is that Mom?" Blake asked after one of the calls.

"Yes. Do you want to talk to her?"

"No!" Blake said.

A "minute" went by and Blake changed his mind. "You know what, can you call her back—I do want to speak with her."

"Can you wait?" James wanted to finish eating.

"No, I want to speak with her now."

James handed his son the phone. Blake took it and walked over to another table while the rest of them ate, not wanting to disturb the family.

As they ate, James kept looking at his watch. The boy was taking a long time. Five minutes had passed. He still wasn't back. Kim was likely giving it to Blake, blaming him for whatever problem she had.

"Excuse me," James said to his mother, sister and brother-in-law.

He found Blake sitting at a nearby table, crying.

"Come on, it's time to get off the phone," James told his son.

"No," Blake said. (*Angrily,* James wrote later in his notes.)

About a minute later, Blake handed his father the phone. Wiping tears from his eyes, he then took off, running into the men's room.

James ran after him.

Blake locked himself in a stall. He sat on the floor, crying.

"What's up, buddy?" James said, encouraging his son to talk about it. What had Kim done now? What had she said to upset the child? James had not put it past her to manipulate her son, who was just about to turn twelve. He was so young. Why didn't she see she was hurting the child with her manipulating and lying and yelling?

"I have to go back to Tyler," Blake said through tears. "My friends miss me."

Kim had plied the kid with guilt.

He was upset for at least an hour, and subdued and withdrawn at least until the next afternoon, James wrote later.

The following afternoon, October 4, Kim started calling for Blake; and, once again, she never stopped. She knew she had the boy on the ropes. One more solid shot and she had him back on her side. She needed to work on Blake some more. She called James at work again the following day—all morning and afternoon long.

"Stop calling me at work, Kim."

She never stopped. In fact, James said, Kim had called his office, on average, twenty-five times in a day when she was in the mood to make trouble. One day, he added, she had called the office sixty times.

"It wouldn't be uncommon for her to call ten to fifteen times during a day," James recalled.

On Friday, October 6, Kim called fifteen times, James documented.

Again the next day, ten more calls. Kim even called Blake's friends and got them to call Blake to tell him to come home. They missed him. They needed him.

James told Blake not to talk to his mother anymore. Not right now. Kim needed to settle down and stop harassing them before Blake could carry on again with her.

Over the next few days James began discussing custody with Kim. There was no doubt that he was going to be granted custody, his lawyer had told him and Kim. James wanted Kim to "make an offer" regarding child support. She was going to have to start paying— another new situation that was going to drive everyone involved crazy.

James had given her his offer.

"That's an insult," she said.

"Well, make me a counteroffer, then, Kim. And stop calling me at work. It's harassment."

She hung up.

Then she called back.

"Stop calling me here, Kim."

James stopped talking to Kim Cargill altogether after that. He decided he wasn't going to allow Blake to speak with her, either. Enough was enough.

Kim began calling Blake's friends once again.

46

THE COURT GRANTED BLAKE PERMANENT residence with his father. After it was official, James gave Kim yet another chance to try and "establish a healthy relationship" with her son for the boy's sake. Blake was still able to visit his mother. Yet, as those visits commenced, James was getting reports back from Blake that she was still abusing him both physically and emotionally. Nothing changed with Kim.

Unfortunately, James wrote in his affidavit seeking a restraining order against Kim on Blake's behalf, *I continue to fear for my child's safety and life.*

Blake's dad wanted to be in a position to make the call whether the boy went with his mom or not. If James felt Kim was not able to behave herself for a visit, he wanted to be able to deny her.

So Kim used the one weapon of hers she'd always turned to when she wanted to make her ex's life miserable.

James listened one night on the other end of the line and realized what Kim was still trying to do to her child.

"I really hate that the new school you're in is so

damn easy," Kim said. Blake had always been smart and attended a science and math magnet school back in Tyler. "The coaches are wondering where you are? Victoria wants you to come back right away for the school dance. Everyone misses you. Please change your mind about coming home, please. Your dad is like Hitler telling me what we can and cannot talk about. . . . You need to set up an e-mail address that your father does not have access to."

Blake listened and responded, "Yeah, okay . . . ," but he sounded confused and conflicted.

The next day Kim called Blake back. She asked him if he had called his friends yet.

"I'm happy living where I am," Blake said.

"Hey, buddy," James said later on when they discussed the phone call. "You handled that really well. The only reason I am listening is because I need to protect you, son."

"She's not going to talk me into anything, Dad. I've made my decision—I'm staying here with you."

Weeks later, when it was Blake's time to go see his mother for a court-ordered visit, he said he did not want to go.

"You have to, though," James said.

Blake would not budge.

"I had to drag him, literally," James said later, "into the car over my shoulder."

There was therapy and missed school days and incidents of Blake causing trouble in school and running out of class and being suspended. Total dysfunctional chaos.

All Kim's fault.

During one visit, no sooner had Blake and Kim arrived back at her house than she snapped, broke into a rage and said (among other disparaging things), "Clean this fucking house, you piece of shit."

Blake knew that when he was forced to clean, all she did was "sit around on her butt," he said later.

Kim once locked Blake inside her porch (it was around 40 degrees) so he couldn't get out. "Me and the other kids are going to the mall—you stay in there!" This was part of a pattern that whenever Blake was over for a visit, Kim would take off, often leaving him to watch the other kids. It would not be for work or an appointment, but mostly for her own pleasure.

"I'm going to the tanning salon, watch them!"

She'd be gone for hours.

"Your son is a monster," Kim would call James and say. "You've created this. He comes over, he refuses to do anything, help me at all."

Kim made Blake sleep on the couch because his bed—in his old room—was piled high with garbage and clothes and other things.

Blake would phone his father to come and get him. Blake would be sitting on the curb outside the house, the house locked, nobody home.

47

A S THE SUMMER OF 2008 progressed, after a year-and-a-half of James dealing with Kim and her drama and emotional abuse, Kim brought the violence to another level. It was an early evening in June. Blake was with his mother. James had given the boy a cell phone of his own, telling him to call anytime there was an issue, or if Blake ever felt he needed to get out of the situation and come home. For James and Blake, the cell phone was Blake's lifeline alert.

"She . . . she attacked me," Blake said after calling his dad that night in June.

He was "hysterically upset," James later said.

"She choked me," Blake continued. "I think she's going to kill me. . . ."

Not the words a father wants to hear from his son.

"I'm coming. . . . I'm coming. . . . Find somewhere to hide until I get there," James said.

"Hurry. Please come now. . . ."

Blake "fled from the house" and away from his mother; he was calling while already hiding out. This much he had known to do already.

James was on his way, he said, and hung up. Before he left his house, he phoned the Whitehouse Police Department and explained what was going on.

After the arrival of the police officers, Blake was back at the house. He was safe. The police were there to watch over him while they sorted out what had happened and what steps should be taken.

Kim was huffing and puffing and being "uncooperative with the police"—her usual self. She tried to explain to the police in her heated, rage-filled voice, "He attacked me"—meaning Blake—"and his younger brother. I want to file a police report against my son for assault."

James was beside himself when he heard this. Kim had abused her child and now wanted to file a report against *him*? It went against everything a mother should do.

The cops took a look at the young boy, Blake's brother.

"We don't see any injuries, ma'am."

Blake would have to, however, be taken into "protective custody" by the police, Kim was told. They couldn't allow Blake to continue the visit with his mother. So Blake took a ride with police to the WPD.

James made it to the police station at 7:18 P.M. and picked up his son. What an ordeal. You try to give Kim the benefit of the doubt, and what does she do? Spit in your face. There was no change in the woman. In fact, looking at the way her life unfolded during the past few years, one would have to say that Kim's behavior was escalating. The question wasn't if she would hurt her children again, but how severely?

Looking at his boy on the way home, James Cargill

could not believe it. Blake had bruises around his neck, as though someone had tried to strangle him. "She put me in a headlock," Blake explained. "[She] choked me and I thought she was going to kill me." The child was beyond upset by now. He was scared to death of his mother and what she was capable of doing if his dad and the police had not been there for him.

After several days passed, Blake wanted an Xbox gaming system he had brought with him during the last visit to his mom's. Within all the confusion and disorder and drama and violence, he had forgotten to grab it when police escorted him away.

"Nope. Not getting it," Kim said. She wasn't budging. End of discussion.

This choking incident was the grand finale in a series of violent and abusive incidents, James explained in his affidavit. The previous month Blake had returned home with his "cell phone literally broken in half." Kim had tried to take it from him and he refused. A struggle ensued and she "deliberately destroyed it" in front of him.

Two weeks later, Blake called from Kim's. "I think my foot's broken, Dad."

"What?"

Blake had kicked his dresser in his room prior to heading over to his mother's that weekend. His eruptions of anger were happening more frequently—Kim's legacy to her child, having shown him by example how to deal with life's difficulties. The reason why Blake had kicked the dresser was because he did not want to go see his mother. James had been forced to allow her visits under a court order, and Blake had to go. Thus, he kicked his dresser and, apparently, broke his foot.

When James dropped him off at Kim's that weekend, Blake had not said anything about his foot hurting. Blake had been "silent the entire way," James later recounted. He could tell his son was less than thrilled by the prospect of another weekend with his mother.

After Blake called to tell his dad he thought his foot was broken, Kim and James spoke.

"You need to take him to PrimaCare," Kim said, "as soon as he returns to your house." Kim was annoyed that this "problem" of Blake's foot had interrupted her weekend and taken up her time.

"Please, Kim, please take him now." At the time James lived about an hour away from Kim. He could not simply head over and do it himself, or he would have.

"No!" she snapped. "I have more important things to do here at home and two *other* children to worry about."

Blake was later treated for a broken toe. He wore a restrictive boot for the next three weeks.

Sometime after this incident, still in 2008, Blake and his dad got into what James later referred to as an "altercation." Because of Kim's constant meddling and messing with Blake's mind, manipulating and feeding him with ideas and thoughts that confused the child, their father-and-son relationship had problems.

"[W]e had another court hearing," James later described, "and the next morning after that altercation, there was a court hearing in which the court placed [Blake] back at his mother's house."

After everything that had happened, everything she had done to the child, much of it documented, the court allowed—perhaps forced—him back into Kim's custody.

Blake began to run away from his mother's house, which became an issue for everyone. When the pressure got too much, Blake would turn up missing.

A frequent call to James from Kim included: "He's run away again. Come help find him."

One day after Kim had custody of Blake back, she called to let James know his son had taken off again. James rushed the hour drive over to Kim's house. There had been some indication that Blake had bolted from the house and gone in the direction of the woods in back of where Kim lived at the time. On the opposite end of those same woods was a Home Depot.

James said he'd begin there.

Behind a "big pile of lumber" outside the store, James found his boy. Blake wore nothing more than underwear: no shirt, no pants, no shoes, nothing but his undershorts. James looked at him. Blake was scratched all over from running through the woods. His feet were dirty and bleeding. He was crying, of course. It was as if living on his own, without clothing or shelter, was better than being in that house with his mother.

48

ONE HAZY, HOT AND HUMID Sunday morning in August (2009), Kim Cargill was in the bathroom inside her Whitehouse, Texas, home. She had the door cracked open. It was close to ten o'clock and Kim was fixing her makeup, getting ready for the day, while talking to someone on her cell phone.

"Can I come in and use the mirror to brush my hair?" Blake asked. He stood in front of the door.

Kim looked at her son. She said nothing. Then she slammed the door in his face.

Blake turned red. He became enraged, banged on the door "a couple of times" with his fist.

With no answer Blake stormed off down the hallway to the bedroom he used while staying at Kim's.

Moments later, Kim came marching—thumping, actually—down the same hallway, walked into Blake's room and began "wailing on" him with her fists. She was hitting and hitting the boy in one of her ferocious and violent outbursts.

Blake pushed Kim off of him. He was a strong kid, growing bigger every day, nearly the same size as his five-three mother. He was tired of taking abuse from her. Enough. It was time to fight back.

As Kim stumbled backward, but not falling, Blake rushed his mother and "pinned her against the wall" in his room.

Kim mounted a few punches to Blake's head and then bit him.

Blake recoiled in pain and backed off.

Kim wasn't done, however. She lunged at her son—who then quickly turned and grabbed a screwdriver on the floor, pointing it at her.

It had been a reaction on Blake's part. As soon as he recognized what he was doing, Blake "realized it was a mistake and put [the screwdriver] down."

Locked inside her own madness, Kim went back at her son with violence in her eyes.

Blake stood his ground and pushed his mother—but this time she fell backward and onto the floor.

Blake walked over. Stared down at her.

"My back . . . it's broken," she said (which was certainly not true). "My back is broken, you little shit. You broke my fucking back."

Little Brian came running into the room to see what his brother and mother were doing. "Call the police. . . . Call the police," Kim told her boy. "Right now. Call 911."

Blake found a spot in the house alone and called his father.

"You run away, find a safe place until I get there . . . ," James Cargill told his son.

"Okay . . . ," Blake said.

The police found no injuries to speak of on Kim, so they gave Blake a ticket for the incident and encouraged them to work it out amongst themselves.

49

BY MID-2010, BLAKE WAS UNWILLING to spend any time with his mother. He wanted nothing to do with her. It was over. Kim never, ever showed Blake any love. She never put her arms around him and hugged him. She never said sorry, I love you, let's work this out. She never expressed an interest in his feelings or showed any care whatsoever.

The less Blake saw of Kim, the better the boy's behavior became in school and at home with James. The healing had begun.

Over the course of Kim abusing Blake, James had seen things he did not think a mother was capable of doing. Beyond the bite marks, Brian later said in court, one of the worst remnants of Kim's violence he'd witnessed were these "big belt welts, kind of long bruises with a curved end that, you know, you might see [made] with a . . . I assume to be a belt."

The walls were closing in on Kim Cargill. Her life was in a constant state of anarchy. She'd lost custody of one boy, Travis, whom she was estranged from entirely. She was losing custody of Blake and would soon be estranged from him, too. Now, as her latest ex-husband, Forrest Garner, removed himself from her madness, he was taking Kim to court to fight for custody of Timmy. And Forrest Garner had one hell of a case against her.

Kim knew, of course, that Cherry Walker's testimony was going to destroy any chance she had at ever becoming the custodial parent of Timmy once again. Though it was hard for Kim to admit defeat, she knew it was over—that is, unless she intervened in some way.

Kim was a tempest. The slightest matter could throw her into a rage—and yet, even with all that she had done to her kids and anyone that had ever brushed her the wrong way, despite all of the abuse and verbal lashings, her worst, most brutal and bloodiest moment of violence was still in front of her.

PART FOUR

*"The beauty of the world. The paragon of animals.
And yet, to me, what is this quintessence of dust?"*

—Hamlet, in *Hamlet* by William Shakespeare

50

TO UNDERSTAND THE MIND-SET OF Kim
Cargill going into Friday, June 18, 2010, the day
Cherry Walker went missing, one has to begin a few
days earlier on June 15. On that day Laura Gillispie,
clinic manager of the East Texas Medical Center, took
several calls from Kim.

Timmy was a patient of a doctor at ETMC. Kim had
phoned on the fifteenth and made her usual demands
loud and clear, telling office manager Laura Gillispie
that she needed information about Timmy and she
needed that information right now or there was going
to be hell to pay.

Gillispie said no. Not a chance. It was against office
policy.

Kim Cargill went ballistic on her and the phone call
ended.

Two days later, on Thursday, June 17, Gillispie took
several more calls from Kim. During all of these
calls Gillispie could not do much more than listen
to a virally "angry, screaming" Kim Cargill, Gillispie
said later. In fact, Kim was so insulting and obnoxious

during all of these calls—a few of which lasted for as long as twenty-nine minutes—that the clinic manager "couldn't talk over her because she was screaming so loudly."

It was the same sort of vitriol anybody in Kim's path had heard during this period. Kim was in the right and everyone else was wrong.

"Are you a mother?" Kim asked Gillispie repeatedly. "How would *you* feel not knowing about *your* son?" Apparently, Kim was blowing this particular gasket because ETMC had information about Timmy they were not bothering to share with his mommy. The other part of this—perhaps what *really* bothered Kim—was that ETMC had scheduled appointments for Timmy (made by Rachel Wilson, Kim's mom, who had temporary custody at this time), since as far back as June 3— of which Kim had not been aware until now. She was calling to find out the significance of those visits and what was going on with Timmy, but nobody was telling her. All Kim had to do, the clinic suggested, was call her mother.

Into that Friday morning, merely hours before Cherry would disappear, Kim was calling ETMC.

"She was in an angry rage," Gillispie later recalled.

Gillispie became increasingly upset because from where she sat inside the office, patients walked in for their appointments. Many could hear Kim screaming on the other end of the phone as she exploded into fits of rage about not being told why her son was seeing a doctor.

"Kimberly, I am going to have to end this phone call, which means I am going to have to hang up now," Gillispie said at one point.

Click.

Kim called back.

Again.

And again.

And again.

As the clinic manager tried to reason with Kim, speaking to her with kindness and resolve, Kim would not have any of it. During one call Kim went on for twelve entire minutes straight, berating the entire staff and Gillispie. The only silver lining was that Kim had not decided to confront the manager inside the office.

Laura Gillispie was very shaken by these calls on June 18. By that afternoon when she got off the phone with Kim, and had decided not to answer any more of her calls, Gillispie told the entire staff to make sure the back door into the facility was kept locked. There was no telling what Kim Cargill was planning to do. She had made it clear that someone would pay for withholding the information from her.

Kim was at a breaking point on Friday, June 18, 2010—and she had just gotten out of bed.

51

CHERRY WAS ALL SMILES AS she walked through the door of Marsha's Place, a small, hometown beauty salon in Tyler, early on Friday afternoon, June 18, 2010. Sonya Burton greeted Cherry with a cordial "Hello, Cherry, how you doing today?" as Cherry opened the door and the bells rang behind her. Outside, pulling out of the parking lot, Sonya could see the woman she knew as Paula Wheeler, Cherry's "provider."

After what turned into a two-hour appointment, in which Cherry was "talking and laughing with everyone, like she always does," Cherry's father, Gethry, picked her up and she was on her way back to her Citadel apartment. After spending all that time up close and personal while doing her hair, talking and laughing, Sonya was certain that Cherry did not show any signs of injury. Not on her neck, face, arms. Anywhere. Additionally, Cherry had her trusty coin purse and cell phone with her.

When Cherry left her salon that afternoon, it was the last time Sonya would see Cherry, speak to her or do her hair. Cherry would be dead within four hours.

Earlier that day, at 10:18 A.M., Cherry had received that subpoena to testify at the DFPS hearing regarding Timmy. Kim had been at work in Athens for approximately three and a half hours already, or since 6:45 A.M. While at work, beyond threatening and repeatedly calling and screaming at Laura Gillispie, throughout that morning Kim also called Cherry several times.

After Cherry left the salon, Kim continued to call her: at 2:14 and 3:29 P.M. specifically, along with at least four additional times throughout the afternoon.

At 5:06 P.M., while still at work, Kim called an old friend. It seemed Kim could not stay off the phone on this day.

It was 2002 when Angela Hardin met Kim at what Angela later called "Nurse Orientation." It wasn't that they became BFFs; more or less, since they'd met, Angela and Kim remained a bit closer than casual acquaintances. They'd call each other from time to time and perhaps hang out once in a while when they were both off. Yet, there would be "long stretches" of time without talking or seeing each other. Angela, for the most part, did not know Kim personally, had never worked with her and saw her only periodically. It's safe to say that Angela did not have a clue as to the *real* Kim Cargill—the danger she was to those around her, or how toxic Kim actually was.

Over the past several years Kim had displayed an escalating pattern of violence and abuse and anger that seemed to be escalating as the third week of June 2010 wound down. Maybe because she was desperate for a friend, Kim called Angela out of the blue. Angela had not seen or heard from Kim in months. But here she was, on the phone, complaining about the problems in her life.

"My fucking babysitter," Kim said. "I'm worried about her being subpoenaed and testifying."

"Why, Kim?"

"She's mentally challenged," Kim said.

"Oh," Angela responded. She didn't know *what* to say. It was the same reaction so many others had to this statement: *Why would you ever hire a mentally challenged person to care for your kids? What kind of mother does that?*

"It's going to ruin me," Kim explained. Her voice revealed great stress and anxiety. She sounded frantic with regard to doing something about this "problem" she now had. As she continued explaining what was happening, Kim grew angrier. Kim felt she was being squeezed, and the one recourse to make things better in the short term was coming into focus for her: get rid of Cherry Walker.

The control that Kim craved had slipped away from her. Cherry—note that Kim did not name her as she spoke to Angela, referring to Cherry only as "the babysitter"—was going to, Kim added, "*destroy* me. . . ."

"I'm so sorry, Kim."

"I need you there, Angela." Not to testify, Kim implied, but for "moral support."

"I can't, Kim. Sorry."

Angela said she had a baseball game to attend and she needed to get off the phone.

They said their good-byes.

Kim left work at 7:30 P.M. Within her twelve-hour shift she had made upward of seventy phone calls on this day—despite the protocol and policy for all nurses that they were not to make *any* phone calls during working hours.

52

CHANDLER, TEXAS, POLICE OFFICER ARTHUR McKenzie was sitting in his familiar Friday night spot near the west end of town on June 18, 2010. It was just before eight o'clock when McKenzie spotted a white Mitsubishi Montero—maybe a 1999 or so— driving by him faster than most of the other traffic. McKenzie was parked by a Dollar General, just down the road from McCain Park on State Highway 31. The posted speed limit was fairly liberal there at fifty miles per hour. But this white vehicle was going about "sixty-one or greater," and so McKenzie hit his lights, took off into traffic and got behind the car.

After he pulled her over, McKenzie approached the woman and asked if she knew how fast she was going.

Kim Cargill explained that she was a nurse and had just left work. "Everybody's told me to slow down between [these two streets]," West Main and North Broad.

"Is there a reason why you're speeding?" McKenzie asked. "Is there any type of emergency going on?"

"No, Officer," Kim said.

McKenzie went back to his cruiser and keyed Kim's name into the system. He found no outstanding warrants, no other trouble associated with Kim's driver's license number. Yes, she'd had some issues with the law, but nothing outstanding. So, staring at the back of her vehicle from behind the wheel of his cruiser, McKenzie thought, *Well, she's a nurse. . . . She wasn't driving crazy. Why not give her a break.*

McKenzie peeled off a warning ticket from his pad and handed it to Kim. "I'm going to give you a warning," he explained. "I need you to slow down, ma'am."

Kim took the ticket. She was in a hurry.

When he was done, McKenzie tipped his hat, reminded Kim once more to slow down and went back to his vehicle. Kim backed up just a little bit, took a look in both directions, pulled back onto State Highway 31 and off she went.

Kim's car was clean. Not a spot or smudge of black soot could be seen in the video accompanying McKenzie's stop and issuance of the speed warning. Within two minutes of receiving that summons from Officer McKenzie, Kim Cargill was on the phone with Cherry Walker, asking Cherry if she wanted to go out to eat, telling Cherry she had some things she needed to discuss with her right away.

It was 8:02 P.M.

53

HE HAD SEEN HER AROUND the Citadel and run into her a few times in the hallway and in the parking lot, but Forrest Garner had no idea that Cherry Walker, his neighbor, had been watching his youngest son, Timmy. At this moment she was locked in a conversation with his ex-wife, Kim Cargill, over the subpoena Cherry received that morning to testify on the following Wednesday in a custody case generated by Forrest. Forrest walked on eggshells himself because of the chaos his ex—a woman he would later describe as "the Devil incarnate"—had caused him.

Kim scared Forrest. He believed she had set his apartment on fire. If she was capable of that type of retaliation, what else would she do if she felt someone, such as Cherry Walker or Forrest, had *truly* wronged her?

Friday nights at the Citadel, Forrest later explained, were an especially stressful time for him. A lot of "younger people," Forrest said, lived at Citadel. On Fridays it was always hard to find a parking spot in the lot because it was filled with young people and cars.

Tenants grilled out there on Friday nights, had beers and, of course, played music loudly. As Forrest left his apartment on Friday, June 18, 2010, he weaved in and out of this scene, noting there were people everywhere.

As Kim Cargill was talking to Cherry Walker, trying to convince Cherry to go out to eat, Forrest took off with a few friends to go hang out at a local bar. He returned home about 9:45 P.M. to the same throng of people in the parking lot, all of them now drunker and louder. Cherry lived directly underneath Forrest. He did not see Cherry or Kim on that night, nor had he heard from Kim. As far as Forrest knew, Kim was at home or working, and Timmy was with Kim's mother.

Forrest unlocked the dead bolt into his apartment, closed the door behind him, making sure to lock it, tossed his keys on the counter, had a glass of water and headed off to bed.

54

BETWEEN THE TIME SHE WAS stopped for speeding (8:02 P.M.) and 12:30 A.M., Kim Cargill was unreachable. No one else could account for where she had gone or what she had done. Kim did not call anyone during this period, nor did she pick up her phone if someone called her. Kim's boss at ETMC had, in fact, been trying to reach Kim all night long (ever since Kim left work) about a patient. Kim had left work in such a frenzied, hurried state that her boss didn't have the opportunity to talk to her then. It wasn't until just after twelve-thirty, a half hour past midnight, that Kim returned the call to her boss, telling her she had been sleeping ever since returning home from her shift.

Her claim that she had been sleeping this entire time was a lie, according to Kim Cargill's account of the hours after she got off work and before the death of Cherry Walker.

Not long after she spoke to Cherry, Kim later claimed, she showed up at Cherry's apartment. It was 8:25 or 8:30 P.M., Kim later said. Cherry was ironing clothes. (Incidentally, Kim just missed bumping into Forrest, her ex-husband, who had left to go out shortly before then.)

"I'll wait for you in the car," Kim claimed she told Cherry.

It took Cherry five minutes, Kim insisted, but she came out and got into Kim's car.

Kim drove with Cherry to her Waterton Circle residence in Whitehouse "because I had left text messages. . . . I was trying to juggle several things at the same time . . . and I had left a text message and called a friend of mine who [mows] my yard."

That would have been Michael Darwin.

Kim claimed she told Michael she'd be home on that Friday night by eight-thirty and she wanted to talk to him. She wanted to wish him a happy Father's Day because they were heading into Father's Day weekend. She could not have done this with her cell phone, Kim explained, because the battery had died—quite conveniently—on the way to Cherry's.

"Cherry, give me a minute," Kim said when they arrived at Kim's house. It was 8:45, maybe 8:50 P.M., according to Kim's recollection.

Kim went into the house while Cherry waited in the car.

Inside, Kim placed her phone on the charger and used the bathroom. She then rifled through her pocketbook and a few drawers to see "how much cash" she had in order to take Cherry out to dinner, as promised.

It turned out she didn't have enough money at home.

Kim got back into her car ten minutes (at most) later and decided to head out to a local gas station.

She was planning on taking Cherry to Posados, on East Fifth Street in Tyler, closer to where Cherry lived.

According to Kim's account, Cherry "was nervous about the situation . . . but happy to be going to dinner." The *situation*, one might guess, being the subpoena.

Kim said she stopped at the Exxon station on Troup Highway and Loop 323 in Tyler (which would be confirmed later). She needed gas and also to check on her bank balance so she could pull out some money for dinner.

After buying $5 worth of fuel for her car (she claimed), Kim withdrew $35 in cash from the ATM for dinner.

They arrived at Posados around nine-thirty, Kim claimed. It was a Friday night; the place was jam-packed with patrons.

Dinner was inconsequential, Kim said. She and Cherry talked. They ate. They left.

During her entire narrative of this crucial time period, Kim spoke as if she and her best friend had gone out on a Friday night to have dinner.

There's only one problem with this blissful picture Kim later painted: every person Kim had spoken to that day—including her boss, who saw her perhaps last before she picked up Cherry—described Kim in a far different state of mind. Everyone said she was angry and full of rage. Moreover, no one in the Citadel parking lot could recall seeing her. Kim never mentioned how many people were partying there that night.

While she later explained the night to her attorney, Kim defined the beginning of it, especially during dinner, as "pleasant."

Imagine: *"pleasant."*

Kim claimed Cherry asked her for a ride "somewhere," but that Kim "didn't feel comfortable taking her there. . . ."

Instead, Kim drove Cherry back to the Citadel.

Along the way, Kim explained, Cherry "was fine until she realized" Kim was refusing to take her where she wanted to go. After Cherry understood Kim wasn't driving her to a certain place Kim never named, Cherry "got upset."

Cherry became increasingly angry because Kim would not take her where she wanted to go, Kim said. So much so that, as Kim turned onto Beckham in order to make the turn left onto Houston, Cherry's street, Kim alleged, Cherry "started to have a seizure."

It had been years since she'd had a seizure. But according to Kim Cargill, as Cherry had a seizure beside her inside her vehicle, things spiraled out of control quickly. They were just one block away from the Citadel, merely blocks away from a hospital, and Cherry, if one is to believe what Kim Cargill later said about this night, was "banging against the glass and the door," thrashing inside Kim's car, having a grand mal seizure.

55

CHERRY WALKER, ACCORDING TO KIM, began to whip herself against the glass and the door inside Kim's car.

Seeing this, Kim claimed, she decided to stop the car. They were just a few feet away from the Citadel parking lot, and so Kim decided to pull in there.

From the time the seizure started until she pulled into the parking lot was "maybe a couple of minutes," Kim said.

A few blocks away, just up the street, was a hospital, but Kim claimed there was far too much traffic to take Cherry to it. That was okay, though, because there were several medical clinic options available all around the Citadel. Still, Cherry was perhaps lucky, because Kim Cargill was a nurse. She had been trained to deal with seizures. She could administer care. She could call 911. She could ask any one of the dozens of people in the parking lot to help.

Inside the Citadel parking lot, which, just an hour before, had been akin to the tailgating section of a sporting complex before a football game, Kim claimed there was now nobody around. She said later that the parking lot was dark and empty.

Kim parked, got out of the car and ran to Cherry's side of the vehicle. She did not call 911: "I left my phone at home," Kim said—a phone she had placed on a charger when she arrived so she could have it for the night. That's not to mention that Cherry Walker never went *anywhere* without her phone.

Kim said she opened the door, and when she did, Cherry fell out and onto the pavement and must have smashed her head.

"The seizure stopped within a few seconds of her hitting the ground," Kim later testified.

Staring at Cherry Walker lying there on the ground, motionless, Kim claimed that she then "ran to [Cherry's] apartment to see if it was locked"—this from a woman who knew that Cherry had OCD issues and would absolutely never leave her apartment unlocked.

"I was looking for a phone," Kim said.

With the gated area of the apartment entrance locked, a fact Kim knew, having been to this apartment complex dozens of times over the past several years, she claimed she went looking for the neighbor, Marcie Fulton, who had introduced her to Cherry—the same woman who used to watch Timmy before Cherry.

"Her [vehicle] wasn't there, but I still tried," Kim said of her alleged frantic search.

When that idea failed, she took a look around and could not find anyone to help her. She had no phone. There was not a soul to be seen: a Friday night, downtown; an ex-husband living in the same building; Cherry, with her own phone in her purse; scores of businesses and doors to knock on nearby. Kim claimed not to have been able to find *one* person to help her with this seizure situation.

At face value alone this was unbelievable.

Running back to the car, where Kim claimed Cherry lay on the ground outside the passenger-side door, Kim said Cherry was "still in the same position." Kim said she "realized that [Cherry] was unconscious."

Not moving.

Kim bent down to check for a pulse.

Nothing.

She checked it again, to make sure.

Nothing.

She listened to see if Cherry was breathing.

Nothing again.

She felt Cherry's chest for a beating heart.

Nothing.

"So I flipped her on her back and I started CPR," Kim said.

Here was a nurse supposedly giving cardiopulmonary resuscitation (CPR) to a 250-pound woman in the middle of a parking lot on a Friday night in a downtown section of the city, but not one person saw any of it.

After Kim drew the conclusion that the CPR failed to work, she decided, "I had to get her some help."

Kim needed to get Cherry into the car and to the hospital, she thought. There was a chance, Kim said she knew then, that Cherry Walker was dead.

"I don't know when I realized [she was dead]," Kim insisted later, speaking to her lawyer during direct questioning. "I know no one was coming. . . . I couldn't keep doing compressions. . . . No one heard me. No one even heard me . . . [and] no one was around. . . ."

Kim said she decided to put Cherry in the car and drive her to the hospital. A woman who was five-three, about 120 pounds then, had supposedly picked up a dead, 250-pound woman and placed her into her car.

Impossible.

As Kim approached the hospital parking lot, she had second thoughts: "I glanced at the clock and realized that she had been nonresponsive for around ten minutes. . . . I couldn't bring myself to take her [to the hospital]. I couldn't. I could not make myself do the right thing. I didn't do the right thing."

The hospital was now directly in front of Kim as she drove. Kim, however, passed by the entrance and turned right, maneuvering her vehicle past the hospital "while trying to figure out what to do" next. Her major concern, she said, adding that it was indeed a selfish one, became how worried she was about "how it would look." She then made the claim that there were "so many people"—including her "family attorney, friends, Cherry's neighbors and friends"—that had supposedly known she "was coming to take her out for dinner."

That was an exaggeration, at best. In fact, Kim might have told her "family attorney," a conversation that would have been protected under attorney-client privilege. Truthfully, no one save for maybe Paula Wheeler and Kim's other friend, Angela, knew that Kim had even suggested dinner to Cherry on that Friday night. Cherry had told Wheeler she did not want to go out with Kim.

Still, in Kim's "mind," she said, "I thought that me opening the door of the . . . [car and] her falling out and hitting her head, I didn't know if that caused her death. . . ."

So a nurse did not know whether a fall from the front seat of a car out the door and onto the pavement could have caused death?

This comment did not make sense.

Kim said she felt it was her "fault" because she did not stop Cherry from falling out of the vehicle.

Regardless, Kim claimed she drove around town for "maybe thirty, maybe forty-five minutes," all while thinking about what to do. She had a dead woman, apparently, sitting next to her the entire time—a dead woman who had been her babysitter and was a witness in an upcoming hearing.

Thus, she said, "I ended up on that country road."

56

ON SATURDAY MORNING, JUNE 19, Kim Cargill walked into the Whitehouse Police Department. Dispatcher Ryan Smith was at the desk. Kim had just had a conversation with her neighbor before heading over to the WPD, and then spent the rest of the morning washing and detailing her car. Just hours before, she later claimed, she was in a terrible state of panic, having been in the presence of Cherry Walker as she had a seizure, fell out of her car and died.

Cherry Walker's body had not yet been found. But here was Kim, inside the WPD, speaking to the dispatcher. Kim sounded calm and nonchalant, behaving like it was just another ordinary Saturday.

Soon word would hit the WPD that a body had been discovered out at the CR 2191 and responding officers would head out, their pulses thumping with adrenaline as they made their way toward the crime scene. And here was *the woman* who had put that body there.

"Well, hello . . . ," Kim said to Ryan Smith after walking through the front door, her every move recorded by the fish-eyed lenses all over the room. "Anything going on today?"

Imagine, out of all the days in her life, here was Kim Cargill inside the WPD, wondering how busy they were.

"Sorry, ma'am?" the dispatcher asked.

"Have y'all been busy today? Are there many police out on the roads? I know tomorrow is Father's Day weekend."

This wasn't actually that odd to Ryan Smith as he understood Kim's query. People walked into police stations all the time and the first thing out of their mouths was usually how busy police were on a particular day.

Still, did Kim Cargill just want to chat with a police dispatcher?

Of course not. Kim even admitted later that she was fishing for information.

Before leaving the WPD, Kim asked the dispatcher another question: "I wanted to see—I wanted to check one more time if anyone has turned in or if you know about a dog that has been missing?" She then described the family pet.

So the woman had lost her dog and was checking all the nearby police stations to see if it had turned up. This made more sense to the officer.

Problem for Kim Cargill was that her dog had been missing by then for two months.

57

KIM WOULD EXPLAIN LATER THAT she decided to burn Cherry's body because of a "panicked" condition she found herself in, not knowing what to do.

One of the reasons Kim gave for burning Cherry's body was that she realized her "sweat and tears and all of me was on the front and back of her from [doing] CPR." She added how scared she was of being "connected" to Cherry by the forensic matter she had left behind. So, Kim insisted later, "I burned her shirt."

This didn't make much sense, either. One is to believe that she was so worried about leaving DNA on Cherry's body, but she actually left a coffee creamer plastic cup between Cherry's legs?

It was interesting that Kim later said she burned the clothing, as if to imply that she never intended to burn Cherry's body. She also said she used "lighter fluid and matches."

That lighter fluid, she insisted, had been inside her car with a lot of other junk for a few months. She had once used the lighter fluid to burn up "ant piles" at her house.

Everything Kimberly Cargill did that night after Cherry died was to cover her tracks and remove herself from being connected to Cherry's dead body in any way. It was selfish and wrong, and Kim said she knew this, but she did it, anyway.

In regard to the accelerant, it might be noted that Kim admitted to buying $5 worth of petrol while driving around with Cherry. Looking at that statement, one might ponder: *Why buy such a low amount of fuel for a car when you had money in the bank?* Playing devil's advocate, one might guess that the $5 worth of petrol was, in fact, enough to fill a small gasoline can, which one could later use to try and burn up a human body.

58

O N SUNDAY, JUNE 20, KIM phoned Angela
Hardin. Now, however, Angela noticed, there was
a pointed difference in Kim's demeanor from the previous conversation on Friday night. It stuck out to
Angela only because Kim's deportment was so different from the previous call. Kim wasn't angry anymore.
She was calm—quite mellow, in fact. It was as if a storm
had passed. Not quite the attitude of a person who had
burned a corpse of a woman who had died in her presence thirty-six or so hours before; not someone who
was, according to her own testimony, deathly worried
that she was going to be tied to an "accidental" death.

"Just calling to see if you would reconsider," Kim
asked. She still wanted Angela to join her on Wednesday, to be at the hearing for support.

"No, I can't, Kim. Sorry."

"Just having a friend there would be great for me. I
feel like I need a good friend."

"No, Kim."

"I tried to get my babysitter to go out to dinner with
me on Friday," Kim said without being prompted in

any way. Angela never brought up the babysitter and wasn't even thinking about that previous call. "I wanted to go over some of the questions I think they might ask her."

Angela wondered why Kim was telling her this. It came out of nowhere.

"I asked her, but she refused," Kim said. "She wouldn't go out to eat with me."

"Whatever happened with her? Are you still upset?" Angela asked.

"She wouldn't go out to dinner with me," Kim said again. Then: "She told me, instead, that she wanted me to go meet her, and she wanted me to find her a white man."

What is this woman talking about now?

"It was kind of an odd statement," Angela said later.

Angela ignored it at first. There was some silence.

"Did you hear what I said?" Kim asked.

"Not really."

"Well, I'll repeat it. She said she wanted me to go out and meet her and find her a white man."

Angela did not know how to respond.

The next time Angela would hear Kim's name, it would be connected to Cherry Walker's murder, coming over the television set in her living room.

59

BY JULY 29, 2010, AN arrest warrant on murder charges had been issued for Kim Cargill. She was in lockup, unable to bail out under that Injury to a Child charge. But now things were far more serious. A day after she had been served with the latest arrest warrant, Kim was arraigned; her bond was set at $1.5 million.

There was no chance she was going to get out of jail.

In her booking photo Kim's blue eyes are penetrating and intense. The look she gave the camera conveyed the firebrand persona she had always projected toward the world. Her lips were flat, her mouth straight, her gaze stoic: *Get ready, everyone, because I am not going down without swinging.*

Defiance.

Diligence.

Determination.

This was Kim's mantra now.

* * *

By the end of October, Kim was indicted by a grand jury on first-degree murder charges. She pleaded not guilty and vowed to take her case to the highest court, if the lower courts did not serve the justice she desired.

Smith County DA Matt Bingham said his intention was to try Kim under capital felony murder charges, which would qualify her case for death penalty status.

Already at issue was the "cause" of Cherry's death, which the medical examiner had listed on Cherry Walker's death certificate as "homicidal violence." More specifically, grand jurors knew only that Cherry's death had been caused by "homicidal violence" because of a "specific means unknown" to anyone. Even the pathologist had been unable to determine "manner and means" of death in Cherry's case. She could guess how Cherry was murdered, but in the end it was all common, educated deduction. Thus, as far as Kim and her attorneys viewed her case, the door to reasonable doubt was opening wider as each day passed and motions were filed.

During one hearing Dr. Meredith Lann, the ME in charge of conducting Cherry's autopsy, testified that she could not "rule out asphyxiation as a possible cause of death. . . . I called it homicidal violence to encompass the nature of the case."

Because Cherry's body had been "found facedown in a remote location and had been burned," Lann did not think "the cause of death was natural, accidental or suicide." She added, "I don't think she did this to herself."

If Kim was going to argue that Cherry had a seizure, she had better make certain that any lab results—the science—backed it up. From where Lann stood looking through her microscope, Cherry's body was "thoroughly tested . . . for medications and to see if her insulin levels were normal, to see if there was any other medical reason for her death"—and the doctor concluded there was not.

Much of Kim's mental health behavior throughout her life was submitted to the court as evidence that she had been diagnosed with personality disorders as far back as childhood. Lucky for Kim, Rachel Wilson, her mother, was back in her camp, vowing to stand behind her daughter as Kim faced a future that could include death.

60

THE COURT APPOINTED JEFF HAAS and J. Brent Harrison to represent Kim. Kim could not have hired many other attorneys more qualified to defend her, had she the money to bring in a so-called dream team.

Haas had over thirty years' experience heading into Kim's trial, having been licensed in Texas since 1981. In private practice he had represented criminal defendants from charges of resisting arrest, all the way up to capital felony, and everything in between—credit card abuse, kidnapping, home invasion, carjacking. Haas promoted the following pledge on his website: *The sooner we get involved, the better your chances are for success.* The sentiment did not help Kim much, seeing how late into the game Haas and his team had taken on the case.

J. Brent Harrison had a résumé that read like an application for Lawyer of the Year. Harrison had taken on cases in well over a dozen counties in Texas since going into private practice as an attorney in the mid-2000s. What would help Kim immensely was that

Harrison had been first assistant criminal district attorney in Smith County from 2004 to 2005 and assistant criminal district attorney in the same county from 1996 to 2004. He knew the ins and outs of how a DA thought and worked.

It was no secret that the evidence against Kim did not look good for her. Medical and forensic evidence, on top of reams of testimony, would point to Kim having means and motive, not to mention painting her in a negative, angry, violent light. One of Kim's most pressing problems was that Cherry Walker's body had been burned to hide identity and evidence. How was Kim going to explain that?

Smith County DA Matt Bingham, the man in charge of waging legal war against Kim Cargill, stated that she senselessly and callously murdered a citizen within the boundary lines of the Texas landscape Bingham's office oversaw, and he was going to do everything in his power to see that she paid dearly for her actions. As he stood before the court on May 7, 2012, after the long and tedious process of choosing a jury and several alternates was finally over, Kim having spent the better part of two years, Bingham had prosecuted five death penalty cases to conviction. In total, Bingham had prosecuted over twenty-five murder and capital murder cases successfully since becoming the DA by the appointment of Texas governor Rick Perry in 2004. He was a proven winner inside a courtroom. For Bingham, part of any successful prosecution began by having the right case to take into a courtroom. Bingham was choosy. He didn't take every case to court. He chose winners.

Matt is known as a crime fighter, Bingham's campaign website stated, *and as a strong advocate for the rights of crime victims. He is a conservative Republican, and a strong supporter of the party's conservative principles.*

Bingham's co-counsel was April Sikes, a polished, calm and tenacious ADA, the perfect balance to Bingham's in-your-face style of going after defendants with passion. Sikes, a Baylor University graduate, had twenty-five years' experience in the courtroom. She had a reputation for using the facts of a case to expose guilt. This was a feat that—although it sounds simple, perhaps even expected—was hard to pull off if the experience wasn't there to back it up.

And so the stage was set.

Pretrial motions and hearings had started back in January 2011. Here they were, almost a year and a half later, ready to square off. Death penalty cases were always double the work—perhaps triple—compared to non–death penalty cases. It's in the nature of the potential result. Every motion and juror question and sidebar and bench conference took twice as long. Still, by 9:00 A.M., Monday, May 7, 2012, all of the paperwork and arguments and evidentiary debate was done. Judge Jack Skeen Jr. was in charge of watching over the 241st District Court of Smith County, with the official court reporter Christy Humphries by his side. Skeen prepared to hand out jury instructions and have the indictment against Kim Cargill read into the record, along with her plea—as a formality—of not guilty.

You'd never know it by looking at Kim's expression as she stared at everyone—a smug grin on her face—

but her life was on trial. As Kim sat looking indifferent
and determined, dressed in a pink-and-white shirt, this
was one situation she could not control. She could not
shout her way out of it. She would have to do what she
was told or a muzzle and restraints would be used to
do it for her.

With that completed, Skeen offered both sides the
opportunity to step forward and begin with opening
arguments.

Standing at a lectern, in a gray suit, white shirt,
black-and-white tie, his shiny bald head reflecting the
lights above, DA Matt Bingham began with the victim,
Cherry Walker. He detailed Cherry's life, focusing on
her low IQ, the fact that she was just starting out in life
on her own at thirty-eight years of age. He reminded
jurors that this was a woman, an "adult," with "the
overall adaptive functioning equivalent to that of a
nine-year-old." However, what Cherry "lacked" in education and ability and everyday functioning within her
age percentile, Bingham made sure to point out, "she
made up for . . . with her heart."

The DA next moved on to Kim Cargill. She was
forty-five years old as she sat and listened. Her dark-
blond hair flowed feathery over her shoulders as she
stared at Bingham without reaction and he tore into
her character.

Bingham went through each of her husbands.
Named each man. He spoke of Kim having four children with four different men. Her oldest child, Travis,
was now a man at twenty-one. Blake, at seventeen,
was ready to turn eighteen and become an adult himself. These were not children anymore, cowing to an

abusive woman beating them at whim; they were tough, strong and ready to testify against the woman who had given them life.

The trial, Bingham explained, was going to focus mainly on Kim's then six-year-old son, Timmy, who "was removed from her home . . . just *fifteen* days before Cherry Walker was murdered."

Bingham talked "timeline" next.

He spoke of the child support "she would be paying" for *two* kids.

How the state got involved and found out she was leaving Timmy with Cherry.

How the court had issued an "order of protection of a child" in Timmy's case.

How Forrest Garner was going to get full custody.

How the walls were closing in on Kim Cargill, come June 18, 2010, the last time Cherry Walker walked the earth alive.

How Kim's anger, narcissism and lack of self-control drove her to commit the ultimate act.

How she tried to cover it up.

How, for Kim Cargill, during that week in June 2010, when her world crumbled, it was "full steam ahead." She needed to react, to do something, to make somebody pay for what had gone wrong in her life.

On the last day Cherry Walker was alive, Bingham mentioned, Kim Cargill spent the entire day, while at work, calling scores of people, spewing her rage. It was Cherry's fault. When Cherry was served with that subpoena in front of Paula Wheeler on the morning of June 18, Kim realized her charade was over—unless, that is, she did something about it.

Her character was put into question repeatedly: "How does a lady [go] to an apartment with a random mentally retarded girl and just *leave* their child with them?"

An opening argument is not considered evidence—and never should be—but it is a statement of the facts as the lawyer giving the argument sees them. As Bingham went on, he focused on June 18, 2010, showing how everything Kim Cargill had done up until that day led to her being faced with the reality that if Cherry Walker gave testimony at the hearing five days hence, on June 23, Kim was going to lose everything.

The lure, Bingham explained, wasn't dinner, as Kim Cargill had told everyone she had contacted that day and night. No, it was offering to pay Cherry to clean her house. Kim Cargill knew Cherry had an affinity for cleaning and cleaning supplies and she used this against her, a trail of crumbs to lure Cherry toward her death.

Bingham moved over to a whiteboard to the right of the lectern and pointed at the cold, hard evidence. He noted how his investigators went to "fifty-eight" different convenience stores that Kim Cargill might have stopped at on the night she killed Cherry Walker. They searched for video. Bingham focused on that window of time between 8:02 P.M. and 12:33 A.M., when Kim called her boss, who had been calling all night long.

Bingham mentioned the "supposed" missing dog, giving a slight indication in his voice that he wouldn't put it past Kim Cargill to have made the dog go away herself, since her son Brian had loved it so much and she would later need a reason to step into the WPD.

The murder scene, or dump site, was up next.

Then all the DNA she left behind.

The way in which Cherry's body was burned.

The autopsy, which "showed asphyxia components . . . because there were hemorrhages within the membranes that overlie the eyes and the eyelids," Bingham told jurors, a fact that proved that Cherry Walker had been strangled. The image was of a strawberry—the inside portion—the white of Cherry's eyes, dotted and speckled with burst red blood vessels, among the white portion of the eyeball.

Many jurors winced at these descriptions, knowing that photos would come when experts took the stand.

Near the end of his opening statement, Bingham told jurors that the defense didn't have to make an opening statement or even present witnesses. However, if they did, Bingham stated with authority, he encouraged each juror to "demand answers" from the defendant and her attorneys regarding the phone calls, the creamer cup and Kim Cargill's statements to Paula Wheeler. Those were the three items that, even by themselves, proved guilt in this case.

61

AFTER BINGHAM FINISHED, JUDGE SKEEN asked Kim Cargill's attorneys if they were going to make an opening statement.

"Your Honor," Jeff Haas said, "we are going to reserve our option."

Interesting approach: no opening statement from the defense. Did it express confidence or trepidation?

With a few legal matters settled, Matt Bingham called the DA's first witness, Dr. Richard Wilson, who had treated Cherry Walker at one time. The reason Wilson was on the stand was to prove that Cherry Walker was mentally challenged.

Brent Harrison focused his cross-examination on pointing out the doctor had not known Cherry by memory. He had to study old reports in order to familiarize himself with her case. Then, grasping at the chief theme of Kim Cargill's defense, Harrison asked the doctor if Cherry had "developed major motor seizures" when she was sixteen years old.

The doctor read from his report, which indicated that Cherry had indeed suffered from seizures then.

With that, Harrison said he was done.

* * *

Bingham brought in a Verizon Wireless analyst, Jennifer Dalmida. Her testimony was tedious, but very necessary. As Dalmida talked jurors through the calls exchanged between Cherry and Kim on June 18, Bingham presented fifteen "blown-up images with cell phone records printed on them," and asked Dalmida to point out certain numbers—Cherry's and Kim's—for jurors.

Brent Harrison stood and said, "Tell me your last name one more time."

"Dalmida."

"Miss Dalmida, how bad would it be if you missed your six o'clock flight? Would it be pretty bad?"

"Yeah."

"You're not going to miss it," Harrison said, before adding he had one question for the witness. "What do your records show when this account was opened?"

"It shows an effective date."

"And what was the effective date that this account was opened?"

"August 25, 2003."

"Thank you, ma'am."

It was rather compelling that just by asking a question, a lawyer could make a date sound as though it meant something—when, in fact, it did not.

The next witness, a cop, talked about text messages and how the police retrieved them. As witnesses came in and testified, Kim Cargill wrote copious notes on a yellow legal pad in front of her, perhaps venting her anger as each witness told his or her story.

As the day wound down, outside the presence of the jury, the lawyers discussed one particular text message. A "family member" had sent Kim Cargill a text that spoke of how morally wrong and unfair it was for her to spend the child support money she received, which came from one husband, on a lawyer to fight charges of her beating one of her children from another husband. That family member was texting Kim to say it just didn't seem right that she was doing such a thing.

What Bingham focused on with this law enforcement witness was how the defendant would delete the texts she had sent, but she would keep many of the responses. It was pure manipulation, Bingham argued. It showed only one side of a conversation.

Ending the day, Bingham said to the judge, "That part [in the text] about beating her child—we can save it for punishment when deciding to send her to death row!"

As his first day of witnesses proved, Matt Bingham was playing for keeps.

62

DAY TWO BROUGHT LAURA GILLISPIE, the ETMC clinic manager who spoke to Kim Cargill on the phone numerous times. Gillispie explained that Kim would not leave her alone and kept calling the office, threatening her, and being vulgar, crass and menacing. Gillispie told jurors she had been instructed not to give Kim any information about her son's care at the clinic. Gillispie detailed one of those June 18 calls in which Kim was explosive and angry and screaming, telling jurors she yelled for almost twenty minutes straight.

Listening, Kim shook her head, as if to say no, that was not how it went down.

Kim's attorneys chose to pass the witness.

From this point forward, Bingham and Sikes paraded a litany of witnesses in and out of the box. Each witness had an anecdote to tell explaining how volatile and violent and angry Kim Cargill was when she didn't get her way. There seemed to be no friend or foe untouched by her routine and repeated acts of aggression.

Jurors heard from Gina Vestal, who placed the nurses at hospitals for Excel Staffing; Sonya Burton, Cherry's hairstylist; Angie Grant, an RN at ETMC, who verified Kim's schedule for June 18; Angela Hardin, who buried Kim with her blow-by-blow account of the phone calls she received from her on June 18. Here, Angela explained, Kim had said "odd" things and planted certain ideas in Hardin's mind. Then, in a complete turnaround, during a second call on June 20, Angela described how Kim had suddenly become a happy-go-lucky, calm and cool friend looking for support.

All of the testimony was damaging to Kim Cargill. The fact that she sat there in her purple blouse and shook her head repeatedly, grimaced and grit her teeth, did nothing to change the facts of this case.

Near the close of day two, one of Kim Cargill's neighbors sat in the witness chair. All April Sikes had to do was ask the right question and stand aside. The facts would explain all there was to understand about Kim Cargill, her demeanor, who she actually was and her movements the day after Cherry Walker had been murdered.

Sikes brought up June 19, 2010, that Saturday morning. Kim's neighbor told jurors that she had worked the graveyard shift overnight and got home around seven-thirty in the morning. As the neighbor pulled into her driveway, Kim pulled out of hers, parked in front of the neighbor's and rolled her window down.

The neighbor approached Kim as she sat in the driver's seat.

"My grass is getting high," Kim said. "Somebody (Kim gave the neighbor the name) is on his way to mow it."

"Okay, Kim. No problem."

The neighbor explained to jurors that it was odd to see Kim Cargill out so early on her day off. She asked Kim why she was up. "And she said that she was going to 'clean her car,'" before adding, "'I didn't sleep well last night.'" Kim also mentioned something about being financially strapped and being late on her house payments.

The neighbor was tired. She wanted to get inside, get cleaned up and head off to bed. But Kim Cargill wanted to chat. She mentioned the imminent custody hearing and asked the neighbor if she would mind coming to the hearing on her behalf. She said how upset she was about her ex wanting custody and she needed all the help she could muster. Then she started crying. The neighbor, a mother herself, hugged her because she felt bad for her.

"So, can you testify on my behalf?" Kim asked after the hug.

"I'll have to think about it, Kim. . . . I really don't feel we're close enough, and I rarely see your kids, you know."

The witness then explained that Kim had texted and called her all that week leading up to Wednesday (the day of the hearing), but the neighbor avoided the calls and disregarded the texts.

Kim Cargill's attorneys asked a few questions—all inconsequential—and passed the witness.

63

ON MAY 9, 2012, PAULA Wheeler told her story of being Cherry Walker's caretaker, seeing Cherry every weekday for months, and being with Cherry on the day in question, June 18, when Cherry received the subpoena. Wheeler noted how Kim Cargill started calling Cherry and badgering her about testifying. From the opening few minutes it was clear that Wheeler's testimony was disturbing in the simple way that it outlined how Kim treated Cherry as her personal babysitter and often left Timmy with her for days on end, without calling or texting or saying where she was or when she would return. It gave the jury a sense that Kim did not care about her child or Cherry. But even more, Wheeler humanized Cherry in a way that only someone who loved her and spent time with her could. It was obvious from the witness's reaction to some of the more personal questions about Cherry that she was deeply troubled by Cherry's death.

One of the more damaging pieces of information Wheeler related to jurors—refuting the notion that Cherry had a seizure and basically died in Kim's arms—

was that when Cherry became upset, she shook. She didn't have a violent, grand mal seizure or an epileptic fit of any kind. Her body simply shook.

Additional relevant testimony Wheeler provided was how Kim had tried to claim that the only reason Cherry was being made to testify against her was "so they could make [Kim] look bad." Wheeler explained how Kim worked hard that day to try and convince Cherry not to testify and also to convince Wheeler that all the testimony would do would be to upset Cherry.

When Paula Wheeler talked about dropping Cherry off at the beauty parlor that Friday, she broke down in tears, reliving that last moment she saw Cherry, adding how nervous and uncertain Cherry seemed to be when getting out of the vehicle. It was devastating for her to learn that Cherry had been the victim of a murder, her body burned.

The defense did not challenge Wheeler much, save for asking her if she knew of any medications Cherry had been taking. Then the defense lawyer asked a few questions pertaining to Cherry's babysitting duties and passed the witness.

On redirect Matt Bingham asked Wheeler if she knew of the medications Cherry was taking and could explain them to jurors. This was an important question for the purpose of showing that if Cherry had been suffering seizures, she would surely be on medications to control them—especially since Cherry was mandated to partake in regular doctor visits.

"Okay. Now, Mr. Harrison asked you about the six meds that Cherry was taking. Two of those were TUMS antacid and one was a vitamin?"

"Yes," Wheeler answered.

"So, if the six meds include the two TUMS and the one vitamin, then I guess . . . yeah, and one is a pill to help her sleep, right?"

"Yes, that's true."

"So, of the six, two are TUMS, one is a vitamin and the other one is a sleeping aid? . . . We have a sleeping pill. We have a vitamin. And either two or three or so have to do with . . ."

"Seizures," Wheeler blurted out.

Kim Cargill's lawyers looked at each other.

"Seizures?" Bingham asked.

"Yes."

"Are all of the rest of them seizure medication?"

"I don't really know if all of them . . ."

"Do you know how many of those are seizure medication?"

"No."

"Because I think one of the questions," Matt Bingham began to say before he was cut off by an objection, "ultimately, that they're trying to insinuate is . . ."

Judge Skeen encouraged the DA to move on.

After he regrouped, Bingham needed a way out of the seizure medication thread. He needed to explain this. So he keyed, smartly, on Cherry's diligence where it pertained to her taking medications.

Wheeler agreed that Cherry was a stickler when it came to taking her meds. She never missed a dose.

"And did you ever see her have a seizure?" Bingham asked.

"No."

Sometime later: "She didn't have 'excitement seizure,' did she?"

"No."

Wheeler went on to make it very clear that she knew the difference between a seizure and the way in which Cherry shook when she became upset or angry, and that she had never seen Cherry have a seizure during the entire time they were together.

They talked about Cherry and her shaking next. The image Wheeler gave jurors was that it was highly possible on the night Kim Cargill picked Cherry up that Cherry became upset and started to shake.

Could this have been that so-called "seizure" the accused was trying to use as her defense?

Nonetheless, the one problem Bingham had was that Cherry Walker was on several medications for seizures, which meant her doctors were aware of the fact that she could suffer a seizure.

Paula Wheeler's boss, Pertena Young, came in next and told her story of Kim Cargill threatening her on the phone that day with the claim that she had friends in the DA's office.

A comment to which Matt Bingham responded, "Oh, *does* she?"

And the courtroom broke out in laughter.

After that lighter moment Bingham was able to get Pertena Young to conclude that Cherry Walker was a person who could be easily manipulated.

As each person who knew Cherry testified, one subtle comment after another built upon a foundation of Cherry's incredibly lovable, however imperfect, character. Cherry was a no-nonsense, free spirit in many repsects, while set in her ways in so many others.

She was someone who deeply cared about people and had a tender, touching uniqueness about her that was hard not to see and become affected by—that is, for perhaps everyone except Kim Cargill.

As the day moved on, the cop who pulled Cargill over for speeding told his story, which set up a timeline that was already touched upon. After that, the pizza delivery driver sat and talked about coming upon Cherry's corpse, which set up an opportunity for the DA to put WPD police officer Joshua Brunt on the stand so he could introduce the crime scene. His statements injected a stark realism into the trial as graphic photos of Cherry Walker's murdered and burned corpse were displayed.

In what could be interpreted as an act of pure Oscar potential, as the disturbing images of Cherry's body presented the courtroom with the brutal depiction of what a murdered and burned body looked like, Kim Cargill turned on the tears and cried. As she did, she hugged herself like a drug addict going through withdrawal. She rocked back and forth in her seat as though the thought of Cherry Walker dead and gone had made her hurt. It was truly embarrassing for some to watch what they saw as an utter display of fakery.

A host of law enforcement witnesses added his or her particular role in the case. Strategically, perhaps, these witnesses' observations were short and scripted on the stand. A highlight from this was Larry Smith, a retired special agent with the Bureau of Alcohol, Tobacco, Firearms and Explosives (ATF). Special Agent Smith had once specialized in investigating fire deaths. He was an expert in liquids used to ignite fires.

The main conclusion the retired agent had come to in this case was that Cherry Walker's corpse indicated to law enforcement that they were looking at an "incendiary fire," which meant it had been "intentionally set with the use of combustible materials, liquid—ignitable liquids." Agent Smith added that the accelerant used in this case could have been "kerosene, gasoline, diesel, heptane, alcohol, rubbing alcohol, wood alcohol, just about anything of that nature."

Near the end of his testimony Larry Smith explained that in his experience most people burned bodies to make them "unrecognizable," and to destroy evidence and identifying markers, such as fingerprints and teeth.

64

THE SMITH COUNTY DAO STUCK to a familiar game plan. Character and expert witnesses shuffled throughout, so as not to put anyone to sleep with long periods of monotonous and mind-numbing scientific testimony that, although necessary, could be hard to sit through. There are only so many credentials one can bear to hear from a witness without thinking, *Blah-blah-blah*. Still, dental records and blood analysis and fingerprint identification on coffee creamer plastic cups (for example), along with a person's knowledge and education surrounding these topics, were part of this case.

Jurors would need to understand that Kim Cargill was at that crime scene, had poured an accelerant over Cherry Walker's body and, after haphazardly leaving her DNA behind, lit Cherry's corpse on fire. This was the real Kim Cargill, a woman who could strike a match, set the world around her on fire, turn and walk away as if it was just another day. Human life meant very little to Kim Cargill—that much, testimony had emphatically proven, was evident from the way she had treated her own children.

Through Kim's June 18 manager at work, the DA was able to show jurors that she had made/sent seventy-eight calls and/or texts throughout her shift. Several of her patients that day, her boss explained, had complained that she was not doing her duty. Kim's boss had to call Kim Cargill into her office and scold her—to which Kim started crying.

As May 10 came, Detective Noel Martin spoke of processing the Cargill home with his crime scene unit. Martin was followed by several police officers (including lead detective James Riggle), each of whom talked about his or her role in the investigation. There wasn't much to discuss besides the evidence because Kim Cargill had never granted an interview and she had been arrested for murder while already serving time for Injury to a Child. As each cop walked in and told his or her story, it was like staring at a puzzle and watching all the pieces connect together.

One dramatic moment came when Noel Martin was questioned by Kim's attorney about the so-called "sheet" that law enforcement uncovered in her washing machine. Among scores of evidence photos taken inside the Cargill house, photos of the sheet and where it had been found were presented. The implication was that Kim had used the sheet to wrap Cherry up in and transport her, or that it contained some blood or other forensic evidence that would have pointed to a crime taking place inside the house. During direct questioning the evidence bag with the so-called sheet sat in the courtroom as the DA asked Martin questions about it.

However, the item was never taken out of the bag by
the DA. When Kim's attorney questioned Martin about
the same piece of evidence, however, asking him if it
was, in fact, a sheet, the lawyer took the item out of
the evidence bag and asked if it hadn't, instead, appeared to be a tablecloth.

"I do not know," Martin answered, shaking his
head. "It looked like a sheet to me. It was a long piece
of linen."

The trial continued on May 11.

Day five of the trial focused on Kim Cargill's life
leading up to the murder. To explain the type of
person she was, the DA had Forrest Garner come in
and tell his stories of dealing with an absolute tyrant
and a hothead. He portrayed Kim as an angry, bitter,
scathing ex who spewed hatred and chaos and violence on what seemed to be a daily basis. Forrest
talked of his apartment catching fire after arguing
with Kim one night, and how he lived nearly next door
to Cherry Walker, but never knew she was watching
Timmy. It was all quite damaging to Kim and her character. In all of his testimony Forrest could not—same
as just about every character witness the DA had called
before him—dredge up one good thing to say about
Kim Cargill. She was a menace; she was a disgrace to
motherhood. She destroyed lives and made day-to-day
living an absolute hell for nearly everyone she came
into contact with.

One chilling point Forrest Garner left the jury with,
if only by suggestion, was that if Kim Cargill had displayed all of this destructive and abusive behavior in

front of people, what had she actually done to her kids when she *knew* nobody was watching?

After Forrest Garner, James Cargill, Blake's dad, took the stand and told of the havoc she had caused him and his child. Kim was like a hurricane that came in, spinning and spinning, and never left town.

In a smart move the DAO ended this day with Rueon Walker, Cherry's stepmother, giving the trial a jolt of sentimentality from the victim's side.

Rueon talked about Cherry and her final days. She spoke of how Cherry was starting off on her own and how proud the family was that Cherry had worked toward her independence.

Then DA Matt Bingham brought up those pivotal dates: June 18, 19 and 20. Rueon detailed those days and the anxiety they began to feel as Cherry had not shown up in church on Father's Day and had not been heard from since Friday. It was numbing, Rueon explained, to learn of her death and how her body had been found on the side of the road, burned like a piece of campfire wood. After all Cherry had been through in her life, to be tossed to the side of the road, it was beyond reprehensible, beyond unimaginable. However, it would turn out for this family that it was *not* beyond forgivable.

Throughout her testimony Rueon was on the verge of bursting into tears.

Near the end of the day Bingham asked Rueon about Cherry babysitting Timmy and how the family and Cherry's doctors had all been against it. They talked about this for some time, with Rueon agreeing that Cherry did not know her own limitations.

"So the fact that Cherry was willing to keep [Timmy] didn't mean that the average reasonable person would think that was a good idea."

"The reasonable person would not—*never*, ever—leave a child with Cherry—" Rueon said as Bingham cut her off midsentence.

"Right."

"—under *any* circumstances."

"Yes, ma'am. That's what I'm getting at. Cherry's willing to do things that Cherry *shouldn't* do?"

"That's correct," Rueon agreed.

"Mr. Bingham?" Judge Skeen said.

Bingham looked at the clock. It was Friday, getting late, and they needed to complete a few legal matters without the jury present before recessing until the following Monday morning.

65

THE SIXTH DAY OF TRIAL began with Rueon Walker concluding her testimony, providing more of the same sentimental candor and victim background every trial should include. Often the victim gets lost in the headlines and the wacky behavior of the defendant takes precedence. Nobody, though, could accuse Matt Bingham and the state of allowing that to happen. The DAO gave Cherry Walker her due respect and had several witnesses spread throughout the trial describe the kind of person Cherry was, the lives she touched and the devastating loss all felt without her in their lives any longer.

Joe Mayo, at one time a suspect, told his stories of being close to Cherry, singing karaoke and enjoying that bright smile and calm demeanor Cherry brought into the world. He expressed her love of horror films and ironing clothes and cleaning her apartment and eating out and living on her own. Joe humanized Cherry Walker perhaps more than anyone else could by simply stating facts about her life: the movies she liked, her daily habits, the food she favored. Joe also had a flair for humor at a time when everyone needed a good laugh.

When Bingham asked him how old he was, the self-proclaimed professional singer said, "I'm thirty-five years old—hard to believe, huh?" Then Joe asked if he could sing in court, but Bingham responded, "Well, probably not, but we know where you're at in case [we] want to go see you. . . ."

"Awesome," Joe said.

Cherry's neighbor, Marcie Fulton, who had introduced Kim Cargill to her, handing off babysitting responsibilities for Timmy, sat next and explained how Cherry had come to meet Kim and then take care of Timmy. Marcie testified that she had *specifically* told Kim that Cherry was mentally challenged, and Kim, learning this, did not let it deter her from using Cherry as a babysitter. All Kim wanted was a place to dump her kid—and in Cherry Walker's clean, small apartment, she found such a place.

Questioning Marcie, April Sikes focused jurors on June 18. Several of those seventy-eight calls/texts Kim had made were to the neighbor. During one of these calls the neighbor recalled Kim being "pretty upset" and even "frantic." It was more evidence of Kim being unhinged and in the frame of mind to do just about anything to save herself. In addition, Kim had asked Marcie if she, too, had received "a piece of paper" (subpoena) and what was she planning to do about it.

Marcie explained to jurors that she had told Kim over the phone she had not been subpoenaed. Not at that time.

Cargill then told Marcie what needed to be done if and when the subpoena arrived.

"And what did she tell you?" ADA Sikes asked.

"She told me to get out of town or go home with her—[because] I *was* going to get a piece of paper, a subpoena."

"Okay," Sikes said, encouraging her to continue.

"And she said, 'I know you don't want to get that piece of paper, because you. . . . If you do, you'll have to go to court.' And that's about the size of it."

In a subtle manner, simply by telling the truth, Marcie Fulton had put into context how manipulative and controlling Kim Cargill could be.

"So it didn't sound to you like she *wanted* you to go to court?"

"No, she didn't."

"Did Kim Cargill ask you to go to her house?"

"Yes."

"But you didn't do that?"

"No . . . ma'am."

The implication here, without being stated, was that had Marcie gone over to the Cargill house on that night, or had she received a subpoena that day, there was a chance she might have wound up next to Cherry, dead and burned, on the side of CR 2191.

Further along, Marcie related that she had spoken to Cherry several times on June 18 and then to Kim Cargill afterward.

Sikes asked, "Did . . . Cherry [talk] like [she wanted] to go to court?"

"Cherry asked me if I was going to lie for Kim, and I said no. She said, 'Well, I won't, either.' That's about what I remembered."

It was clear to jurors that Cherry Walker knew exactly

what was going on and what Kim Cargill was asking her to do.

"Okay," Sikes continued, "do you remember Kim Cargill saying, 'Cherry talks like you *want* to go to court. . . .' Do you remember that?"

"Yes, I remember that."

"And you told her you *didn't* want to go to court?"

"No, I don't want to be here."

"Did Cherry tell you Kim was trying to take her out to dinner?"

"Yes."

After taking the pass from ADA Sikes, Kim Cargill's lawyer said, "We have no questions, Your Honor."

66

SUZANNE JONES-DAVIS NEXT TOOK HER place in the witness-box. After telling jurors she had been arrested and charged for tampering with evidence, Kim Cargill's so-called friend explained how she had been swallowed up into the black hole of Kim's madness after reconnecting with her. They had met in the eighth grade, Suzanne recalled here, but they had not seen each other in many years. Then that wonderful social media invention, the Internet, brought them together for a class reunion. Suzanne had not, she said, been indicted thus far, nor had she cut any deal for her testimony. However, everyone paying attention to her words knew that if she played nicely in the sandbox with the DA, she would catch a break down the road.

As Suzanne testified throughout the morning session, it became clear that Kim had made up stories about her life in order to draw Suzanne into being a pawn in Kim's plot to get around how abusively she had treated her kids. Suzanne walked into the situation blind, not knowing anything else besides Kim's version of events—and she fell for it.

The witness discussed the letter to the court she had written under Kim's direction, rewriting and editing, several e-mails they had exchanged, and then explained that she decided to help an old friend, by stretching the truth.

She and Kim talked on the phone for hours, Suzanne told jurors. One of the main topics was Kim's worry that she was going to have to pay support for a second child. This was not something Kim was going to be doing, she told her friend. After those conversations Kim would always sign off by saying things such as, "Love you . . . and may God be with you," plying Suzanne with the phrases she knew she wanted to hear. In Suzanne's mind Kim Cargill was a sincere, God-fearing woman in need of a sympathetic ear. It seemed that everyone in her old friend's life was against her.

As ADA Sikes and Suzanne went back and forth, it was obvious that Kim had used Suzanne, abused her, lied to and cheated her, finally convincing Suzanne to do things Kim Cargill knew were illegal and morally corrupt. True, Suzanne could have said no. She could have walked away, like the Waterton Circle neighbor who stood her ground. However, Kim knew a mark when she saw one. Where Suzanne was concerned, Kim layered on the superficial charm, with large helpings of glibness. She was a master sculptor shaping and molding Suzanne Jones-Davis into the perfect soldier.

The one bombshell Sikes brought in through Suzanne was how, on Monday, June 21, Kim called her and asked if she had seen the news about her babysitter being found dead the previous Saturday.

Only problem with that information: It had not been news yet. Thus, jurors were left with the question:

How would Kim Cargill know her babysitter was dead if she had not killed her?

The state next brought in Dr. Meredith Lann, the ME in charge of determining how Cherry Walker died and by what manner. As Lann began her testimony, detailing her long list of credentials, she explained to jurors that she no longer worked for Smith County. In fact, Lann had taken a new job and was now the ME for Alaska. A monumental task, essentially—but a new job that spoke to the respect Meredith Lann had within her field.

There had been some indication that Lann would wrap up the state's case. It would be hard to imagine a better way to end than once again introducing jurors to photographs of Cherry Walker as Dr. Lann had last seen her: at autopsy, on her table, in death. The stark images would remind jurors a dead human being was at the center of the trial. Not a name. Not some mentally retarded woman for Kim Cargill to blame her life on. Not a number on a toe tag. But a woman, a sister, a daughter, a friend, a churchgoer, an incredibly special person who was loved and missed.

After Lann told jurors about manner of death, cause of death and how she drew her conclusions, DA Bingham asked, "And what kind of . . . um, is there a limit on the amount of information that you want, or do you want as *much* information relevant to . . . [the] case as you could get?"

"Being a very thorough person, I like to have as much information as possible, especially if there's a homicidal nature to the death."

From that point Lann showed how, through the

process of "many phone calls" with law enforcement, whose "field agents do a lot of work there on the front line," the doctor was able to gather more information that helped her determine cause of death. "And I can spend most of my time just collating all the information to be able to come up with an opinion and my final conclusions."

Lann studied X-rays. She scoured medical records. She conferred with detectives. She photographed Cherry Walker's body and studied the case every which way she could. Although her methods (or the methods of any ME) are never 100 percent guaranteed, she made certain she hadn't missed anything. Finding out how a person died was a careful process of deduction. Medical examiners took into account every possibility and every potential medical condition and scenario that could have led to a person's death. Lann left no stone unturned. It was her job to do so.

Bingham went through a list of the medications Cherry was taking and asked Lann if those would have made a difference in the way the doctor determined manner or cause of death.

She said certainly they would, adding that she knew Cherry Walker had been treated for seizures and was on meds that could cause seizures. This was not a secret to anyone.

After discussing how Lann knew about Cherry's meds and potential seizures, and how Cherry had been treated for seizures in the past and had suffered mild tremors, when all was said and done, it did not matter to Lann. Cherry Walker, in Lann's opinion, had not died from a seizure. That was clear from the examination of the body and the evidence Lann had collected and analyzed.

"Do any of those records change your opinions that you've made in this case?" Bingham wanted to know.

"No," Lann testified.

The conclusion Lann had come to—and would stand behind with her career—was that Cherry Walker died by means of "homicidal violence." It was the only conclusion Lann could come to after taking every other scenario and possibility into account.

"Do you have any question about that in your mind?" Bingham restated.

"No," Lann reiterated.

Bingham asked about the idea Lann had posited from day one indicating there was a chance Cherry Walker might have been asphyxiated. The DA wanted his expert to explain this for jurors so they understood exactly what Lann was saying.

"At autopsy," Lann said, "I had a few findings, which although not specific, they're suggestive of a possible asphyxiation, and they point toward that she *might* have had a compression to the neck or some sort of portion of her body, which allowed for these small capillaries in her eyelids and eye-lining. . . . The lining which covered her eyes, called the conjunctiva, had small hemorrhages in them." She added that when she saw "those little hemorrhages or bleeds in the membrane," it gave her pause to "wonder. So, like I said, it's not specific, but it *does* make me wonder."

"Okay. And so . . . I want to make sure I state it correctly . . . the manner of death was ruled homicide."

"Yes," Lann said again.

Cherry Walker was murdered; there were only so many ways one could articulate that finding.

In addition, Lann offered, when she checked the

toxicology reports, looking for any other sign of what could have been in Cherry's system and led to her death, Lann found "low" levels of the seizure medication Cherry had been prescribed. The thermal burns Cherry had received from being set on fire had altered Cherry's blood levels. So it was hard to tell how much medication was actually in her system, but Lann was certain Cherry had indeed taken her seizure meds on the day she died. That fact was clear in the blood work.

Lann walked jurors through each photo, painstakingly and heart-wrenchingly, detailing what each represented to her in terms of the autopsy and Cherry's death. As each photo, which was unbearably graphic in nature, came before the courtroom on computer screens, Kim Cargill could not bring herself to look up. She had that yellow notepad in front of her and either doodled on it or simply kept her head down. Here was the end result of Kim's work on display for everyone to see, and she did not want to be judged for looking at it herself. Instead, she could only squirm in her chair once in a while and look to the side or down at the floor—anywhere else but at the result of what she had done to Cherry Walker.

Dr. Lann was "confident" in her opinions. She stood by them. Before passing his witness, DA Matt Bingham made the point that Cherry Walker had *not* died as the result of a seizure. Cherry Walker, according to the ME, was murdered.

Jeff Haas took over the questioning. This was one of the defense's only chances to present its "seizure" defense during the state's case. If he could get Lann to admit she had no idea how Cherry died and open up the opportunity for her to have died of a seizure, just as his client had claimed, he would be on the road leading to a verdict of not guilty.

Within his cross-examination Haas alluded to several theories. One was that Dr. Meredith Lann knew law enforcement was "very interested" in her autopsy results as she worked on Cherry Walker's body; another was that the ME knew law enforcement had a "person of interest" in the case—a woman who was a nurse.

Lann said yes to both, adding that this was not so much different from any other homicide case she had been involved in. Cops were always eager to know the results of an autopsy when they suspected foul play. Their interest was typical; it was not an anomaly, as Haas had made it sound in the way he phrased his questions.

Haas focused on the bruises found on Cherry's body. Finally he asked if any of the bruises Lann noticed during autopsy would have been "consistent with defensive wounds"?

"No."

Then it was on to the abrasions Lann found on Cherry Walker's body. The way Haas asked each question made it sound more important than it was. For example, he'd preface his queries by saying, "Now, you said something" or "All right, let's talk about . . ." These types of phrases, along with the tone Haas used, gave the false impression that what followed was significant—but jurors were smart. They knew smoke when it stunk up a room, and they understood what truly mattered in the end: evidence.

"All right," Haas said at one point, "now, you did a *real* diligent search, I would imagine, to try to determine what the cause of death was, correct?"

"Yes."

"And you weren't able to make a determination, correct?"

"The cause of death was homicidal violence."

How many times did Lann need to say this?

"But the manner and means or mechanism?" Haas pressed.

"The manner is homicide. The mechanism, unknown."

For instance, the bullet is what kills; the gun it was fired from—or mechanism—becomes insignificant in terms of the outcome.

"Now, you found no ligature marks around the neck, correct?"

"Correct."

"The windpipe or trachea, was that crushed?"

"No."

"Were there any bruises around the neck that you could see?"

"No."

"What kind of . . . What does 'undetermined' mean—just don't know?"

"Correct."

Another common tactic defense attorneys leaned on was the hypothetical, which Haas then posed. "Are there ways for people to die that you're not able to determine *how* they died?"

"Yes."

A few questions later, another wild question that

had little to do with the case: "Have you ever heard of sudden-death syndrome?" Haas wanted to know.

"Yes."

He asked Lann to explain.

"I've heard of . . . sudden *infant* death syndrome," she corrected, "as a use of a diagnostic tool. But I don't ever really use it in my practice. It's a way for people to describe a collapse or cessation of life without any known means or mechanism. . . ."

"I know you're talking about homicidal violence, but as far as the means of death, [you] just don't know, correct?"

"Yes."

"Now, is it possible for someone to die of a seizure?"

"Yes."

"And if someone dies of a seizure, is that able to be determined?"

"It's a diagnosis of exclusion. Seizure is a key cause of death in many circumstances of epileptic individuals, but it requires a full study of previous medical history, account of the individuals present at the time of seizure, as well as review of the autopsy findings and toxicology."

Emphasis, perhaps, on the *"account of the individuals present,"* because several mitigating factors went into a medical examiner pronouncing seizure as the cause of death. Just about all of which, in this case, led Lann to believe, she said again, that it just didn't happen.

After her careful, considerate and detailed autopsy, Lann did not believe that Cherry Walker died from a seizure. The evidence just wasn't there. No matter how the defense attorney presented his case for death by seizure, how one tried to talk it up, which phrases one used and questions one asked, which potential scenarios one hypothesized, the end result was always going to remain the same from where Dr. Lann saw it: Cherry Walker died of homicidal violence, not a seizure.

Jeff Haas was doing his job as best he could with what he had to work with. A mountain of evidence pointed to Kim Cargill murdering Cherry Walker. No evidence—besides what Kim Cargill suggested— indicated Cherry Walker died of a seizure. When Haas pressed Lann on Cherry perhaps biting her tongue and some potential bruising found on the inside of her mouth—common injuries associated with seizures— Lann said that "evidence" was indeterminate and unsubstantiated. There was no definitive proof that Cherry had any of those injuries, and the minor scarring and bruising inside her mouth could in no way be associated with biting from seizures.

After a long lunch break Matt Bingham took to the floor again. This time, however, he said simply, "Ladies and gentlemen of the jury, the state rests."

Judge Skeen recessed until the following morning when, he said, the defense would have the opportunity to present its case. It was clear from what had transpired over the course of the state's case that the only chance Kim Cargill had was to get up there and tell jurors her story. Would this narcissistic sociopath feel confident enough to spin her tale of woe for jurors?

67

A S SHE SAT IN THE witness-box, with her eyes blinking slowly and repeatedly, one could almost sense the uncontrollable, internal spasm of rage bubbling up inside Kim Cargill. A sheriff's department deputy stood in back of her, just in case she allowed her inner wrath to manifest into something more outwardly physical. Looking at Kim Cargill as she sat in the witness chair and took questions from her attorney on May 16, 2012, one could feel that negative, frenzied energy issuing from her pores. Here was a defendant livid and unnerved by the accusations made against her. She was embarrassed. She was impatient. She was being forced to bite her tongue when her nature was to lash out. Kim Cargill was on the hot seat, feeling the temperature rise through her body like an electric current—and the one thing Kim hated more than perhaps anything else was giving up control.

Her lawyers had motioned before she sat down for a "directed verdict"—in which the judge would "direct" the jury to come to a particular verdict—of

not guilty, but it was a formality that was quickly denied
by the judge.

Brent Harrison, with the polished, gentle and manicured good looks of a soap opera star, took on the task
of questioning his client. Kim wore a floral-patterned,
long dress, multicolored and soft and soothing, no
doubt by design and advice from her lawyers. She
spoke softly, in contrast to her regular bombastic and
loud voice. Her Texas accent was played for effect,
sounding much sweeter than it actually was.

Harrison asked her to settle in and speak loudly and
clearly into the microphone. After she introduced herself, Kim admitted—in dramatic form—to dumping
Cherry's body on the CR 2191. This admission came
before telling jurors that story of Cherry having a
seizure inside her vehicle and falling onto the ground
unconscious, where Kim eventually determined Cherry
was dead. She spoke of running for help, but she just
could not find a phone or person anywhere. She said
she panicked and decided to try to cover it all up because of what people would think, especially since she
had that upcoming custody hearing. It was a story that
sounded rehearsed and contrived.

Kim Cargill answered her attorney for about thirty
minutes—with the main body of her testimony focused
on that tale of Cherry dying inside the car and Kim hitting the panic button four blocks away from a hospital.

Harrison finally asked, "When you called Suzanne
[Jones-Davis], knowing Cherry Walker was dead, did
you tell her you *hadn't* seen [Cherry on] Friday?"

"Yes."

"Was that a lie?"

"Yes."

"You were with Cherry Walker on June 18, 2010?"

"Yes."

"Were you with her in Smith County, Texas?"

"Yes."

Strangely, Harrison then asked: "She is a deceased individual?"

"Yes."

Ever more strangely: "She was a living individual prior to the time . . . prior to that time on June 18, 2010?"

"Yes."

"Did you kill her?"

"No."

That was it. All finished—at least from the defense's point of view.

Now the real test would begin as DA Matt Bingham stood.

68

MATT BINGHAM WORE A PATTERNED tie, with alternating dark and light stripes, white shirt and a dark-colored suit jacket. He stood behind the lectern with a determined look on his face. Bingham knew that less was more here. Although it would be hard to quell his emotion, he'd want to avoid a heated cross-examination as much as he could. There was no need to go through and ask Kim about every piece of the story and pick apart her lies, one by one. There would be nothing to gain from such a tedious replaying of the evidence. The best strategy was to pick his arguments smartly and go straight at the facts that would prove Kim Cargill was guilty. The truth, any prosecutor knew, has a way of rising to the surface. All one needs to do when confronting a lying defendant is present the opportunity for her to cut her own throat and she, eventually, will drag that knife across her own skin.

Bingham began with the obvious. Prior to telling the courtroom, just moments before during her direct examination, who else had Kim Cargill told tales to about Cherry Walker's seizure?

There was a thunderous objection from Brent Harrison to the question.

The judge allowed the question, as long as Bingham kept it to what Kim had told anyone else *but* her attorneys. That information was, of course, covered under attorney-client privilege.

Bingham went through a list of possibilities.

Suzanne?

"No."

The neighbor?

"No."

Michael Darwin?

"No."

"Anyone?"

"No," Kim said. She had not told anyone the seizure story.

"As a matter of fact, your first explanation—*one* of your explanations—was that she was going out to eat with . . . what?"

Bingham indicated he needed some help from Kim Cargill.

"Boyfriend," Kim finished.

"'White boy'? 'White boy,' right?" Bingham finished, repeating what Kim had testified to during her direct examination "Remember that?"

"Boyfriend" was all Kim would divulge.

"Yeah. And *why* did you come up with *that* lie? . . . It's a lie, isn't it?"

"Yes."

"And *why* did you come up with that?"

"Because that's actually who she wanted to find that night," Kim said, contradicting her own testimony.

"So she still wanted to find the 'white boy'? Is *that* your testimony?"

"Her boyfriend."

"Okay," Bingham conceded, his point clearly made. "Her boyfriend."

Kim began to sniffle, sounding as though she was on the verge of tears.

Bingham seized upon her emotion. "And let me ask you this—You're up there, and you're . . . you're making crying sounds. . . ."

After an objection, "I'm trying not to," she answered.

"Let me ask you then—When you went into the Whitehouse Police Department and you went in there to gather information, where was Cherry Walker's body?"

"She was on that country road."

"Yeah. She was on the country road burned up, wasn't she?"

"Yes."

"Why aren't you crying on the Whitehouse PD video? . . . It's a lie, isn't it?"

"Well, not . . ."

"Well, is it or *isn't* it?"

"Not exactly."

"Oh, *really*?"

Kim claimed she was in denial while standing inside the WPD talking about Father's Day, her two-month-missing dog and how busy the police were on that day.

Bingham shrugged, knowing he'd revisit the denial comment.

Kim told jurors she had no idea Cherry was "MR," adding, "I did not know she had that diagnosis."

It was laughable. There were plenty of witnesses on record saying Kim had known this about Cherry and mentioned it on several occasions. That was the thing about chronic liars, Bingham knew. They often had a hard time keeping track of all the lies.

Bingham let that slide and went back to the denial comment, asking, "Cherry Walker's life on this earth is over. Why aren't you crying on that video?"

"It was an act."

"So you're that good, huh?" Bingham paused. "Is this an act today?"

"No."

"No, it's not?" Bingham asked, before he added, "So, in front of the jury, when you're looking at being convicted of *capital* murder, this is *not* an act. But you went to the Whitehouse Police Department—knowing that you've taken her out there, dumped her body, set it on fire—you're able to set *that* aside, right, and just be happy-go-lucky? You're *that* good?"

Kim did not respond.

"Is it just an act?" Bingham asked again, demanding an answer.

"I was trying to appear normal."

"Well, you *did* appear normal. . . ."

This passionate prosecutor, standing in the courtroom as a voice for Cherry Walker, was keen to make clear that Kim Cargill had watched a woman, whom she knew personally, die in her presence the previous night, dumped that same woman's body on the side of the road and lit it on fire, watched it burn, but then walked into a police station about twelve hours later (by her own account) and acted like a carefree housewife and mother looking for a lost dog, wondering how busy the police department was. If she had been so distraught, as she had now claimed, if she had been so upset and "in denial" over what had transpired just a half day before, here was solid evidence in the form of a videotape showing that it did not take her long to get over it. Thus, why would it be bothering her in this courtroom so many years later? After all, she had spoken to several people after that Friday night and came across as nonchalant and normal, as she had in the video. Why was she feeling that pain so many years later?

Kim had no answer. However, she did respond to every scenario posed by Bingham. For example, Bingham focused on the lighter fluid she said she'd just happened to have inside her car on the night she needed it to burn Cherry's body. Bingham, like many, had an issue with this stroke of convenient fortune. Most believed Kim had taken the lighter fluid from her home with the intent to use it on Cherry after she murdered her, or had used that $5 worth of gas she'd purchased that night. So, if she had the lighter fluid inside her car, lighter fluid she had said she used to kill fire ants around her house, Bingham wanted to know why it was in the car.

"Why didn't you leave the lighter fluid in your garage, since you burn things around your house?" Bingham asked.

"Because I-I-I had a little one (meaning Timmy) that I didn't want-want-want him to get-get-get into it," Kim answered, nearly stuttering.

Bingham knew she was lying. But you don't come out and call the defendant a liar—you show by example.

"Really?" Bingham said with a sarcastic chuckle. "Well, you had a hypodermic needle sitting on your [kitchen] table. Were you concerned about that?"

"That probably came from my nursing scrub pockets and he wasn't there at that time."

"And he wasn't there, either, when it was in your car—the lighter fluid—*was* he?"

"It had been in there for quite a while."

"Yeah . . . and . . . you want these people to believe sitting here . . . that you left the lighter fluid in your car so your little one *wouldn't* get into it?"

"I had a bunch of stuff in the back of my SUV."

This type of ridiculous answer to what were common-sense questions went back and forth, with Bingham winning every time. Kim repeatedly came across as insincere and untrustworthy, answering questions with whatever came to mind.

Another point Bingham brought up was that on no other day in her phone call history—which law enforcement had checked—had Kim Cargill made so many calls while at work. Why was it that she had made so many phone calls the day Cherry Walker had received a subpoena to testify against her?

After Kim failed to answer, Bingham left jurors with the impression that she was going insane on that day trying to figure out how she could stop Cherry from testifying—the sole reason why she had made so many calls.

Another solid fact Bingham brought out was how, on that Saturday after Kim admitted to knowing Cherry was dead, she called her neighbor and talked about the hearing scheduled for the following Wednesday. The reason she called, Bingham shouted, was because "You're still moving on with the hearing. . . . Cherry

Walker is dead, laying [sic] in the dirt, just what you wanted. . . ."

The defendant said that wasn't what she wanted.

"And so what do you say to [your neighbor] when you see her that morning? 'Hi, how are you doing,' right?"

"Yes."

"Not crying then, either, *are* you?"

"I was pretty stressed."

"Oh, I *bet* you were!"

Later, Bingham stated in a sardonic tone that Kim was so stressed and upset on that morning after talking to her neighbor that she even went out and washed her car.

Kim played down every bit of what she did and said and how she acted in front of people throughout that weekend. When backed into a corner, she answered Bingham with "I don't remember" and "I cannot recall."

Under questioning Kim then submitted to Bingham that she was mostly concerned about the court humiliating Cherry—and this was the real reason why she didn't want her to testify.

Bingham shook his head. "Well, I know you were real concerned about that," he said. "It's just like when you poured the lighter fluid on the back of her body and set her on fire, right? Pretty concerned about her. . . ."

Kim claimed she never said she wanted Cherry to "hide out" at her house. Paula Wheeler had misconstrued what she had said. Instead, Kim claimed, she had asked Cherry to come "hang out" at her house. There was some confusion about the two words.

It was nonsense. The jurors, looking bored but alert, were not at all fooled by Kim Cargill and her lies.

* * *

Matt Bingham and Kim Cargill went toe to toe all day long. Most of what Bingham wanted the jury to understand was implied in his questions. It was a solid strategy. If she didn't answer the way in which Bingham wanted, he'd rephrase the question as a statement and move on.

During one of his longer declarations, after detailing what Kim had said during direct questioning regarding what happened to Cherry inside her car, Bingham ended, "And it's just because you just had . . . dang, you just had *bad* luck. She happened to die on the *very* day that she got subpoenaed to testify against you in court."

"No," Kim said.

"Well, what is it? I mean, isn't that it, basically? That you're coming back from a happy meal at Posados and, all of a sudden, you start hearing something, and she's having a seizure, banging her head against the window, and you're like, 'What the . . .' You didn't kill her. It's just bad luck, right? Just a *bad* chain of events. All of it culminated just on that one night."

"She got subpoenaed—" Kim began to say, but her own lawyer cut her off.

"Judge, I would ask . . . There's not a question there."

Kim said, "I made some tragic and desperate choices that night."

"Well, I mean, you're saying you *didn't* kill her," Bingham went on to note. "You're saying she had a seizure, right?"

"That's correct."

"Okay. And how do you *know* she had a seizure?"

"Because I know what a seizure looks like."

"You do? Well, how?"

"I've seen many at the hospital."

"All right. And are you trained to help with seizures?"

"Yes."

"And is it your testimony that you're in a turn lane, and the reason you *don't* go to a hospital, as a trained LVN who's seen many seizures, that you're just blocked by traffic?"

"Yes. I was in the left turning lane with the other traffic coming forward and two lanes . . . with cars. I was blocked in."

"Okay. So let me get it straight. You're . . . an LVN sitting in your car on the *very* day that she gets subpoenaed to testify in court. You've gone by and you've picked her up, and all of a sudden you're in the turn lane. And so if . . . you go to the left, you go to her apartment. If you turned right, you'd be on a street that's right next to a hospital, wouldn't you?"

Kim did not know what to say to that.

"The fact of the matter is," Bingham added, demolishing her left-turn explanation, "the reason you didn't is because that never happened. What you did is, you pulled her into the garage at your house, you shut the garage door and you *killed* her."

The courtroom went church silent.

"That's a lie," Kim said defiantly.

"That's a hoot," Bingham said with a laugh. "Calling *me* a liar."

Throughout the day Matt Bingham caught Kim Cargill in one lie after the next. Kim must have lost track of how many lies she had told. She just couldn't keep track of them all. At one point Bingham wanted Kim to talk about dumping Cherry's body, adding, "So you pull her out. And how do you get her away from your car?"

"I just pulled her with her arm."

"Right. So you [dragged] her basically?"

"For about a foot, yes."

"About a foot? So how does it feel to reach down and put your hands under the arms of Cherry Walker and pull her a foot, knowing that you're fixing to put lighter fluid on her body and set her on fire? How do you do that?"

"I don't know, but I did."

"I mean, what kind of person *does* that?"

"A desperate person."

"Desperate for what?"

"To not be blamed."

"To hide evidence, right?"

"Yes."

"So you pull her a foot. And when do you realize that you have the lighter fluid in your car?"

"When I'm driving around, trying to figure out what to do."

"And you think, 'Good. I don't have to stop. I've got lighter fluid in my car,' right?"

"Well, yes."

"Yeah. And you got matches in there?"

"I had some in my purse."

"Okay. Why do you have matches in your purse?"

"I . . . I . . . always have . . . ," Kim said, stumbling through her answer, finally saying, "I pick up matches when I go to restaurants or different places," as if an answer suddenly came to her.

"Okay. You don't smoke, do you?"

"No."

Bingham then asked Kim to explain every detail she could with regard to lighting Cherry on fire and fleeing the scene. At times Bingham would ask the judge to remove the jury so they could discuss something the defendant had said that contradicted the record. In other words, Bingham would catch her lying. He'd call up the transcript, or a transcript from a hearing or interview with one of her kids, and read from it. Then she would be hit with an epiphany— *"Oh, geez, that's right. . . . How silly of me to confuse things."*

The judge would call the jury back into the courtroom and correct the record. Bingham would prove once again that Kim was not to be trusted because she was a pathological liar. Kim Cargill was trying anything and everything she could to save herself from a date with death.

69

BINGHAM COULD HAVE PROBABLY questioned Kim Cargill for a week and would have gotten her to crack eventually. But he didn't have the time frame to do that. She'd done a fair job over the course of a day showing jurors that she not only had an answer for everything, but she was not going to admit to murdering Cherry Walker. She adamantly—and despite illogical appearances—stood behind the lie of Cherry having a deadly seizure in front of her.

On May 16, 2012, Bingham finished his cross-examination of Kim Cargill during the morning session. Brent Harrison called his second witness, Detective James Riggle.

Harrison focused on Riggle's visit to Cherry Walker's apartment after she had been found on the side of the road. It was a transparent attempt to make something out of nothing. Harrison asked Riggle how he got into the apartment.

"A key," the cop said.

Harrison then encouraged Riggle to explain what the apartment looked like.

"Fairly neat," Riggle opined.

Harrison moved on to a "pill organizer" Riggle found inside Cherry's apartment, plastic multicompartment container with the days of the week stamped on the top of each lid. Harrison wanted to know if there were still meds inside any of the sections. As Riggle began to say there was no way for him to know the answer to that question, that they had collected the container as evidence, Harrison moved on to another topic and then indicated he was done.

Riggle's testimony lasted all of five minutes.

Harrison called two more witnesses, who added no strength to Kim Cargill's defense. For many inside the courtroom, her defense felt like a car heading for a cliff, its driver recognizing at the last moment what was about to happen and now searching for s*omething* or s*omeone* to grab hold of, but realizing, in the end, there was nothing and no one there.

The following morning, May 17, the defense rested its case.

The state called a few rebuttal witnesses to seal the deal, then closed its case a second time. The defense did the same, and the judge adjourned, letting everyone know that closing arguments would begin on the following morning after a few court-related matters.

Late in the morning of May 18, just before noon, after the judge read the charges against Kim Cargill, DA Matt Bingham stood at the lectern in front of jurors. There was a poster-size, blowup photo of Cherry Walker on an easel to his right; an American flag, framed in gold, was on the wall over his shoulder. April Sikes looked on from the state's table, and Judge Skeen perched on his bench, listening.

"I want to start off by telling you how much I and Mrs. Sikes, the family of Cherry Walker seated here in the front row, appreciate your service in this case," Bingham began.

The idea of a closing argument is to condense the highlights of your case and place an aesthetically pleasing bow on your package so jurors can understand exactly where you are coming from. Before doing that, Bingham talked through the charges the judge had read, making sure the jury understood it had choices with regard to a verdict: murder and capital murder.

Life or death.

As Bingham led into the state's case, he talked about the previous night as he sat alone and wondered how he was going to fit what turned out to be "a week-and-a-half worth of testimony" into what the court wanted as no longer than an hour of closing argument. He then put the state's case plainly. He explained that if the jury believed that Cherry Walker just happened to have a seizure on the exact day she had received a subpoena, and that the evil and madness and cruelty she endured following that was a mere coincidence: "All the talking in the world is not going to change your mind."

As he talked, Bingham made his points clearly and concisely—and this was one of Bingham's greatest assets to the DAO: his ability to show how subtle evidence that exposed itself in the realm of a defendant's lies was all that jurors needed in order to see the truth through the dust of manipulation.

He asked jurors to take a look at Kim Cargill's yard—they had plenty of photos to go through and study the grounds of her home—and think about how Michael Darwin had testified that he took care of her mowing and other landscaping needs, which sort of proved that her fire ant story for that lighter fluid was a lie. She never killed a fire ant in her life. She could not have cared less about fire ants or done anything else having to do with her yard. The inside of her home was a Dumpster, the outside no better, Bingham suggested. That alone indicated she lied about the lighter fluid.

"She hasn't done anything in her yard or house for months . . . but she has to come up with *something*. So she just *happened* to have lighter fluid and matches. And she's the kind of person that could pull that out, pour it on the body of Cherry Walker, a sweet, mentally retarded girl, and set her on fire. She can do that. . . ."

He then encouraged jurors to "go back" and watch the WPD video of Kim Cargill walking in and talking to that cop just hours after she admitted dumping and burning Cherry Walker. Her demeanor and how she approached that cop—"When she thought nobody was watching"—said a lot about who she was at the time Cherry Walker lay dead and burned up. This was the real Kim Cargill, nonchalantly walking into a police department, asking about her dog, how business was going, talking about Father's Day, trying to find out how much the WPD knew at the time.

These comments set the theme of Bingham's closing: Look at the evidence. Don't listen to me. Don't listen to her. Don't listen to her attorneys. See for yourself in the truckload of evidence presented during testimony. It was all there: the truth, the lies, the cunning and conniving ways of Kim Cargill and, of course, the sheer evil she was capable of.

Another lie she got caught up in, without realizing it, was her story of pulling out of the Citadel parking lot that night. Kim Cargill said she turned left—and that was, Bingham smartly noted, the opposite direction of the hospital, a little fact she overlooked when constructing her story of Cherry dying inside her car.

Bingham called Kim Cargill "kooky."

Manipulative.

Paranoid.

A control freak.

Someone who didn't give a "hoot" about Cherry Walker or anybody else.

A woman "filled with rage."

A "fruit bag."

Someone whose life was "unraveling" at the time she committed this cruel murder.

As Bingham listed all of the lies and stories Kim Cargill told throughout the trial, it was a wonder she didn't slink down in her chair and try to hide underneath the table in embarrassment. But Kim Cargill, the true narcissist, sat and stared sternly at the prosecutor, shaking her head.

Bingham reminded jurors that Dr. Meredith Lann testified that she was "absolutely sure" Cherry died of homicidal violence. Bingham did not want jurors to be fooled by any other theory. The defense had the opportunity to call rebuttal witnesses against Lann, but they had chosen not to.

"A seizure is not a homicide," Bingham said at one point.

Also, Kim Cargill claimed she took Cherry out for Mexican food that night, Cherry's favorite place to eat. Yet, Bingham said, "Why wasn't there Mexican food in her stomach at autopsy?"

Another lie exposed by the *evidence*.

"Either you believe Dr. Lann . . . or you believe the defendant," Bingham said. "That's what this comes down to."

Bingham had a knack for making the obvious appear as devastating as it was: "Her lies are evidence of homicidal violence," he said. Why? "I know *this*," he added. "The defendant did kill Cherry Walker by homicidal violence. She was able to burn her body. And, you know, that hurt the case some, and she knows it did. She burned evidence up around [Cherry's] head and neck."

Matt Bingham then thanked April Sikes for her years of work on the case and for basically putting all the pieces together. The DA concluded by stating, "I just want to end by saying this. . . . Don't forget Cherry Walker. [Kim] sat in here, listened to the evidence, taking that stand, and spit her venom out and lied to you. That's why I put that picture up. . . ." He pointed to Cherry's photo. "I just want you to remember *her*."

Brent Harrison stood and attacked Bingham's version of the events, saying many of the reasons Bingham had just given were indications of how panicked Kim Cargill was on the night Cherry died, and why she decided to do what she did.

Then Harrison brought in part of Paula Wheeler's

testimony, trying to say that it showed evidence of a woman, Kim Cargill, who was not trying to hide her anger or any of her feelings about Cherry testifying. Fundamentally speaking, if she had planned on killing Cherry, why would Kim have a conversation with Paula Wheeler such as she had? Why, moreover, Harrison posed, would she then "kill the primary witness against her" in a custody case, knowing that Paula Wheeler and the other people whom Kim spoke to that day could talk about how pissed off she was?

"It doesn't make any sense! It does *not* add up."

The difference, Bingham and Sikes knew, was that what Harrison had just told jurors was speculation and grandstanding. It was not evidence that jurors could wrap their minds around and take to the bank. What's more, when jurors went back and read through her testimony, Kim had said she wasn't angry or mad on that day—that everyone had pegged her wrong.

Harrison called it an "anti-alibi"—Kim's movements and the conversations she had throughout that entire day and night and what she did was in contrast with a presumed guilty woman

After talking about how complicated the case was, as opposed to Bingham's "simple" argument, Harrison launched into Cherry Walker's medical history, focusing on her history of seizures.

But if jurors believed that Kim Cargill was a pathological liar—a fact that had been unmistakably proven during the trial—they would have to take into consideration that she was lying about Cherry having a seizure, on top of a medical examiner telling them Cherry did *not* have a seizure and instead died of homicidal violence. If jurors looked at the case in that manner of speaking, every point Harrison made in his impassioned, intellectually stimulating and clever closing became a moot point. It did not matter. The end result would come down to the fact that Kim Cargill lied.

To her husbands.

To her mother.

To her kids.

To the court.

Just about to everyone she ever met.

As he talked through the case, Harrison fixated on Lann's testimony. He read from it. Near the end of his reading, Harrison intoned, "And Dr. Lann testified that she believed there was a possible bruise inside the cheek of Cherry Walker. And she testified on cross-examination that that would be consistent with a seizure."

To which, Bingham—rightly so—interjected, "That's a mischaracterization of the evidence."

Judge Skeen asked jurors to "rely" on their "recollections and memory of evidence." They could also request Lann's transcript and have a look for themselves.

Ending where he began, Harrison said, "Nobody wants to stand up here and say Kim Cargill's an angel. She is not. What she did is reprehensible." He talked of the "decisions she made after Cherry Walker's death" and how "awful" those were. However, he pointed out, "Where is the proof that she caused the death of Cherry Walker?" In a bizarre metaphor he then encouraged jurors to be "sure" of their decision before jumping "out of that airplane."

* * *

April Sikes and Jeff Haas offered their closings, both of which followed, for the most part, the same path each of their predecessors had carved before them. Each lawyer made his or her case, asked jurors to reach a verdict in his or her favor, then sat down with the understanding that arguing until the Texas sunshine came up the next morning would not sway a jury one way or another. Most jurors, everyone knew, make up their minds before the closings even begin.

In what seemed to be no more than an hour, the jury foreman, Jeff Shaffer, declared they had reached a verdict.

The swiftness of this jury was not a good sign for Kim Cargill.

"'In Cause Number 241-1510-10 verdict form, we, the jury,'" the judge read without emotion, "'find the defendant, Kimberly Cargill, guilty of the offense of capital murder as charged in the indictment. . . .'"

After all of the chaos and pain and conflict and violence she had caused those in her circle throughout the past twenty years, Kim Cargill had been found guilty of the worst crime the United States had on the books. She would now face the same jury during the sentencing phase, men and women who would decide whether Kim Cargill lived or died.

Staring blankly and standing stoic and defiant, not a smidgen of emotion or a slight reaction on her face, Cargill looked at the judge as he read the verdict. It was as if Kim Cargill did not care about being found guilty of capital murder.

70

THE PENALTY PHASE OF A capital murder trial can become cumbersome on jurors, weighing heavily on their emotions and moral compass. Most community members serving on a capital case entering the penalty phase will say it is the hardest thing they have ever done in their lives.

DA Matt Bingham opened on Monday, May 21, 2012, with the state's argument for death, promising jurors his opening here would be quicker than his closing the previous week.

In what could be called nothing short of a brilliant legal move, Bingham said right away, "Ultimately, you're going to be asked to decide three special issues. The first one being, what is the probability that the defendant will continue to commit criminal acts of violence that will constitute a continuing threat to society?"

Here was Bingham at his finest, leaning on his signature form of using the law against Kim Cargill— same as he had done throughout the trial. She was a killer of the most despicable kind, a cruel and vicious sociopath who cared only about her own wants and needs. Bingham had proven that repeatedly. But none of that mattered, the DA was saying with this opening line. What mattered now was following the law and the judge's instructions regarding determining life or death—and if you followed those rules, Bingham insisted, as a juror *you* had to come to one conclusion.

Death.

Kim Cargill's lawyers passed on the opportunity to give an opening at this time. A strategy of "less was more" was probably the best way to go. The defense needed to humanize Kim through testimony, not by shallow words that the jury could twist and turn into what it wanted, or overlook, or be offended by. That was all behind them now. She was guilty.

Still, how does one put a shine on a woman who had murdered a mentally retarded person? How does a defense attorney make jurors believe that Kim Cargill, who did not value human life, deserved to live?

As Harrison and Haas sat and listened, one witness Bingham called on the first day of testimony was a fourth-grade teacher. She had taught one of Kim's sons, Travis. She said Kim Cargill was the type of malicious taskmaster who, if the child got below a 96 on anything, would come into the class and ask the teacher to give the child extra work—which the teacher would always refuse to do.

The teacher said the child came across as fearful

and scared. However, after leaving Kim's home and going to live with his dad, Travis changed, becoming much more relaxed in class, able to focus on his studies. She also mentioned seeing bruises on the child from time to time.

Nailing the way in which Kim could change her demeanor in an instant, another teacher referred to her as "sweet as sugar one minute and mad as a hornet the next. . . ."

These two witnesses preceded a long line of others that came in and told stories of Kim Cargill destroying lives, physically assaulting people whenever she felt like it, threatening anybody she chose, lying, cheating, screaming at her kids in public, hitting them and hiding them out from her husbands. It went on and on.

Kim's mother sat in the witness stand and did what she could to try and put a sparkle on her daughter's image. She tried to explain why her daughter was the way she was, but it all felt desperate and scripted. Forced. Kim Cargill was a psychopath and, unfortunately, no matter what anybody said or how many stories doctors and family members told of her days struggling with depression and feeling unwanted, her medication changing her, there was nothing anybody could say or do to file down those figurative horns protruding from the top of her head.

Kim's ex-husbands and ex-boyfriends, and even her own children, told story after story of her abusing them, lying to them, manipulating them, threatening them and making their lives a living hell. The woman destroyed lives as routinely as washing clothes or taking a walk. It meant nothing to her to hurt someone, physically or emotionally—and the people around Kim Cargill were at the constant receiving end of her torment.

The state, staying true to the thoroughness it had displayed with utter authority during the guilt portion of the trial, spent a week providing witnesses—doctors and neighbors and family members—all of whom described Kim as a person who cared only about herself and her selfish needs.

All of this testimony contrasted with Rueon Walker's positive stories. She spoke of being a stepmother who presided over a family that was grieving and missing a gentle soul, who was the most special person they had ever known. Contrary to what some might have thought, Rueon made it clear that they were *not* asking themselves why Kim Cargill took Cherry's life. The proverbial "why people kill" being at the forefront of trials and true-crime talk. Instead, they had come to the stark and pious realization that Cherry's death was part of a greater plan.

Acceptance has a way of allowing forgiveness to enter the soul.

Brent Harrison gave an impassioned opening on May 28. The task of trying to save Kim Cargill's life was as tough a job as he was ever going to face. Harrison and Haas called several defense witnesses, mostly doctors who had treated Kim Cargill for her personality disorders. The collective claim was that a change in her medications throughout the years might have caused a psychotic break. It was a last-ditch effort on the defense's part to save their client's life.

What else, really, could they do?

By May 31, 2012, after closing arguments, the jury was dismissed into deliberations, clearly not looking forward to the duty at hand. Everyone looking on could feel the weight the jury carried with them as they exited the courtroom.

Late into that same day the jury presented a question to the court, which offered some insight as to where they were: *What are our options or what happens if we cannot decide?*

The court indicated it could not give any further instructions.

Making it obvious they were taking their responsibility seriously, jurors went back to the table.

Deliberations went on into the night.

By 9:00 P.M., the jury indicated it had come to a decision.

One of the questions the jury faced while deliberating Kim Cargill's fate put the entire case into perspective: *Taking into consideration all of the evidence, including the circumstances of the offense, the defendant's character and background and the personal moral culpability of the defendant, is there . . . sufficient mitigating circumstance or circumstances to warrant that a sentence of life imprisonment rather than a death sentence be imposed?*

This type of question, which the jury could deliberate on, made their decision a bit easier than a life-or-death verdict. It put into context how they should view their decision and took, for the most part, morality out of the equation.

As it was read into open court, the jury's mutual answer shocked just about everyone: "'We, the jury, unanimously find and determine that the answer to this Special Issue Number 2 is no.'"

Thus, after two years of intense preparation on both sides, four weeks of jury selection, eighteen days of courtroom testimony, with that decision Kim Cargill became the first woman to face execution and begin what was left of her life on death row in the state of Texas since 2005. She was only the fourth female since 1863 to face such dire circumstances.

As a formality an appeal was filed in the days after the verdict.

It was finally over.

In a direct statement to Kim Cargill while on the stand talking about Cherry's life, Rueon Walker summed up, perhaps, what mattered more than anything else to the Walker family. With great humility and a sincere appearance, Rueon stared at Kim Cargill, who had no reaction and showed zero emotion as Rueon spoke: "Mrs. Cargill . . . Cherry *loved* you. She did not *deserve* the terrible thing you did to her." Rueon let Kim know that Cherry's father, Gethry, did not hate her, contrary to what maybe many had presumed.

"We have to accept what God has allowed," Rueon concluded. "He allowed this to happen for a reason. . . . We don't hate you because we're not made out of hate. We only have love and pity and compassion for you."

EPILOGUE

I WROTE TO KIM CARGILL and her mother. Neither responded. Instead, I heard from Kim's appellate lawyers that Kim and Rachel were not interested in speaking to me until the case was completely adjudicated and I understood that they all believe Kim Cargill is innocent. These were the same two lawyers who had prepared that *Initial Application* habeas corpus document I quoted throughout this book.

Every convicted murderer I have spoken to believes that he or she will win his or her appeal.

It never happens.

Kim Cargill's new lawyers, along with Kim and her mom, I was told, were not at all interested in talking to me unless I bought into the argument that Dr. Lann totally botched this case. They claimed to me that there was plenty of evidence pointing to the fact that Cherry Walker died of a seizure, but that attorneys Harrison and Haas did not present all of it during trial and, in turn, acted as incompetent counsel for Kim Cargill. In addition, one of Kim's new lawyers insulted me and my career as a journalist, noting on the phone during a call (with a scathing, how-dare-you tone in his voice) something to the effect of, "I've seen you on TV. . . . I saw your website. . . . I know about those crime shows and what you do." He mentioned *Snapped* in particular—an episode dealing with Kim Cargill, of which I was not a part. The implication was that I had made up my mind about Kim Cargill going in, without knowing all of the facts, and wasn't interested in changing my mind. This is common when dealing with appellate attorneys, save for a few I have met and have come to respect greatly.

After spending a year on this book, studying every piece of available information, I would be in denial of the obvious if I came to the conclusion that Kim Cargill did not murder Cherry Walker. It is so obvious based on the evidence; to overlook this is tragic.

When I asked her appellate lawyers for accompanying documents cited in the *Initial Application,* one of them e-mailed me, explaining that I could find those documents at the courthouse: *We are hoping you will write a book that argues for Ms. Cargill's innocence.*

That story—of Kim Cargill's innocence—does not exist, I'm afraid. To quote a phrase Wally Lamb drew on as the title of one of his novels: "*I Know This Much Is True.*"

As I wound down my interviews and research for this project, I sent an e-mail to Kim's new lawyers, letting them know that if she or her mom wanted their voices heard, they had two weeks to respond. It had been months since my first request. A journalist writing a book has to put a deadline on closing out interviews. I do it with all my books.

I never heard from them.

* * *

Kim's new lawyers found an expert (in Ohio) that agrees with her argument of Cherry having a seizure and dying from it on that Friday night in June 2010. Not some hack, paid to testify to what you ask him to, mind you, but rather a bona fide expert in his field. Dr. Samden Lhatoo is the director of the Epilepsy Center in the Department of Neurology at University Hospitals Cleveland Medical Center. His credentials are impressive; his résumé is stellar. He is respected and knows his business of epilepsy. His conclusions and reputation were put to the test when he was summoned to testify for Kim during her habeas hearing based on that *Initial Application*.

I will say up front that I don't see how a second, thorough examination of Cherry Walker's supposed "condition," or how she died, could be done without exhuming her body.

That's number one.

Number two, in Lhatoo's twenty-three-page report, dated August 14, 2014, he says that Cherry's "death was sudden" and had been "unexpected" and there was a witness to it.

All salient facts.

But the credibility of that witness is not discussed in the document Lhatoo generated to support his claims. In fact, that witness is a convicted murderer sentenced to death.

Not the best witness to substantiate facts.

When she died, Cherry was in what Lhatoo called a "prone position," as are a "majority" of the victims he's studied that ultimately died from SUDEP, a rare condition Lhatoo defines as follows: *[It is] sudden unexpected, witnessed or unwitnessed non-traumatic and non-drowning death in a patient with epilepsy with or without evidence of seizure. . . .*

The Epilepsy Foundation website describes SUDEP more pointedly: *Sudden Unexpected Death in Epilepsy, [a condition wherein] a person with epilepsy dies unexpectedly and was previously in their usual state of health.*

Dr. Lhatoo attacked the autopsy conclusion Dr. Lann had come to as a matter of Lann taking most of the facts at face value. He said there was "possible evidence of seizure" that was missed at autopsy: *Even if we were to discount the evidence of the defendant. He added, The postmortem examination did not reveal a toxicological or anatomical cause of death.*

Thus, Lhatoo's report noted, *in the absence of an identifiable toxicological or anatomical cause of death, Cherry Walker's death is likely to have been a SUDEP death.*

Lhatoo claims the most likely age of the SUDEP death is a person between twenty and forty years of age. He also said in his report that between three thousand and five thousand people a year die from SUDEP. He even explained how George Washington's daughter had died from SUDEP, as provided by Washington's explanation of what happened to her in his presence, adding how SUDEP is not a "new phenomenon" and it is "widely accepted."

The Epilepsy Foundation's website states: *Each year, more than 1 out of 1,000 people with epilepsy die from SUDEP. However, it occurs more frequently in people with epilepsy whose seizures are poorly controlled.*

This contradicts the facts in Cherry's case. What's more, as the Epilepsy Foundation further states, the person found dead from SUDEP is often "in bed and doesn't appear to have had a convulsive seizure." One third of SUDEP victims exhibit evidence of a "seizure close to the time of death." Those victims are frequently found lying facedown.

The cause of SUDEP is still unknown: *Some researchers think that a seizure causes an irregular heart rhythm. More recent studies have suggested that the person may suffocate from impaired breathing, fluid in the lungs, and being [facedown] on the bedding.*

Again, all of this is in total contrast to the autopsy results, toxicology and how Cherry was alleged to have had a seizure (according to pathological liar Kim Cargill).

Lhatoo then went on to attack the homicidal violence conclusion by Lann, saying the "minor" injuries she described were "insufficient" to be categorized as "cause of death." In contrast, he said, the injuries described were "consistent with circumstantial evidence of a seizure," where a person's "biting the tongue, lip or cheek is a common occurrence."

Dr. Richard Ulrich, who had treated Cherry, was called as a state witness during Kim Cargill's trial and he talked about SUDEP under cross-examination from Kim Cargill's attorney, Jeff Haas. SUDEP was clearly outlined in the trial for jurors and they rejected it.

In the end, after arguing his case for seven pages, Dr. Lhatoo concluded that "based" on his review of "all the materials provided" to him: *I am under the opinion that Cherry Walker's death is likely to have been a SUDEP death.* He went on to say that had he been contacted by her former attorneys: *I would have been able to testify consistent with this report.*

Of the twenty-three pages in his report, seven focused

on the doctor's argument; the remaining sixteen consisted of his curriculum vitae.

In October 2014, Kim Cargill's appellate lawyers, Derek VerHagen and Brad Levenson, from the Office of Capital Writs, went public with their *Initial Application* and claimed to have "new evidence" in their client's case (mainly, Lhatoo's conclusions). They also claimed that Kim's attorneys at trial knew about Lhatoo and should have put him up on the stand, with Brad Levenson calling Lhatoo a "nationally renowned expert" on epilepsy. The idea was that Haas and Harrison put Cargill on the stand to explain what happened to Cherry in her presence, but they did not support her admission/Cherry's death narrative of that seizure with an expert.

Matt Bingham said in a statement responding to the *Initial Application: Kim Cargill was convicted by a Smith County jury of Capital Murder and sentenced to death based on the overwhelming evidence, including DNA evidence, as well as her own admissions regarding her dumping and setting the body of the mentally retarded victim on fire in order to destroy evidence.* Bingham went on to note that Cargill had been "afforded every right under the law to which she is entitled," and would continue to be under the appellate process. Bingham praised Judge Skeen. *The facts at trial showed the extreme brutality and heinous nature of this crime and what Kim Cargill is capable of doing to another human being,* Bingham concluded.

Levenson and VerHagen maintained that their client had what they termed "ineffective trial attorneys" and argued for her writ of habeas to warrant a new hearing on the matter.

As of this writing, the matter has still not been decided. (Please Google this after reading the book to see if a final decision has been made.)

In November 2014, however, the highest criminal court in Texas denied Kim Cargill's automatic trial appeal (separate from the habeas) and upheld the jury's decision and sentencing. In that appeal the legal team for Kim Cargill argued to the Texas Court of Criminal Appeals that the evidence against Kim was "insufficient to justify a capital murder charge." It maintained: *[Skeen] improperly allowed testimony about how she acted enraged and screamed during phone calls to state child welfare officials and about how she had choked her two children and her mother.*

Tacked onto this appeal was an accusation that her trial attorneys did not do a sufficient job of defending her and did not call expert witnesses that could have helped explain several important factors to the jury.

Kim Cargill remains on death row at Mountain View Unit in Gatesville, Texas. No execution date has been scheduled, as of this writing.

She can still appeal to the Supreme Court of the United States, if she can find a lawyer to take on such a monumental task.

Experts on both sides can argue about the specifics and science of seizures, while medical examiners can weigh in on what they believe happened to a particular individual and how the science backed up their opinions. But in this case a jury weighed all of those opinions, heard the science, all under the careful tutelage and watchful legal eye of a competent judge, and found Kim Cargill guilty.

For me, personally, I have to believe there is a bit of truth in every lie. If we apply that theory to Kim Cargill's story, when considering what happened to Cherry Walker, I ask myself one question. Could Cherry have had a seizure while Kim was strangling her to death? In my opinion that is *exactly* what happened.

There is one major factor that all of Kim Cargill's supporters, I feel, either entirely missed or consciously overlooked. Kids don't lie about the things Kim Cargill's children admitted to have happened to them throughout the years. They don't make up those types of stories. In addition, each of the kids' separate stories back each other up. Do these truths of abuse make Kim Cargill a killer? No, of course not. But it does, without a doubt, show by example what she is capable of and how far she is willing to take matters—even where her own children are involved. There is no doubt, based on those abuse stories alone, that Kim Cargill is a cold, callous, vindictive, violent sociopath, who is capable of the worst crime imaginable.

I could have included a dozen additional stories exemplifying Kim Cargill's psychotic, abusive behavior toward her husbands, boyfriends and children. However, room in the manuscript and redundancy stopped me from going further than the samples I chose to use.

I wish to conclude where I started—with Cherry Walker. By all the accounts I read and those individuals I spoke to about Cherry, she was one of those people others viewed, as Gethry would later put it, within a prism of unconditional love—someone to whom we could all look and learn so much about ourselves.

Where Kim Cargill is concerned, one could speculate that she and Cherry were polar opposites: one representing every good thing that makes the human soul what it is (the light); the other representing the true madness and evil within the human soul (the dark). One would, I assume, bring out the best and the worst in the other.

ACKNOWLEDGMENTS

There is really only one person to thank for this book: Donna Dudek, a producer from Jupiter Entertainment, a great friend who sent me an e-mail long ago to the tune of, *Phelps, you* have *to do a book on Kim Cargill.* She outlined just a small fraction of Kim Cargill's extraordinary life of crime—the pain she caused everyone around her—and the ultimate crime of murder she committed. I looked into it. I was hooked from the first few moments I began to learn about Cherry Walker's life. I felt Cherry needed a voice. I felt Kim Cargill needed to be exposed for the monster she is, despite fooling two new lawyers and others in her life. Without Donna's help and encouragement I could not have written this book.

Also, Natasha "Knoxy" Horton at Jupiter has been a friend and incredible talent to work with.

To everyone I interviewed and those who helped with documents and other source materials, a big thank-you! Equally, I appreciate James Cargill contacting me and verifying several things.

To my readers: I adore you and thank you for returning, book after book. I am constantly in awe of your dedication. I put my heart and soul into every manuscript and I hear from a lot of you that it is fully appreciated. I am humbled and honored to be able to write these books.

Don't miss M. William Phelps's
next compelling real-life thriller

DANGEROUS GROUND

Coming soon from Kensington Publishing Corp.
Keep reading to enjoy a sample excerpt . . .

SHE IS DEAD.

On a metal slab. A sheet covering her body. A tag hanging from her big toe. Soon manner and cause of death will be determined.

Murder by strangulation.

He is, contrarily, alive. Standing in my kitchen.

I walk in.

He appears to be waiting for the *ding* to tell him the Howard Johnson's Macaroni & Cheese dinner in the plastic frozen boat he placed inside the microwave has been fully nuked. But I notice the carousel inside the oven is not making that squeaky noise it does when it is on. Also, he is not moving. His head is bowed, as if he's trying to touch his chin to his chest, the folds of his neck fat exposed like rising dough. His eyes are closed. His right hand is on top of the microwave; his left is by his side. The familiar smelling richness of the melting cheese is not there, and this is an aroma that permeates the kitchen air whenever he cooks this meal. In a strange moment of reflection I don't see my oldest brother nodded out in a methadone-induced coma while standing erect in front of the microwave, but a corpse—a dead man standing. All he cooks is mac-n-cheese and those baked stuffed clams, full of bread crumbs, in the half shell. He lives off pills, methadone, beer, cheese and gluten.

"Mark?"

He does not answer.

"Mark?"

Nothing.

I toss my keys on the kitchen table. Walk over. Shake him.

It is April 12, 1996. I am twenty-nine, and I am separated from my wife for the past two years. In a few months I will be officially divorced. Nine months from now, on New Year's Eve, I will be married to a woman I haven't yet met. Mark is living with me in a house the bank is about to foreclose on; we're both biding our time, waiting for the sheriff to come and tell us to leave. He has recently split with his "wife," Diane, who is living in Hartford, Connecticut, on Garden Street, not far from Asylum Hill. A forty-one-year-old woman was murdered the previous year on Huntington Street, just a mile away. Unbeknownst to any of us then, a serial killer is on the loose in the Asylum Hill section of Hartford, plucking women off the street, raping, beating and killing them. Hartford is twelve miles from my house.

Last I hear, thirty-four-year-old Diane (her actual name is Diana, but we all call her Diane) is pregnant. Mark isn't sure if it is his child—and this tears him apart. He tells me he's done with her, for good this time. It's over. Yet, in the twenty years they have been together, we have all heard this a zillion times: after each fight; after each one has had the other arrested;

after they hit and scratch and berate each other in front of their kids at retail stores, restaurants and all sorts of other public places.

"Hey, man, wake up," I say, and shake him again.

Mark is thirty-nine. That's young, I know, but he looks fifty, maybe older. The life he's led has taken its toll. "The silent killer," hepatitis C, is coursing through his veins.

"Mark . . . wake up, man."

A snotlike length of drool hangs from his mouth.

After he comes to, figures out where he is, acclimates himself to his surroundings as if he is on a boat, trying to manage large swells, he takes his mac-n-cheese and heads down the five flights of stairs to his space in the house. He mumbles something I cannot understand. I can decode what he says about 20 percent of the time. Later on, I will have to clean up after he spills the macaroni all over himself, on his bed, the floor, before passing out again. The used boat his food came in will be on his lap, now an ashtray, and the juxtaposition of the ashes and leftover cheese, a cigarette butt stabbed into a piece of elbow macaroni, will remind me that life is, in the end, about choices.

Several hours later daylight has given itself to night. Mark is standing in my kitchen again, staring out the window. He is waiting, anxious as each car drives by the house, headlight beams looking like a Hollywood premiere strobing across the greasy wallpaper. He is somewhat coherent. His belly is full of cheese and pasta; the methadone and pills have worn off. After he leaves, it will occur to me that as he stood in the kitchen, an image of his face was reflected in the windowpane as he waited for a ride. I saw myself standing in the same spot, at fifteen years old, waiting for my friend, older and able to buy liquor, to come and pick me up so we could go get loaded.

"Shopping," he says after I ask where he is going. "A friend is on her way."

"Don't come back all drunk and high," I warn. "I won't let you in."

He looks at me. Doesn't respond. Lifts his cigarette up to his mouth, his fingers stained Listerine-yellow from the nicotine, hep C or both. He inhales deeply, blows what's left of the smoke at the windowpane, fogging it up.

His disability check and food stamps allow him to feed himself, but he also trades some of the food (or sells the food stamps at a 50 percent loss) for booze and Newports. As a kid l liked the Newport package with the upside-down Nike symbol. But stealing and smoking his cigarettes came with a Tic-Tac–like, cold burn in my lungs, so I wound up switching to Marlboro, which I considered more macho cigarettes, anyway.

He'll be broke in two days, will be eating my food, calling and begging our mother for money. She'll give it to him. He'll buy pills with that money because his methadone is regulated. A taxi—paid for by the state of Connecticut—picks him up every morning, brings him into Hartford and returns him home. At the clinic they give him his dose of "Kool-Aid." Sometimes he stores up several doses so he can go on a bender. It is a cycle, one we've been on most of our lives. No one tries to stop Mark anymore because we can't.

It is while he is shopping that I get the call—the fucking call that will not be a shock to most in my family, but it will change Mark forever, send him on a new course and initiate a suicide that will take him eight years to complete.

Several days before the call Mark came upstairs. I asked him to sit down. "I need to tell you what I have told you a dozen times since you moved in." As calm as I could, I explained: "I know that while I am at work, Diane is coming over." Knowing Diane all my life, I knew she was rummaging through my house, looking for things to pawn or information about me to hold over my head. "I don't want her in the house. She cannot be in this house."

He said something about being the older brother, more experienced in life, and how I should respect that. "And you never have. I love her. We're getting back together."

It's hard, however, for me to look up to a man with burn marks all over his chest from nodding out while smoking, all his shirts with tiny burn holes on them, the bed he sleeps in and his sheets the same. He is a man who spends fifteen hours a day basically unconscious, takes opiates and methadone together, while drinking cans of Busch beer, and has not been a father to his three kids since they wore diapers. I love him, but I am perpetually furious with this man. He gave up on life long ago for reasons I do not understand.

For a response I go to my emotional childhood bank and withdraw something our father would have said in this same situation: "But this is *my* house, Mark. My rules if you want to live here. And I don't want Diane over here."

He is nodding as we speak. In and out. His eyes languid, tired, Marty Feldman–bulged. His skin is slithery; the shiny texture of a salamander, with a subtle hue of yellow, like a healing bruise, same as the whites of his eyes, a strange, dull urine color. He is sickly-looking, gaunt and emaciated. At times he resembles a Holocaust victim staring back at me through an invisible fence between us. He has an anesthetic smell to him, same as a patient in a hospital.

You walk down into the area of my split-level, ranch-style home, where he lives on the bottom floor, and it reeks of a rich, cigarette-butts-stuffed-inside-a-can-of-beer, stale tar odor that is part of the house forever. He sleeps on one of *those* pullout couch beds, with the springs that stick into your back. There are empty see-through-orange pill containers all over the place. Beer cans. Dishes. Drinking glasses. Old newspapers. Greyhound racing programs. Pencils. Pens. Two-liter Coke bottles, fruit flies hovering. Cigarette butts. Silver-gray ashes. So many ashes: the remnants of his smoking covers everything, like dust. The carpet around where he sleeps is dirty and worn, same as any runner into a home during winter. There are small burn holes all over the area surrounding his worn Archie Bunker chair, and these look similar to tiny craters on the surface of the moon. I have installed four smoke detectors in an area the size of a one-car garage.

In this moment of our lives, if there is one thing about my brother I can count on, it has to be his predictability. His addiction runs his life and has him on a strict schedule. When we were growing up, and when he lived with Diane and the kids, everything about his life was unpredictable. You never knew what he was going to do next. Here, I can say that with his abnormally and enormously bloated hep C stomach, frail arms and old-man, saggy-skin legs, the wires of his tendons exposed, white fingernails, dry lips, cracking and sometimes bleeding, his greasy black hair from not showering regularly, my brother is, if nothing else, confined to some sort of controlled insanity that only he comprehends.

"Did she kill that man?" I ask after we agree that Diane cannot come into the house ever again.

He stares at me. Looks down at the kitchen table. He knows what I'm talking about.

A few years before this conversation a man was found stabbed to death inside Diane's vehicle. She had driven him to Hartford on the night he was murdered. It is unclear what happened. He was a man she met at a bar while she was living with my brother at a nearby scuzzy motel. Diane was not in the car at the time the man was murdered, she claimed.

"Not talking about that with you," he says. "She would never kill anyone."

Mark leaves to go shopping. I put on some music and try to relax.

The phone rings.

That fucking call.

It's our other brother, Thomas (whom we call Tommy). He and I are closest in age and get along same as good friends. Tommy lives a few miles away—two of Mark and Diane's kids live with him. First it was me and my soon-to-be ex-wife; now Tommy is their official foster parent. Mark and Diane's other child, the oldest, lives with an aunt in a neighboring town.

"She's dead," Tommy says. "Strangled to death."

It doesn't register. "What do you mean—who's dead?"

"Just heard. Ma called me. She heard, too. Someone murdered Diane. Where's Mark?"

"Shopping . . . Shit, dude. Are you sure?"

"Yeah, we're sure."

"What are you going to tell the kids?"

"I don't know."

I couldn't have known at the time, but fifteen years after that phone call, my relationship with a man who had strangled eight women to death would set me on the road to resolving some of the issues I faced when my familial and personal worlds unraveled. That early evening when my brother Tommy called and told me Diane had been murdered was the Phelps family's introduction to the ripple effect murder would have on all of us forever. Like so many other families I'd become involved with through my work, as murder became part of our lives that night, we would never be the same people.

"You mentioned a little bit about your loss," my serial killer tells me one day. "A death wakes up the family. Maybe some good can come of it. Maybe a Scared Straight course for the Phelps clan."

In September 2011, I wrote to this man, one of the nation's most notable, nicknamed serial killers. My goal at the time was to convince him to act as a consultant, an anonymous profiling source on my Investigation Discovery television series, *Dark Minds*. Concerned about glorifying his crimes or revictimizing the people he murdered, his identity remained secret throughout his tenure on the series and after. He was known to audiences only as "Raven," a disguised voice on the telephone explaining what was going through the mind of the serial killers I hunted and profiled each week. But as the series aired and our relationship progressed, something happened.

We became "friends."

"I can help you look at your sister-in-law's murder," he continues, "and offer my understanding. Hard to believe a convicted serial killer has something valuable to say, but what I offer is insight into the mind of how this killer thinks. I see through cases because I have witnessed this kind of evil firsthand, lived with evil twenty-four hours a day."

I had no idea how to respond to this.

He encouraged me to "listen and learn."

As we began, the true emotional, physical and spiritual impact this relationship would have on my life, or how his "insight" would affect my everyday thinking, on top of the relationship with my family, was hidden—a series of blows I could have never imagined.

"Sorry for your loss," he says. "Don't make excuses for her. She was doing what she wanted to do. We play at a cost. Then someone dies and we look at ourselves for answers."

My five-year friendship with a serial killer, like my relationship with Mark and Diane, would not only change who I was, but break me.